GREAT IS
PEACE
A Modern Commentary on Talmud Bavli Tractate Derek Eretz Zuta

by Rabbi Dr. Arthur Segal
and Sara Davies

Cover Illustration: *Cherubim*. Detail, stained glass window by the famous 20th century Jewish-French-Russian artist, Marc Chagall, courtesy of Union Church of Pocantico Hills, NY.

Book design by Sara Davies

Portions of this book were published in *The Path & Wisdom for Living at Peace with Others* and *Love Peace and Pursue Peace*.

Contents

5 **Acknowledgments & Dedication**

6 **Introduction**

9 **Chapter One**

85 **Chapter Two**

116 **Chapter Three**

135 **Chapter Four**

152 **Chapter Five**

164 **Chapter Six**

176 **Chapter Seven**

188 **Chapter Eight, the Lost Chapter**

189 **Chapter Nine**

225 **Chapter Ten, the Chapter on Peace**

268 **Conclusion**

271 **Appendix A**

330 **Appendix B**

335 **About the Authors**

Acknowledgments & Dedication

Only God can bring something out of nothing—*Ex Nihilo*. Everything I am today—every word written—is wrought by God my Creator, and by the nurturing, love, and wise teachings I received from my parents, grandparents, aunts, and uncles, many of blessed memory.

Unlimited thanks to my rabbis and teachers, including C. Potok, J. Kohen, A. Belzer, R. Wolkoff, A. Waskow, B. Bloom, T. Levy, Z. Schachter-Shalomi, G. Milgram, G. Steinberg-Caudill, who all played an important role, as did my devoted friends and talmidim, to my sister who always stood by me with devotion and love, and most especially to my wife, Ellen, my *beshert*. She is indeed an Eshet Chayil, a woman of valor.

This text is also dedicated to Asher Ezra ben Seth v' Sarah Dreyfuss, born Wednesday, July 11, 2012, Tammuz 11, 5772. May he and his generation grow in a world of derek eretz and shalom.

Introduction

With what is he to be compared who possesses more knowledge than good deeds? With a tree of many branches and but few roots. A storm comes and plucks it up and turns it over....But what does he resemble who can show more good deeds than learning? A tree of few branches and many roots. Even should all the winds of heaven rage against it, they could not move it from its place.

—Rabbi Eleazar ben Azariah
(First century C.E., Judea)

The book you hold in your hands is the first modern commentary on Talmud Tractate Derek Eretz Zuta, which was written over 1500 years ago. Derek Eretz literally means 'the way of the land.' In Aramaic, *zuta* means small, or for our usage, Part One. Derek Eretz is not about Jewish ritual, but about how we are to treat one another, and the traits of character, *middot*, we should try to develop. In order to simplify the study process, I have broken the chapters into subsections labeled as 'verses,' although they do not appear as such in the original text.

Through the study of Derek Eretz we learn how to get along with others, even difficult people. The development of good character traits and transformation through Jewish spiritual renewal is called *mussar*. "Derek eretz comes before Torah" (*Midrash Vayikra Rabbah 9:3*). One cannot personify Torah until he demonstrates *derek eretz* in all that he does.

Beresheit, Genesis, tells us that "In the beginning, God created...". One may infer that God created only the beginning. How we humans choose to treat our fellows and the planet is up to each of us to decide, as God created us with *bechira*, free will. We can choose to live our lives with derek eretz, or we can allow our *yetzer ha ra*, the evil inclination, to lead us.

Two of the many important maxims in Derek Eretz:

> *If others speak evil of you, let the greatest thing seem unimportant in your eyes; but if you have spoken evil of others, let the least word seem important.*

> *If you have done much good let it seem little in your eyes, and say: 'Not on my own have I done this, but through the good which has come to me from others'; but let a small kindness done to you appear great.*

Chapter Ten, known as the Chapter on Peace, teaches us to "Seek peace, and pursue it," which means that we are to seek peace where we are, and if we do not find it, seek it in other places. The rabbis were so impressed with this chapter, so dedicated to its message, that some of them wanted to make it a Tractate of Talmud by itself.

In my years as a teacher and rabbinic counselor, I have seen my *talmidim* (students) transform their lives through the study and practice of Derek Eretz. May you enjoy the learning process and come to shalom.

Todah rabbah.Shalom uvracha. Thank you very much. Peace and blessings,

Rabbi Dr. Arthur L. Segal
Hilton Head Island, SC, USA
August 2012; Av 5772

Chapter One

VERSE 1

The qualities of the sages are modesty, meekness, eagerness, courage, bearing wrongs done to them, and being endeared to everyone; submission to the members of their household, fear of sin, and judging everyone according to his deeds.

Modesty

In traditional Judaism, *tzni'ut*, modesty, usually refers to the way one dresses or relates to the opposite sex. In the study of derek eretz, however, modesty means humility. The rabbis teach that a man who thinks he can live without others is mistaken; one who thinks others can't live without him is even more deluded. Humility creates in us the capacity to truly love. It is one of the desired character traits of the Jewish People (*Yevamot 79a*).

Moses is referred to as "exceedingly humble, more than any man in the world" (*Num.12:3*). Humility is a sign of Godly strength and purpose, not weakness. "God opposes the proud but gives grace to the humble" (*Proverbs 3:34*). Humility allows us to understand that we are all connected with a transcendent unity. We experience this connection with the universe, or with the Divine, by becoming egoless.

Ego separates us from God and our fellows. If we resent someone, chances are that we see in him a defect of character that we possess. We prefer to shun him or to hold a grudge than to work on ridding ourselves of that defect.

"I stood between God and you" (*Deuteronomy 5:5*). Moses tells Israel that he was an intermediary between the Israelites and God at Sinai. *Anochi* is the Hebrew word used for 'I'. If we look at the verse literally, 'I' (ego) forms a barrier between God and ourselves.

While pretending he was Esau, Jacob said to Isaac: "It is I, Esau your firstborn" (*Genesis 27:19*). *Anochi* was also used here. The sages teach that wanting to be the big man, wanting to be an 'I,' is a trait of Esau. Esau is not one of our seven shepherds, *ushpizin*, who visits us in our sukkot. Jacob's humility was better expressed in his statement "I am too small [undeserving] of all the kindnesses You have done for me" (*Genesis 32:11*).

We earn self-esteem by doing God's will. "A vain person is one I cannot bear" (*Psalms 101:5*). Dr. Robert Smith (20th century, United States) wrote:

> *Humility is having perpetual quietness of heart. It is to have no trouble. It is never to be fretted or vexed, irritable or sore; to wonder at nothing that is done to me, to feel nothing done against me. It is to be at rest when nobody praises me, and when I am blamed*

or despised, it is to have a blessed home in myself where I can go in and shut the door and pray to God in secret and be at peace, as in a deep sea of calm, when all around and about is seeming trouble.

Meekness

Meekness, the second *middah*, trait, discussed in Verse 1, is often used pejoratively in literature: "Exist unthinkingly like a slave, like a working animal"—*Iris Murdoch*; "Like an ox, his head bent meekly, he waited for the blow of the axe which was raised over him"—*Leo Tolstoy*; "Like a victim: meek, like a sacrifice"—*Margaret Drabble*. Based on its common associations, who would want the trait of meekness?

The rabbis do not ask us to be like unthinking, obsequious farm animals, ready for sacrifice or victimization. True meekness seems to have been lost in our aggressive, self-centered culture. Because people associate it with weakness, most today do not admire others for being meek. Yet it is a quality of character very noticeable in our greatest sages, *zekher tzadik livrakha*—may the memory of the righteous be for a blessing (*ZT"L*). It is a trait we need to develop.

Meekness, *anav* in Hebrew, means subdued in mind (gentle) or circumstances (needy, especially saintly): humble, lowly, meek, poor. In Talmudic terms, to be meek is to be egoless, loving, kind, forgiving, and gentle—the opposite of flamboyant or charismatic. The best of our sages could not have attracted a TV audience with televangelism.

To be meek is to understand that the spark of the Divine, the *yetzer tov*, is within us, and to allow it to be expressed. True love of God and our fellows softens our stiff-necked rebellion and our hearts, so that we become receptive to the Creator and aware of His image in us. Therefore, meekness is also defined as being malleable, receptive, and teachable.

Meekness enables a person to bear patiently life's insults and the injuries he receives at the hands of others. It makes him ready to accept that, as the Talmud teaches, "A wise person is one who can learn from anyone." It allows him to endure provocation without being inflamed by it. We find an example of this in the story of R'Hillel, whose students place a bet to see if they can get him to lose his temper. They taunt him with silly questions. He demonstrates meekness by remaining cool while others become heated.

Meek people seek no private revenge; they leave that to God's sense of justice while they try to remain true in their calling and meet God's standards. The spirit of meekness enables its possessor to squeeze great enjoyment from his earthly portion, be it small or great. Delivered from a greedy and grasping disposition, he is satisfied with what he has. Serenity of mind, *shalom*, is one of the fruits of meekness.

This misunderstood virtue is the antidote to most of the nervous anxiety that intensifies the day-to-day stresses of modern life. God commands us to "Seek the Lord, all you meek of the Earth, who have upheld His justice. Seek righteousness, seek meekness" (*Zephaniah 2:3*). "The meek shall eat and be satisfied; those who seek Him will praise the Lord. Let your heart live forever!" (*Psalms 22:26*). "The Lord lifts up the meek; He casts the wicked down to the ground" (*Psalms 147:6*). "The meek also shall increase their joy in the Lord, and the poor among men shall rejoice in the Holy One of Israel" (*Isaiah 29:19*). "But the meek will inherit the land and enjoy great peace" (*Psalms 37:11*). We are to be *ma'abir 'al middotaw*, of a forgiving, yielding disposition (*Bava Kama 99b*).

Eagerness

Eagerness, *zerizut*, means enthusiasm or zeal, the desire to move forward. Its English root comes from the Latin *acer*, for sharp or biting. The Talmud refers often to sharpness as it relates to the eagerness to do *mitzvot*, the commandments, and to study Torah. "The words of Torah shall be sharp in your mouth so that if someone asks you something, you shall not fumble and then tell it to him, rather you shall tell it to him immediately" (*Kiddushin 30a*).

Pirkei Avot 5:20 quotes Rabbi Ben Teima: "Be brazen as a leopard, light as an eagle, quick as a gazelle, and strong as a lion in performing the will of your Father in Heaven." Eagerness comprises the middot of boldness (leopard), speed and alacrity (eagle and gazelle), and strength (lion).

In the 15ᵗʰ century mussar classic, *Orchot Tzaddikim, Ways of the Righteous* (originally entitled *Sefer ha-Middot, Book of Traits*) author Yom-Tov ben Solomon Lipmann-Muhlhausen (d. ca. 1425, Germany) devotes an entire chapter to the trait of zerizut, stating that it is the foundation of all other traits. We cannot do acts of *ahavath chesed*, loving kindness, if we don't have the eagerness, the zest, to get out of our houses and do these acts. Yet zerizut also depends on another trait we today refer to as 'mindfulness.' *Orchot Tzaddikim* says: "Zerizut depends upon the state of a person's heart. When a person frees his heart of all other thoughts that reside in it, and seizes upon one thought, then he will be a *zeriz*, one without doubt."

When we follow our own will instead of single-mindedly seeking to follow God's will, we are not integrated. When we don't have integration, *shlema*, we do not have *shalom*, serenity. We are in conflict with ourselves, and find ourselves in conflict with others. A life of spiritual disconnection is what the rabbis call *pizzur ha nefesh*, the scattered soul.

We may rationalize about our laziness or procrastination rather than do what is right and just in God's eyes. "A lazy person considers himself to be wiser than seven sages" (*Proverbs 26:16*). Jewish spiritual renewal is for those who want it, not for those who need it. Many need it, but do not yet wish to transform.

Rav Yosef Karo (1488 Spain–1575 Safed), in his introduction to the *Shulkhan Aruch, The Set Table*, writes only about the strength of a lion which awakens us to do God's will. Where are the leopard, eagle, and gazelle? The Taz, also known as Rav David Halevi Segal (1586–1667, Poland), wrote a critique of Karo, entitled *Turei Zahav, Rows of Gold*. Segal observes that the strength of a lion is the most desirable characteristic when in combat with the *yetzer ha ra*, the evil inclination. Thus, he explains, Rav Yosef Karo left out the other three traits to emphasize the trait of spiritual eagerness. Eagerness, in Derek Eretz, leads one to approach life with the perspective *Shiviti Hashem le-negdi tamid*, "I place Ha Shem before me always" (*Ps. 16:8*).

"R' Ben Azzai would say: Run to pursue a minor mitzvah, and flee from a transgression, for a mitzvah brings another mitzvah, and a transgression brings another transgression, for the reward of a mitzvah is a mitzvah, and the reward of transgression is transgression" (*Pirkei Avot 4:2*).

Courage

Courage is the opposite of giving in to fear. To overcome our fears, we must recognize that we only go around once in life. This is not an audition or a dress rehearsal; this is the big show. If we let our fears get the best of us, we are going to bomb, but if we triumph over those fears, we will bring the house down.

Our sages tell us to list all of the fears that have held us back throughout our lives. When we do, we will probably find that we have many fears in common with other people. We fear living. We fear dying. We might fear failure, success, not being loved or accepted, or not being good enough. Is there anything else we can think of? We are advised to include all of our fears—those we have now, and those we had in the past. We are taught to take our time and to be rigorously honest.

When we review the list we will probably notice that most of our fears are irrationally based. Most fears are of events over which we have no control. Worse yet, many of them, like the fear of not having enough money, will lead to the *chet*, the sin, of coveting. Coveting inevitably leads to resentment. To hold a grudge is a sin, as we may further sin by acting against those we envy. Fear is a process of the mind that can have ruinous consequences and drive us to hurt others.

Although many of our fears are irrational, there may be a few that have a rational etiology. For example, we might fear poverty, because our parents, who lived through the Great Depression, were always talking about it. Some people develop a fear of the opposite sex because at some point they were made to feel sexually inadequate. Others fear, in the depths of their hearts, that they are just not good enough, which leads to a fear of other people whom they perceive to be superior. Jealousy ensues, as does the desire to undermine, gossip, or otherwise lash out.

We are asked to determine the reasons for each fear. Where did it come from? Did somebody teach it to us? Is it the result of a traumatic experience? We skip no fear. We skip no reason. If, while doing this, we recall another fear, we add it to our original list.

We are asked to think about the behaviors that each fear causes. For example, if we have a fear of poverty, we might hoard our cash, avoid making charitable donations, shoplift, or pad our expense accounts. Do not be ashamed;

none of is a perfect angel. Again, we need to be rigorously honest.

Next, the sages teach us, for each of our fears, we ask ourselves this question: 'If I trusted in, had faith in, had experience with, and believed in God, could I let go of these fears and the behaviors that stem from them?' Via *mussar*, ethical and spiritual transformation, we learn that the answer is yes. When we learn to stay in conscious contact with God, our covetous thoughts and all other fear by-products become objectionable to us. We know that we can ask God to remove our fears and to end the destructive behavior they cause. He will, but we will be the ones doing the work.

> *There were seven clouds, four on the four sides of them, one above them, one beneath them, one before them to prepare the road before them, raising the depressions and lowering the elevations to make for them a plain, as it says: 'Every valley should be lifted up and every hill and mountain shall be made low and the rugged shall be made level, and the rough places a plain.'*
>
> —Isaiah 40:4

The sages teach that God will always raise valleys and flatten mountains during times of trouble, and that belief in God gives us a life free of fears and full of courage to do "what is right and just in God's eyes" (*Deut. 13:18*).

We learn in the Talmud that because of their experience

with God, our sages gained the courage to stand up to tyranny, for Judaism, and for their people. We see the same in the TaNaK with Moses, David, Esther, Job, and most central figures. "Who can protest and does not, is an accomplice in the act" (*Shabbat 54b*). By wearing the armor of Ha Shem, we rarely lack courage, nor give in to fears. We truly cannot "stand idly by while our neighbor's blood is shed" (*Lev.19:16*).

The opening prophecy that God communicates to Joshua after the death of Moses is: "Only be strong [*hazak*] and be very courageous [*ematz*] to observe [*lishmor*], to act [*la'asot*] according to all the Torah which Moses My servant has commanded you; do not depart from it to the right or to the left, so that you will prosper wherever you may go" (*Joshua 1:7*). Our sages explain that the heartening *hazak* (be strong) refers to Torah learning, while the encouraging *ematz* (be courageous) indicates the practice of good deeds (*Berachot 32b*).

Our sages offer the following verse as another source of courage: "Be strong, and let us strengthen ourselves [*venithazak*] on behalf of our people and on behalf of the cities of our Lord, and God will do that which seems good in His eyes" (*II Samuel 10:12*). The verse is taken from General Yoav's tactical discussion with his brother and fellow general, Avishai, during the battle against Ammon and Aram. Yoav offers encouragement before the two generals depart with their separate armies. "Hope to God, be strong, and He will give your heart courage [*veya'ametz*], and hope to God"

(*Psalms 27:14*). These words are read at the conclusion of every book of Torah by the entire congregation.

To develop the middah of courage, it is important to surround ourselves with spiritual and ethical people from whom we gain encouragement and inspiration. There will be times when we need encouraging words, and times when we need to offer them.

Rebbe Nachman of Breslov once said, "If you won't be better tomorrow than you were today, then what need do you have for tomorrow?" We can always improve and grow ethically and spiritually.

Bearing wrongs done to them

Often we hear that Judaism is a legalistic religion, as opposed to a way of love. Although Judaism certainly has its rules, which stem from its Hebraic roots, all of Torah and Talmud are meant to teach loving kindness. The Talmud Tractate Berachot clearly states that any ritual commandment must be waived to preserve the honor and well-being of another.

Rabbi Akiva says that the two most important commandments are love of one's fellow and love of God. Rabbi Hillel defines both: "What is hateful unto you, do not do to your fellows." The Midrash teaches that all Jews are *ma'aminim b'nei ma'aminim*, believers who are descendants of believers, but more important than faith itself are the actions which point to one's faith. Rebbe Levi Yitzchok of Berditchev (1740–1810, Poland) said, "Whether a man really loves the Divine can be determined by the love he bears toward his fellow men."

How can we love the neighbor who mows his lawn at 6 AM on Sunday? Leviticus 19:17–18 tells us not to hate, not to revenge, not to resent, but to love, and to gently instruct someone who is on the wrong path. The verse ends with "I am God." Only via God's love do we become able to love those who annoy us.

> The Holy One, Blessed is He, said to Israel: My beloved children! Is there anything I lack that I should have to ask of you? All I ask of you is that you love one another, that you honor one another, that you respect one another. In this way, no sin, robbery, or base deed will be found among you, so that you will remain undefiled forever. Thus it is written, "He has told you, O man, what is good, and what Ha Shem seeks of you—only to do justice, to love kindness, and to walk humbly with Ha Shem, your God" (Mic. 6:8).
>
> —Midrash D'Vrei Eliyahu Rabbah
> Ch. 28.

> Not only did Yosef not repay his brothers in kind [for having sold him], but he acted toward them with kindness and truth. Such is always the way of the righteous. Therefore,

*the Holy One, Blessed is He, forever watches
over them, in this world and in the next.*

—Kabbalah from the Zohar Genesis
on Parasha Mikeitz 201b

The Torah tells us: "You shall not take revenge and you shall not bear a grudge; you shall love your fellow as yourself" (*Lev. 19:18*). If someone behaves improperly towards us, we must erase the matter from our hearts, and behave correctly in every way with that person, just as we would with anyone else, as if nothing negative had ever come between us. Judaism requires no less from us. To seek revenge or to carry a grudge is not Judaic, and shows we are spiritually disconnected. Why let someone who is not paying rent live in our heads? Why hold a grudge when it only harms us, like an acid eating away at its container?

I have been saying the bedtime *Shema* for years, and it has helped to change me. The first paragraph goes:

> *Master of the universe, I hereby forgive any-
> one who angered or antagonized me or who
> sinned against me—whether against my body,
> my property, my honor, or against anything
> of mine; whether he did so accidentally, will-
> fully, carelessly, or purposely; whether through
> speech, deed, thought, or notion; whether in
> this transmigration or another transmigration.
> May no one be punished because of me. May
> it will be Your will, Ha Shem, my God and the*

God of my ancestors, that I may sin no more. Whatever sins I have done before You, may You blot out in Your abundant mercies, but not through suffering or bad illnesses. May the expressions of my mouth and the thoughts of my heart find favor before You, Ha Shem, my Rock and my Redeemer.

The last line is from the TaNaK, Psalms 19:15. Only in the third paragraph do we say the actual *Shema*, the acknowledgment that God is One. The man-to-man mitzvot take precedence over the man-to-God mitzvot.

Being endeared to everyone

What do the authors of *Derek Eretz Zuta* wish to convey when they tell us to be endeared to everyone? Well, first of all, we do not need to parse the word 'everyone.' It means what it says: *every* human being we encounter.

Being endeared means that we find in every person something dear, something valuable. "Every person contains something precious that cannot be found in anyone else," observed Rebbe Pinchas of Koretz. That 'something precious,' is what we find endearing. If we do not see it right away, our job is to mine for it, as we would for a precious gemstone.

When we are spiritually connected, we know that we are all made from Divine sparks. We know we are interconnected. We understand that when we hurt another person, we also hurt ourselves. All of Torah, including Talmud, is meant to bring us to ahavath chesed, and to help us to repair ourselves and our world. For this reason, *derek eretz*, the correct way to treat others, precedes Torah's rituals.

"Two eyes were given to man: one with which to see his fellow man's virtues, and another with which to see his own faults," taught Rebbe Meir of Premishlan. We must see and point out the beauty in every person instead of his imperfections. Faults we are to find only within ourselves. We are to take our own daily *chesbon ha nefesh*, an inventory of our soul. Never are we to take another's inventory.

It's impossible for a physical being to be devoid of faults; everyone has his share. We must not flee or hide from them, nor resign ourselves to them, but face up to them, and systematically chase them away. It's our responsibility to recognize who we are, and to gradually clean up our acts. What we see in the mirror may seem ugly at first, but our Divine path is to look.

Few rules are mentioned in Derek Eretz about human relationships with the Divine. The *talmidim*, disciples, of Rabbi Schneur Zalman of Liadi once asked him: "Which is greater—to love God, or to love one's fellow?" Replied the Rebbe: "The love of God and the love of a fellow are equally ingrained in the soul. God loves every person. So to love a fellow is to love what God loves, which is greater than to love Him Himself."

Remember, the rabbis call us hypocrites and liars if we say the *V'Ahavtah* prayer to announce our love for God, Whom we cannot see, but then we ignore or harm another person, the image of God, whom we can see.

Submission to the members of their household

At first glance, this quality of the sages appears absurd, especially to those of us with teenaged children. The sages say: "Whoever acquires a servant, it is as if he has acquired a master!" They go on to state that if the master has a pillow and the servant does not, the master must give the servant his pillow. In the Gemara, the rabbis debate the issue and conclude that a person with derek eretz could not sleep well if he had a pillow and his servant did not. Hence, if the master gives his pillow to the servant, both sleep well (*Kiddushin 20a*).

The middah of selflessness means putting the needs of others before our own puny desires. When we understand that God always provides for us, we can put our needs aside to care for our spouses, our children, and our employees. Rabbi Israel Salanter, father of the mussar movement, describes ego deflation as "killing one's self" in order to obtain the knowledge in Torah. Ego, as observed elsewhere, Edges God Out; it separates us from the Divine and our fellows.

To submit to the members of our household means to be humble, compliant, to make the needs of others a priority, and to promote *shalom bayit*, peace in the house. Our rabbis teach that if our home is not peaceful, we will have a difficult time being peaceful or productive in the workplace, or in our friendships. Is it worth sacrificing peace to fight over which movie to see or at which restaurant to eat? One of the very few times we are allowed to tell a white lie is to promote peace at home.

Our obligation to love our fellows is even greater with regard to our spouses and children. "He who loves his wife as himself, but honors her more than himself, is reassured that his home is based on underpinnings of peace" (*Yevamot 62*). "Parental love should be impartial; one child must not be preferred to the other" (*Shabbat 10b*). "It is a father's duty not only to provide for his minor children, but also to take care of their instruction, and to teach his son a trade and whatever is necessary for his future welfare" (*Kiddushin 29a*).

Jewish law forbids us to create an atmosphere of fear in the home. We must address our families in a quiet, gentle way (*Gittin 6*). Husbands are under special directive "not to bring tears" to their wives (*Bava Metzia 59*). In the Talmudic era, although wife-beating was a common, accepted, and legal practice in both Christian and Muslim Europe, it was considered a grievous sin for Jewish men to treat their wives in such a manner (*Shulchan Aruch Even Ha'Ezer, 154:2, Rabbi Moshe Isserles, co-author of Rabbi Karo*).

King Solomon advises us to "Relish life with the spouse you love each and every day of your precarious life. Each day is God's gift. It's all you get in exchange for the hard work of staying alive. Make the most of each one!" (*Ecclesiastes 9:9*).

Fear of sin

Fear of sin has been discussed in many of our Jewish texts. *The Path of the Just, Mesillat Yesharim*, by the Ramchal (AKA

R'Moshe Chaim Luzzatto, d. 1746, Italy) contains a mussar chapter on *yirat chet*, fear of sin. The traditional perspective is that fear of sin comes from the fear of Divine punishment.

Here is the difficulty. Many, if not most, Jews today deny a God who punishes, and also deny an Olam Ha Ba where God corrects this upside-down world. Some of our sects have truncated God, if they even promote experience with the Divine. Hence, we end up with people who sin openly. "Are they ashamed of their loathsome conduct? No, they have no shame at all; they do not even know how to blush" (*Jer. 6:15*). "The ox knows his master, the donkey his owner's manger, but Israel does not know, my people do not understand" (*Isaiah 1:3*).

It is discouraging to see that gossip, pettiness, mean-spiritedness, elitism, and *sinat chinam*, baseless hatred, are more present than ahavath chesed in many so-called houses of God.

How can we reach the modern Jew? We cannot effectively hold the sword of a vengeful God at his neck, and demand that he be good. If we read the TaNaK, that strategy didn't work then, and it doesn't work now. Transformation requires nothing less than spiritual renewal and awakening. We must affirm the desire to live a good life according to the fundamental rules of common decency described in Derek Eretz. As the Talmud says: "Do not be as slaves who serve their master for the sake of reward. Rather, be as slaves who serve their master not for the sake of reward" (*Pirkei Avot 1:3*).

Each person must decide for himself if he is willing to investigate his ways, and to do a chesbon ha nefesh. He must find his own defects of character abhorrent. He cannot change because others tell him that what he is doing is wrong.

We need to discover this for ourselves. When we do, we can confess to God, Who already knows, and to our rabbi (if we can trust him or her). We can ask God to remove our defects via *tashlich*, which means 'to cast away', and we need not wait until Rosh Ha Shana. We must make *teshuvah*, amends, to those we have hurt over the years. Living free of character defects benefits us, as well as our fellows. It is truly a universal win-win.

Judging everyone according to his deeds

Although our Talmud and other texts advise us not to judge, we need to remember that our sages, as rabbis, had duties we would find atypical in today's world. They did not serve as congregational rabbis, nor did they appear on the *bimah*, pulpit, often. Lay leaders led services and gave d'vrei Torah. Rabbis gave d'vrei Torah on two Shabbatot a year: Shabbat ha Gadol, right before Pesach, and Shabbat Shuvah, between Rosh ha Shana and Yom Kippur.

One of their duties was to serve on a *beth din*, a rabbinical court. Often these courts ruled on matters of *halakha*, Jewish law, or approved conversions or *gettim*, divorces. They also decided matters of business or criminal law. For their role in the courts, the sages were taught to judge a person only by his deeds—in other words, by the facts in the case. They were instructed not to base their opinions on the reputation or past deeds of the defendant.

The rabbis who served as judges were not to separate themselves from the community. They needed to know what was happening outside of their Talmudic academies. For example, if a person was brought before them for stealing a loaf of bread, and they were aware that the local economy was bad, they might have ruled leniently.

In our current society we can still apply the concept, albeit somewhat differently. As Hillel said, let us not judge another until we can stand in his place (*Pirkei Avot 2:4*). Since it is impossible to stand in another's place, knowing all of his history, his problems, his loves, his deepest thoughts, it is best not to judge. We may see that someone is a horrid gossip, but we know that gossips put others down to make themselves feel better. "A vain person seeks to compensate for his feelings of lack by thinking himself superior" (*Rabbeinu Yonah al HaTorah, p. 156*). When we judge, when we are cliquish, we not only deny God, but worse, play God. The Talmud teaches, however, that we can be discerning; we can avoid a neighbor with bad character traits.

Their thought concerning this world is: "All that is in this world is of no importance to me, for this world is not mine." They are occupied in teaching others, and no one can see in their teaching anything wrong. Their questions are to the point, and their answers are according to the Law.

The 'Law' referred to above means Torah, including the TaNaK, Talmud, Midrash, and Zohar. In the Gemara, the rabbinic commentary on the Mishna (Oral Law), the Aramaic word *mammon* is used to describe non-essential worldly possessions. The rabbis witnessed conspicuous consumption in ancient Babylon, Greece, and Rome, and would see the same today in our 21st century. They believed that one could not serve God while also serving mammon.

They did not oppose capitalism, however. They eschewed monasticism and vows of poverty, and felt little affection for the Jewish sect of the Essenes. They limited the amount of *tzedakah*, charity, one could give, so as to not allow oneself to become impoverished. Many of our rabbis were very wealthy. Judah ha Nasi, the Prince (ca. 175 CE), was rich enough to befriend Caesar Antoninus Pius.

The rabbis intend to convey that chasing after worldly possessions is not the most important activity in life. They understood that nothing in this world truly belonged to them; everything was a loan from God. Nothing could be earned without Divine aid. Anything accumulated could be lost. They understood they were to share their wealth with others who had less, as are we.

A comparison of Talmud Yerushalmi and Talmud Bavli reveals a rivalry between the rabbis of Judea and Persia. What follows below is a vignette that illustrates how the Judean rabbis felt about their wealthier and more ostentatious Persian counterparts.

> *Rabbi Hiyya bar Abba and Rabbi Assi were sitting before Rabbi Johanan, while Rabbi Johanan was sitting and dozing. Now, Rabbi Hiyya bar Abba asked Rabbi Assi, "Why do the sages in Babylonia dress distinctively?" He answered him: "Because they are not very learned and consequently enhance their status through distinguished, costly clothing."*
>
> *Rabbi Johanan awoke and said to them, "Children! Didn't I teach you the verse: 'Say unto wisdom, Thou art my sister'(Proverbs 7:4)? If the matter is as clear to you as the knowledge that your sister is forbidden to you sexually, say it; but if not, be wise enough not to speak."*

They said to Rabbi Johanan: "Then tell us, master. Why do the scholars of Babylonia dress distinctively?" And Rabbi Johanan answered: "Because they are not in their original homes, since they are now in Babylonian exile. Some say: 'In my own town my name is sufficient; away from home, the way I dress indicates my status.'"

—Shabbat 145b

While R' Johanan defends his Persian colleagues' academics and hermeneutic methodology, he still gives a *zetz* to their worldly means of dressing.

It is fine to work hard and to earn money, even to become wealthy, but we should not allow ourselves to become deluded by mammon. We should not allow ourselves to lose conscious contact with the Divine.

The next part of the verse teaches us that a rabbi's primary role is to teach others. *Pirkei Avot*, in the very first verse, tells us that one of a rabbi's three major obligations is to "establish many talmidim" (students). It is a relatively recent phenomenon to find rabbis weekly on the bimah, leading prayer services, sitting in board meetings, collecting money for building funds, and acting the role of both Master of Ceremonies and *maitre d'* from the Borscht Belt. Few, if any, of our sages would meet the requirements of a modern rabbinic search committee. The lesson for each of us is to share what we are best at doing, and not spend our energies doing what others can do.

Furthermore, our rabbis must teach correct material. Failure to do so is a grave matter that meets one of the definitions of *lifnei iver*, putting a stumbling block before the blind. For those who are not rabbis, this part of the verse reminds us to share accurate information, and to avoid *lashon ha ra* (gossip, slander, talking about others). Rabbis need to remember to keep our egos out of what we teach. We must label our opinions as such, and teach the sages' lessons on a topic thoroughly before going off on tangents. Everyone needs to remember humility, as well as modesty. "Rabbi Zeira said in the name of Rava bar Zimna, 'If the earlier Sages were the sons of angels, then we are the sons of men; but if the earlier Sages were the sons of men, then we are donkeys'" (*Shabbat 112a*).

When we ask questions, we are not to make speeches. How many of us have attended a Q&A at the end of a lecture, and found ourselves listening to a speech someone launched in the guise of a question? Such a person, driven by ego, wants to show us how smart he thinks he is. I was guilty of this for years. It is selfish. The Talmud tells us that a jar with one coin can still make a lot of noise (*Bava Metzia 85b*).

Here is a cute exchange that illustrates how a son is to ask his father a question:

> Rabbi Elazar asked Rabbi Shimon bar Yochai, his father, "Why did the blessed Holy One see fit to send the Israelites down to Egypt?"

He replied, "Are you asking me one question or two?"

Rabbi Elazar responded, "I'm asking two questions: Why were they sent into exile, and why down to Egypt?"

Rabbi Shimon answered: "Actually, the two are connected and become one question."

—from the Zohar 2:14b
Rabbi Shimon bar Yochai
(ca. 140 CE)

Our words are as precious as coins. Use them wisely. My dear friend Rabbi B. Bloom taught me that less is more. Words can hurt and words can heal. Let us strive to only use our words to uplift others.

CHAPTER ONE, VERSE 3

One shall always be like an air-bag which is open to receive the air, and as a deep excavation which preserves the water therein contained, and as a glazed jug that preserves the wine therein; as a sponge that absorbs everything. Be as the lower threshold that all tread upon, and as a nail in the wall that is within the reach of everyone to hang his clothes on.

As *Derek Eretz Zuta* was written 1500–2500 years ago, the above verse cannot refer to an automobile safety device. When the rabbis said 'air bag,' they likely meant a dead animal's lung or bladder, which would be filled with air and used as a bellows.

The sages, *ZT"L*, teach us that before we can learn, before we can listen, we must rid ourselves of preconceptions and prejudices, so that we can be empty to receive. The Hebrew word for 'receive' is *kabbalah*. In modern usage, an air bag is someone who is full of himself, who dominates a conversation, pontificates and spews his air. In English, to bellow means to roar. We have all met folks who know little, but because of their loud voices or charisma, speak nonsense that many, unfortunately, believe. Spiritually, if we want to change, we must let go of worn out concepts that do not work for us, and open our hands to receive the gift of a new way of living, through Jewish spiritual renewal.

When someone talks to us, we should actively listen, not think about what we will say when it is our turn to speak. If we need to respond, the best way is to say, 'If I understand you correctly, you are saying…'. We let the speaker know we have been listening, and give him a chance to correct us if we misunderstood.

In our studies, we must be like a deep well dug into bedrock, where lessons (water) don't drain into the earth, but are retained. How to best remember what we learn is unique to the individual. I was not one to sit in a two-hour lecture with 500 students, listening to a professor and taking notes. My best results came from studying one-on-one. Ironically, this is the traditional method of studying to prepare for the rabbinate.

A glazed earthenware jug is not porous. The glaze keeps the wine, a precious liquid, from being wasted. Note, please, that the verse doesn't say 'water.' We are now at a level of learning beyond water. The deep well kept the water. Much of what we learn is water and is necessary, but the wine, the wisdom of each lesson, needs to be kept in an accessible glazed jug, from which we lose not a drop.

To be as a sponge is to absorb everything. When a sponge is squeezed, it empties and dries out. We need to absorb, but we also need to retain. We must separate air (common sense), water (mitzvot that a society learns without

Torah, such as a prohibition against murder), and wine (the precious teachings of our sages, ZT"L, in what we now call the Oral Torah, Talmud, and Midrash).

As sponges, we absorb all, but we must go farther; we must also be like sieves (*Pirkei Avot 5:15*). We must separate the coarse wheat from the fine wheat germ, the finest part of the flour. We are not to accept anything on blind faith. Whether we listen to a rabbi's sermon or watch the so-called news, we must discern the truth for ourselves. We should not even accept the existence of God on blind faith. "One who is quick to understand and slow to forget—his is a good portion" (*ibid. 5:12*).

Be as the lower threshold that all tread upon

The sages are referring to a door frame—in today's terms, the place where we would lay a doormat. Are the rabbis telling us to be doormats, to allow people to step on us? No. During the time *Zuta* was written, the lower threshold of a door, especially to a house of worship, was considered holy. People were to step over it without touching it. This is still done today in Muslim mosques and Hindu temples.

The rabbis tell us not to be like a holy lower threshold, which people cannot touch, but to be like an ordinary wooden threshold, which people may step on. In other words, we should not act 'holier than thou' because we have knowledge. Although we have learned Torah and Talmud, and have become rabbis, we're no different from anyone else. We are not to be inaccessible, as were the Hebrew priests. We need to keep our doors of knowledge open to all who wish to learn. The Talmud, quoting Torah, reminds rabbis that the Torah is an inheritance to all of Israel. Torah was given to all humankind. If we refuse to teach it, the sages explain, we are stealing another's inheritance.

Be as a nail in the wall that is within the reach of everyone to hang his clothes on.

Derek Eretz Zuta does not say to be as a cloak or as a hat, nor does it say to be as a fancy armoire. We are to be as a plain, humble nail, within reach of everyone. We are not to hide in an ivory tower, or to behave like the rabbis in the Coen brothers' movie, *A Serious Man*. The rabbis Larry Gopnik consults are obtuse, oblivious, and obscure. His synagogue's senior rabbi is never available.

> *Larry Gopnik:* Please, I need help! I've already talked to the other rabbis. Just tell him I need help.
>
> [The secretary rises, goes to the door behind her, opens it, and shuffles into the dimness. She speaks quietly with the aged rabbi, who sits idle. She shuffles back, closes the door and sits down.]
>
> *Rabbi Marshak's Secretary:* The rabbi is busy.
>
> *Larry Gopnik:* He didn't look busy!
>
> *Marshak's Secretary:* He's thinking.

We are to allow people to 'hang their clothes' on us, not just their hats. We are to help them with their dilemmas, their conflicts, and their 'dirty laundry.' We are to help them to see themselves as beautiful, pure, and beloved by God when they are vulnerable. We are to help them see themselves without the trappings, the 'clothes,' of society. We are meant to help our fellows recognize that in their unguarded form, they are lovable and capable of loving others.

CHAPTER ONE, VERSE 4

I f you have sustained a loss of your property, remember that Job lost his property, children, and health. Be careful about all that you see with your eyes, for the principal deception is by the eye. Be careful with your teeth [with your meals], that you should not eat too much. Do not discuss with the Sadducees, so that you shall not fall into the Gehenna. When you hear others insult you, do not answer them. If people are praising you for having done a great thing, you shall nevertheless consider it of no importance.

If you have sustained a loss of your property, remember that Job lost his property, children, and health.
Few of us could suffer like Job, who lost everything but his faith in God. We must remember to be grateful, even if we have lost property, our livelihoods, or our homes. The majority of people on our globe do not own property, nor do they have a reliable income. Many have neither their health nor their families.

Why do we perform a Rosh Chodesh ceremony at the beginning of the lunar month? Our sages teach that, like the moon, we experience periods of waxing and waning in our lives. No human has ever lived as a fully waxed moon. Each of us must overcome challenges and circumstances. *Derek Eretz* teaches that although we may have lost material possessions, God, in His time, will give us the strength, *koach*, and wisdom, *kochmah*, to rebuild. Rabbi Yisrael Salanter wrote:

> *It is harder to change one bad character trait than to learn the complete Talmud. It is just as great a distance from knowing something to not knowing something as is the distance from knowing something in your head alone to internalizing it into your heart....As long as one is still alive, one can still work on perfecting himself.*

When our hearts are connected with our minds, we are integrated and know true *shalom*, *shlema*, wholeness and oneness with God.

Be careful about all that you see with your eyes, for the principal deception is by the eye.

In Judaic and Hebraic literature, the eye is the gateway for the *yetzer ha ra*, the part of us that wants to do our will at the expense of others. Our eyes allow us to see, but cannot give us complete understanding. Our eyes can entice us, and cause us to forget that actions have consequences.

An examination of the Hebrew tells us that the mitzvah of wearing *tzitzit*, fringes on the four corners of our garments, is intended to remind us not to allow our eyes to wander. "And it shall be unto you for a fringe, that ye may look upon it, and remember all the commandments of the Lord, and do them; and that ye seek not after your own heart and your own eyes, after which ye use to go a whoring [*zohnim*]" (*Numbers 15:39*). How many times have we foolishly coveted another's big house, fancy cars, and sexy spouse, only to find out later that our neighbor's possessions were mortgaged to the hilt, and the trophy wife was sharing her affections with her golf teacher and her tennis coach?

The rabbis ask us to use our minds to investigate, rather than to rely on what we see. They also warn us about the yetzer ha ra. "The yetzer ha ra starts as thin as a spider web strand, and if one does not conquer it, it grows thicker than a cart rope....The bigger that one spiritually is, the bigger his yetzer ha ra is" (*Sukkah 52a*). "The strongest trick in the storehouse of the yetzer ha ra is to take what you know to be truth and make you come to have doubts about it. If you are not careful, this can cause you to come to sin, even where you are spiritually strongest" (*Duties of the Heart, Rabbi Ibn Paquda, 1050 C.E. Spain*).

Be careful with your teeth that you should not eat too much.
At first glance, the rabbis seem to be advising us to avoid gluttony. Throughout the Talmud, we are told to do everything in moderation. The Talmud provides details regarding

which foods to eat and when to eat them, and even contains recipes. Rabbi Hillel (ca. 100 BCE) says: "One who increases flesh, increases worms" (*Pirkei Avot 2:7*).

I believe there is a deeper spiritual lesson. Throughout rabbinic literature, the teeth are called the guardians of the tongue. The tongue is an organ that the rabbis spend much time discussing.

> *Rabban Gamaliel said to Tavi his servant: 'Go and get me good food from the market.' He went and bought him tongue. He said to him: 'Go and get me bad food from the market.' He went and bought him tongue. Said he to him: 'What is this? When I told you to get good food you bought me tongue, and when I told you to get bad food you also bought me tongue!'*
>
> *Tavi replied: 'Good comes from it and bad comes from it. When the tongue is good there is nothing better, and when it is bad there is nothing worse.'*
>
> *Rabban Gamaliel made a feast for his disciples and placed before them tender tongues and hard tongues. They began selecting the tender ones, leaving the hard ones alone. Said he to them: 'Note what you are doing! As you select the tender and leave the hard, so let your tongues be tender to one another.'*

Tavi teaches Gamaliel about *lashon ha ra*, literally 'bad tongue,' and Gamaliel passes the oral teaching to his students (*Midrash Leviticus Rabbah 33:1*).

The sages tell us that we need to use our teeth, our intellects, and to be careful what we allow into ourselves. We also need to use our teeth to make sure that our tongues speak words of truth, tempered with kindness. Hate speech, whether encountered at Oneg Shabbats, or heard in the news, affects us. Hate speech can inspire hateful thoughts, which may lead to hateful action. Judaism recognizes that when we speak lashon ha ra, using the tongue for evil, we kill not only the subject, but also the listener and ourselves. I believe that the rabbis are asking us to use our teeth as a wall, to guard our tongues from swallowing evil and speaking it.

Do not discuss with the Sadducees, so that you shall not fall into the Gehenna.

What is *Gehenna*? We might answer that Gehenna is Hell, but because Judaism teaches that all of Israel has a share in the World to Come (as do the righteous of all nations and religions), Gehenna is, at most, a 12-month boot camp for the soul (*Sanhedrin Ch.11*). Those who rid themselves of character defects while still alive will run fewer spiritual laps in Gehenna. Those who don't will wear out a pair of Nikes each week.

Who are the Sadducees, and what is wrong with talking to them? The term *Sadducees* is derived from the name of Zadok, the first High Priest of Solomon's Temple (ca. 950 BCE.) Sadducees practiced the religion of Hebraism. Hebraism accepts only the *Five Books of Moses*; it discards the Prophetic texts as well as the Rabbinic texts (including the Talmud.) The Hebrews did not believe in corporeal resurrection, in an afterlife, or in a messiah. They did believe in a cult god who punishes, but this was not the universal God of Judaism. The Sadducees didn't believe in direct prayer to God, but in the intercession of the priesthood through animal and grain sacrifices.

When the Temple was destroyed in 586 BCE, the two remaining Hebrew tribes, Judah and Benjamin, were captured and taken to Babylon. They could no longer worship as Hebrews. Over time, Talmudic rabbinic Judaism emerged. And this split, this separation, labeled them Pharisees (separatists).The word *pharisees* comes from Hebrew, and means 'to separate.'

For as long as the rabbis were in what we now call Iraq and Iran, and the Hebraists, with their Temple by Ezra, remained in what we today call Israel, the two religions didn't clash very much. After the Hashmonian-Maccabean revolt (ca. 165 BCE), both groups became prominent in various parts of Israel.

To say they didn't get along is an understatement. The rabbis say: "A learned *mamzer* [bastard] takes precedence over an ignorant High Priest" (*Horayot 3:8*). They agreed on very little. For example, the Pharisaic-Rabbinic understanding of "an eye in place of an eye" was that the value of an eye was to be paid by the perpetrator (*Bava Kamma,*

Ch. 8). The Sadducees interpreted the phrase literally: the offender's eye would be removed.

The Hashmonean Hebrew kings and priests, descendants of the Maccabees, were Sadducees who slaughtered Jews and their rabbis. We Jews used to celebrate the Shevat 2, 76 BCE death of the Hebrew Hashmonean King Alexander-Yannai (Jannaeus). He was an avowed enemy of the Jewish sages and our people. So ruthlessly did he persecute the rabbis and their followers (some 50,000 were killed between 82–76 BCE), that the day of his death was declared a holiday. King Yanni was neither a Roman nor a Greek puppet. The Romans didn't come into Judea until 63 BCE (13 years after Yanni died). The Greeks had been expelled circa 165 BCE. Yanni practiced Hebraism.

Thus, in this verse, the rabbis counsel avoidance of Sadducees, as discussions with them might lead to death. The descendants of the Sadducees are known as Karaites. They get along well with the Jews of Israel and Turkey, where most of them live today.

The rabbinic injunction against debating religion with those who want to kill us extended into the Middle Ages. Rabbis were forced into Disputations with the Catholic Church. More often than not, the rabbis lost, and they and their congregations suffered. Nachmanides (the Ramban) of Girondi, Spain, won a debate and a case of gold in 1293. The Pope forced King James to change his ruling, and sentenced the Ramban to exile in Palestine.

Thank God we can today have gentle discourse with those of other religions, and emphasize our similarities instead of our differences. Everyone has opinions. We don't need to argue.

When you hear others insult you, do not answer them. Falsehoods spoken about us require no response; we remain silent. Why? From a spiritual point of view, we don't need to explain ourselves. Our friends know the truth; our enemies won't believe it. We use the bedtime *Shema* every night to ask God to allow us to forgive anyone who has harmed us: "Master of the universe, I hereby forgive anyone who angered or antagonized me or who sinned against me... whether through *speech*...".

We also remain silent when negative truths are spoken about us. In that moment, the gossiper, despite the sinfulness of his behavior, is our best teacher. We must spend time alone in quiet reflection. We need to make a chesbon ha nefesh, and own up to the truth of our defects of character.

The word 'insult' in Verse 1:4 does not necessarily refer to gossip. When verbally abused, we Jews, as our fellows in other faiths, are to turn the other cheek. (Physical assault, however, is a different issue; Judaism is not a pacifistic religion.) When someone insults us, we respond with loving kindness. Arnold Toynbee (1889–1975, England) said: "Love is the ultimate force that makes for the saving choice of life and good against the damning choice of death and evil. Therefore, the first hope in our inventory must be the hope that love is going to have the last word."

We must remember humility. "Know from where you came and to where you are going and before Whom you are destined to give account and reckoning. From where have you come? From a putrid drop. Where are you going? To the place of dust, worms, and maggots" (*Pirkei Avot 3:1*). When we truly understand and believe we are nothing more than a putrid drop from our fathers, and that our end is food for worms, what insult can top it?

If people are praising you for having done a great thing, you shall nevertheless consider it of no importance.
If we are blessed in life to do something 'great', we must give all credit to He Who gives us the skills, intellect, wisdom, and understanding to achieve. We acknowledge God, our teachers, and all those who have aided us. It would be nice if we said, 'You know, anyone with the same skills as I could have done an even better job.'

Although I understand the need for synagogues and charitable organizations to obtain donations, when we laud over others too much, put their names in our newsletters repeatedly or call them Man (or Woman) of the Year, we are not helping them with ego deflation. Those with ego believe their own press; good PR becomes a drug for them. When we look at any organization's bulletins, we tend to see the same volunteers year after year. We recognize them as the folks who take full credit for their achievements. Although we describe them as volunteers, they get paid with kudos. The practice of derek eretz requires ego deflation.

If we act according to God's will, we understand that others' opinions of us are none of our business. We no longer have skin like Velcro. Nothing sticks to us, neither praise nor insult. Our skin becomes like Teflon. Remember, Moshe Rabbeinu, Moses our Teacher, could not please everyone, and neither will we. The only One we are truly accountable to is God. Gaining the approval of others is just icing on the cake.

CHAPTER ONE, VERSE 5

An ordinary man shall be considered to your eyes great, if you have insulted him, until you have asked him to forgive you. If others say something bad about you, even if it is of a serious nature, treat it as insignificant. On the other hand, if you say something bad about others, even if it is insignificant, you should regard it as serious and have no rest until you beg pardon. Your behavior shall not be bad, for this is no praise for the Torah, which you possess, but let your behavior be good, for this is praise for the Torah.

Our rabbis admitted they were human. Sometimes they hurt others, and sometimes they were hurt by others. Verse 1:5 tells us that human beings haven't changed much in 2500 years.

It is impossible to get through life without encountering someone who treats us with disrespect or tries to cause us harm. It is equally impossible, even if we pray every day to do God's will, not to slip and allow the *yetzer ha ra*, the ego, to rule us, and to end up hurting someone else.

Let's examine the last line first:

Your behavior shall not be bad, for this is no praise for the Torah, which you possess, but let your behavior be good, for this is praise for the Torah.

The purpose of our Holy texts is to teach us *ahavath chesed*, loving kindness. Again, to paraphrase Rabbi Hillel (ca. 100 BCE), all of Torah, all of Judaism, is meant to teach that what is hateful to us, we should not do to another (*Shabbat 31a*). Rabbi Akiva (ca. 100 CE), said that to love our fellows is the most important mitzvah in the Torah (*Kidoshim 4*). Akiva further said: "He who esteems himself highly on account of his knowledge is like a corpse lying on the wayside: the traveler turns his head away in disgust, and walks quickly by" (*Avot of Rabbi Nathan*). We can quote the Torah from the last letter in Deuteronomy, *lamed*, to the first letter in Genesis, *beit*, but if we don't have a loving heart, we haven't learned anything from our Torah studies (lamed-beit spells the Hebrew word for 'heart').

When we hurt another, we do *chillul ha Shem*—we hollow out God's Holy name. We possess Torah to teach us how to behave. When we misbehave, we curse Torah as well as God.

> *If one has been guilty of profaning God's name, chillul ha Shem, then penitence has no power to suspend punishment nor Yom Kippur to procure atonement, nor suffering to*

finish it, but all of them together suspend the punishment and only death finishes it. As it is said: "And the Lord of hosts revealed Himself in my ears; surely this iniquity shall not be expiated by you until you die" (Is. 22:44).

—Yoma 8a

The Gemara continues:

You shall love the Lord your God (Deut. 6:5) that the name of Heaven shall become beloved through you. But as for one who learns [Scripture], studies [Mishna], and serves Torah scholars, but his business transactions are not conducted faithfully, and whose manner of speaking with people is not pleasant—what do people say about him? "Woe unto his father who taught him Torah; woe unto his teacher who taught him Torah. See how perverse are his deeds and how ugly are his ways." Regarding him Scripture says: "They came among the nations... and they profaned My holy name when it was said of them, 'These are the people of the Lord, but they departed His land'" (Ez. 36:20).

Judaism takes the mistreatment of others extremely seriously. One never sees part of the Talmud damning someone to hell for failing to eat kosher or to keep the Sabbath.

Why is Parashat Mishpatim, which is about the mitzvot between one person and another, immediately after Parashat Yitro, in which we read about the giving of the Torah? The Talmudic sage Rabbi Chanina ben Dosa put it best: "If the spirit of one's fellow is pleased with him, the spirit of God is pleased with him; but if the spirit of one's fellow is not pleased with him, the spirit of God is not pleased with him" (*Pirkei Avot 3:15*). Thus, Mishpatim appears right after the giving of the Torah to emphasize the importance of mitzvot that pertain to proper conduct and love.

Rabbi Yechezkel of Kuzmir said: "People are compared to a box full of glass dishes. If the dishes are packed tightly, the box can be moved about and transported, and none of the dishes will break. But if the dishes are packed loosely and bang into each other, they will easily break."

Our behavior must be good, so that we don't harm anyone (and harm ourselves in the process). We must also behave well in order to praise Torah, God, and the way of life taught by Judaism.

If others say something bad about you, even if it is of a serious nature, treat it as insignificant. On the other hand, if you say something bad about others, even if it is insignificant, you should regard it as serious and have no rest until you beg pardon.

No matter how well we live our lives, others will treat us badly and behave unpleasantly toward us. The more spiritually centered we become, the more we frighten others; they know that the way we are living is the way that they should be living.

The media love to see an evangelical TV preacher or a group of Haredi Orthodox rabbis get busted in a scandal. Some folks use this as an excuse to paint all clergy or spiritually connected people as dishonest.

We must ignore those who say negative things about us. They are jealous, fearful, selfish, arrogant, and spiritually disconnected. Pray for them. If, God forbid, we who try to live spiritually, with derek eretz, do speak lashon ha ra, even if a minor remark, we shouldn't rest until we have made teshuvah.

Love the Law, and respect it; love all creatures, and respect them. Subject your will to the will of others, as was done by Leah for Rachel, and by David for Saul. But ignore your will, and even the will of others, for the will of Heaven, as we find that Jacob did not kiss Joseph (because he was engaged in prayer). Love doubtfulness (i.e., everything shall be doubtful to you until you convince yourself of it), and hate the expression: "And what of it?" (i.e., even of the most unimportant things you should not express yourself thus). Keep aloof from everything that may bring you to sin, and from the abominable, and from what is equal to it, so that others do not suspect you of transgression. Do not slander your neighbor, because he who does so has no remedy. Keep aloof from grumbling, for by grumbling you may come to growl at others, and it will be added to your transgressions. With seven patriarchs covenants were made, and they are: Abraham [Gen. xv. 18], Isaac [ibid. xvii. 21], Jacob [Lev. xxvi. 421], Moses [Ex. xxxiv. 271], Aaron [Numb. xviii. 19], Pinchas [ibid. xxv. 12], and David [Ps. lxxxix. 41]. Seven patriarchs are resting in glory, and worm and maggot do not affect their earthly remains, and they are: Abraham, Isaac, Jacob, Moses, Aaron, Amram their father, and, according to others, also David, as it is written [ibid. xvi. 9]: "Therefore is rejoiced my heart, and my spirit is glad; also my flesh shall rest in safety." Nine entered the Garden of Eden while they were still alive, and they are: Enoch (Chanoch) the son of Jared, Elijah Messiah, Eliezer the bondsman of Abraham, Hirom the king of Zor, Ebed-melech the Cushi [Jer. xxxviii. 7], and Jabetz the son of R' Yehudah the Prince, Bothiah the daughter of Pharaoh, and Serech the daughter of Asher, and according to others, also R' Yehoshua b. Levi.

Love the Law, and respect it

What is 'the Law'? Unfortunately, the word Torah has been poorly translated into English. We hear of Moses the Law Giver; his *bas relief* is chiseled on the façade of the building that houses the United States Supreme Court. In non-Jewish texts, the word *rabbi* is often translated as 'lawyer'. In Hebrew, however, the word *torah* means 'instruction.' In the traditional rabbinic sense, Torah includes both written and oral portions, both of which were given to Moses at Sinai. The rabbis did not reveal or teach the Oral Torah until circa 586 BCE, during Babylonian captivity.

Why do we need not only to study Torah, but to love and respect it? "The world only exists because of the breath of children learning Torah in school" (*Shabbat 119b*). Torah preceded God's creation of the universe; He used Torah as

His blueprint (*Shabbat 88b*). Torah, deeds of loving kindness, and prayer sustain the world (*Pirkei Avot 1:3*).

In ancient transcriptions, such as those found in the 1500-year-old Jewish community of Kaifeng, China, in the 2500-year-old Jewish community of India's Malabar Coast, and the 2000-year-old Dead Sea Scrolls of the Jewish sect of the Essenes, not one copy differs by so much as a single letter. Rabbi Yishmael cautions his student Meir (who becomes the great Rabbi Meir), as Meir transcribes a new Torah scroll: "My son, be careful in your work, for your work is Heavenly. If you delete even one letter or add even one letter, you may destroy the whole world!" (*Eruvin 13a*).

The Torah is a Tree of Life, *Aitz Chaim*, to those who grasp onto it firmly (*Prov. 3:18*). We first encounter the Tree of Life in Genesis 2:9. It is one of two special trees in the Garden of Eden; the other is the Tree of the Knowledge of Good and Evil. The fruit of the second tree is forbidden to Adam. Eve eats from the Tree of Good and Evil, and Adam soon follows her example. Consequently, they lose their angelic purity, and become human. They acquire a *yetzer tov*, a good inclination, and a *yetzer ha ra*, an evil inclination.

Our Midrash tells us God intends for Adam and Eve to eat from the Tree of the Knowledge of Good and Evil, but not until after they eat from the Tree of Life. In other words, God wants them to first learn the ethical and spiritual message of the Torah, so that they will be able to listen to the yetzer tov and ignore the yetzer ha ra. Torah provides instructions for living a happy and joyous life. When we understand its value, we cannot fail to love and respect Torah and its Giver.

Love all creatures, and respect them.

The Torah contains many passages regarding the fair treatment of animals. For example, two animals that differ in strength must not be forced to pull the same wagon, because the smaller animal cannot keep up with the larger (*Deut. 22:10*). We are forbidden to prevent an ox from eating while it works in the field (*Deut. 25:4*). Animals are allowed to partake of the produce from fields that lie fallow during the Sabbatical Year (*Ex. 23:11*). Animals rest on Shabbat, as humans do (*Ex. 20:10*); we cannot ask the dog to fetch the newspaper on Shabbat. One who races pigeons cannot serve as a witness in a trial (*Sanhedrin 24b–25b*). The Talmud beautifully illustrates Jewish spirituality with the instruction to feed our animals before we feed ourselves. We can get our own food; our animals cannot (*Berachot 40a*). The Talmud also tells us not to purchase an animal until we buy its food and prepare a place for it to live. One of the kindest commandments in the Torah is to move a hen away from her nest before taking her eggs (*Deut. 22:6–7*).

Although Judaism is not a vegetarian religion, we learn in Genesis 9:3 that humankind was vegetarian until after the Flood. When we read the Torah, Talmud, and Midrash, and see how horribly humans treated each other and their farm animals, we understand Judaism doesn't say that vegetarianism *alone* makes one a better person. From the Midrash we learn that in the Messianic Age, humans will become vegetarian again (per Rav. Avraham Kook, based on Isa. 11:6–9), but will not be vegan. We will live in a *sukkah shalom*, a dwelling of peace, made from the skins of the Leviathan. We actually say a prayer to this effect on the last night of Sukkot: *Kein ez'keh l'shanah haba'ah leisheiv b'sukat oro shel Liv'yatan*—May I merit next year to dwell in the sukkah of the hide of the Leviathan (*Talmud Bavli Tractate Sukkot*).

The Talmud is filled with recipes, most of which explain how to cook vegetables and grains. Bread is the main course, so we say a *berachah*, a blessing to God, to thank Him for bringing forth (*motzi*) bread (*lechem*) from the earth (*ha eretz*). A blessing for bread covers all food other than wine. Rarely do we say a blessing for meat (only when it is served without bread.) Meat was a precious and limited resource reserved for Shabbatot and Yom Tovim (sabbaths and holidays). Blood and milk sustain life; thus, the Torah asks us not to eat meat and milk together.

The kosher method of slaughtering animals was far ahead of its time. Judaism asks us to take life from animals only on rare occasions. The man who brought a cow or lamb for slaughter would first make certain his knife was sharp and had no nicks. He would then cut the animal's jugular vein quickly.

All animals lived free range. Our rabbis could not have imagined the so-called kosher death factories that exist today. Although quick slaughter complies with the letter of the law, it does not fulfill the spirit of the law. An animal must be treated with loving kindness for as long as it lives. The workers must be treated with justice as well.

"A righteous man knows the soul of his animal" (*Proverbs 12:10*). Jewish law requires us to prevent *tza'ar ba'alei chayim*, the suffering of living creatures. The ancient *Chazal*, the sages, understood what psychiatrists and criminal behaviorists have since proven: one who harms a helpless animal is more likely to harm a helpless human.

The Talmud tells the story of our great rabbi, Judah Ha-Nasi, who was punished with years of kidney stones and other painful ailments because he was insensitive to the fear of a calf being led to slaughter. He cruelly told the calf: "Go—for this purpose you were created." He was relieved years later from his illness when he showed kindness to baby weasels (*Bava Metzia 85a*). If we are supposed to treat weasels with kindness, how much greater is the demand to treat other humans with kindness?

Subject your will to the will of others, as was done by Leah for Rachel, and by David for Saul.

One of our highest values is *shalom*, peace. "*Gadol ha shalom*," the Midrash Rabbah teaches: "Great is peace." One of God's names is Shalom (*Shabbat 10a*).

To use a mundane example of *shalom bayit*, peace at home, if my wife and I are watching TV, and she wants to watch one show and I another, I agree to watch her show with her, rather than go to a different room to watch my show on another set. Good relationships trump individual will and wants.

We see a great example of this with Abraham and Lot. Their herds have grown, and Lot believes they need to go their separate ways. Abraham handles the situation calmly and lovingly: "'Let's not have any quarreling between you and me, or between your herders and mine, for we are brothers. Is not the whole land before you? Let's part company. If you go to the left, I'll go to the right; if you go to the right, I'll go to the left'" (*Gen. 13:8–9*).

Abraham calls Lot his brother, but Lot was actually Abraham's nephew. We are to treat all of our fellows as siblings. As Malichi says: "Have we all not one Father? Hath not one God created us? Why should we deal treacherously, every man against his brother?" (*Mal. 2:10*). Yet how many of us can tell stories of siblings who no longer speak to one another because of fights over family estates?

In Verse 1:6 we learn of two Biblical figures who make their wills secondary to the wills of others. Leah and David begin full of ego, living according to the philosophy 'my way or the highway,' thus it is significant that they change their behavior.

Leah continually competes with her sister Rachel. She steals Rachel's husband, and seeks to produce more sons for him than Rachel does. In Chapter 30 of Genesis, we find Leah with six sons. Her maid has two, and Rachel's maid has two. Leah is pregnant again. She knows Jacob wants and *will have* twelve sons. If Leah gives birth to a seventh son, Rachel can have one at most. As a result, Rachel's status will fall below the maids'. Leah prays to God for a miracle, and God changes the male fetus she carries into a female.

Leah gives birth to Dinah for Rachel's sake. Rachel goes on to bear Joseph and Benjamin (*Berachot 60a*).

Saul is the old king, and David will become the new king. A civil war occurs in Judea. Each man tries to kill the other. David and his men hide in a cave in Ein Gedi. Saul, who does not know they are there, enters the cave, one of hundreds in Ein Gedi, to urinate (the Torah euphemistically says "cover his feet"). David has the opportunity to kill Saul, but he doesn't. While Saul is concentrating on the task at hand, David sneaks up and cuts a piece of Saul's robe (*I Sam. 24:1–6*). David puts Saul's will to live above his own will to win the war.

Many business relationships and marriages end with strife, *makloket*. To avoid strife is a Torah mitzvah, as we are commanded not to be like Korach (*Num. 17:05, Sanhedrin 110A*). Because of ego, people fight over the silliest things. This can destroy long-term relationships and wreak havoc upon synagogues and other organizations.

But ignore your will, and even the will of others, for the will of Heaven, as we find that Jacob did not kiss Joseph (because he was engaged in prayer).

This line troubles me a bit, for Berachot 19b–20a teaches that all negative mitzvot are set aside for the honor or well-being of another. In the Torah, Gen. 18:1, we see that Abraham interrupts his prayer, meditation, and conversation with God to attend to the needs of three travelers who are hot, tired, and hungry.

When we study Tractate Berachot we find many rules against interrupting prayer, but the rabbis decide that although we cannot begin a long conversation, we certainly should stop for a second to say shalom to another. They tell the story of Rabbi Yehoshua ben Perachiah (ca. 88 BCE) who was engrossed in prayer. A student approached to greet him, but the rabbi ignored him. The student took this as a rebuff, left Rabbinic Judaism for Hebraism, and became an enemy of the Jews and their rabbis (*Sotah 47a*).

Judaism teaches that there are two situations in which God's will trumps our will to live. The first is if we are asked to participate in rape or incest. We should rather die. The second is if we are told we have to kill someone (this does not refer to war, nor to a *rodef*, stalker). The Talmud tells us that no one's blood is redder than another's. We should rather die than kill another innocent person (*Pesachim 25b*).

The early sages taught of a third circumstance: if one is forced to worship another God. Soon it became clear that life is more important. If someone puts a sword to our throats and tells us to convert, we convert. The purpose of *Kol Nidre* (All Vows), a prayer on Erev Yom Kippur, is to negate forced conversions.

To ignore the will of others for the will of Heaven means that when our friends say to us, 'Hey, we are at the Super Bowl, our wives are back home, let's go…,' God's will for us comes first, and we decline.

The story of Channah and her seven sons, each of whom died one at a time because they wouldn't eat pork, is

Hebraic, not Judaic (*2 Mac. 7:2*). If someone puts a gun to our head and demands that we eat pork, we eat it.

In my opinion, Jacob's refusal to interrupt his prayer to kiss his son Joseph (whom he hadn't seen in many years and believed to be dead) is Hebraic and foolish, not Judaic and loving. When Jacob and Joseph meet after 22 years of separation, Joseph falls on Jacob's neck and weeps greatly and continuously. Rashi explains, however, that Jacob does not fall on Joseph's neck and does not kiss him. Instead, he says the *Shema* (*Genesis 46:29*). The Ramban disagrees; he says Jacob does fall on and kiss Joseph's neck, because a parent's love for his child is greater than a child's love for his parent. Note that the *Shema* is given to the Hebrews in Deuteronomy, during the last month of Moses' life and in the final weeks the Hebrews remain in the Wilderness. The above kissing event takes place before Joseph dies, about 400 years before the Hebrews become slaves.

The Talmud repeatedly teaches that when we follow our own will, we live with dread. We step on the toes of others, and they retaliate. We live like wild dogs, constantly watching and marking our territory. Our will, the ego, is mismanaged by the *yetzer ha ra*, the inclination to do ill.

I use this prayer at least three times a day: "Make that His will should be your will, so that He should make your will to be as His will. Nullify your will before His will," (*Pirkei Avot 2:4*). If I do not ask God for His help to do His will rather than my will, I will make a mess of things with my puny wants.

We learn from this part of *Derek Eretz Zuta* 1:6 that Judaism wants us to put the honor, wishes, respect, and love of others before our own will.

Love doubtfulness (i.e., everything shall be doubtful to you until you convince yourself of it)

One of the greatest gifts given to us by God is wisdom, according to Rabbi Ibn Paquda, in *Duties of the Heart*, written 950 years ago. God endowed us with sophisticated faculties of perception and intelligence. Wisdom is the life of mans' spirit and the light of our intellect. It leads us to be able to discern for ourselves.

Paquda teaches that blind faith in the existence of God is not Judaic. We must use our intelligence, wisdom, and rationality to arrive at the conclusion that God exists and that He is One. Our love of doubtfulness, if doubt leads us to investigate, brings us to *emet*, truth.

Note that the verse says 'everything.' We are not meant to passively accept the opinions expressed by television pundits today, just as we were not meant to accept rabbinic sermons 950 years ago. We are to study, explore, ask why, and ask for proof. The concept of a guru or rebbe providing all the answers is not Judaic. Our rabbis should challenge us, teach us how to study, teach us to question, and if we walk out of their classes more confused than when we entered, so much the better. Judaism was not meant to be a religion in which we attend a Shabbat service once a week, or maybe even once a month, listen to a sermon, and accept it as truth. The love of doubtfulness—the love of critical thinking—leads us to the love of study.

Dogma is the established belief or doctrine held by a religion. It is authoritative and not to be disputed, doubted, or diverged from by the practitioner or believer. Our Talmudic rabbis disputed, doubted, diverged, and disagreed on most everything. Dogma doesn't exist in *pure* Judaism. In Morocco, in 1166, the Rambam wrote his creed for Judaism, listing 13 dogmata. His fellow rabbis rallied against him. His *Principles of Faith* were controversial when first proposed, evoking criticism by both Rabbi Hasdai Crescas and Rabbi Joseph Albo, and were effectively ignored by much of the Jewish community for the next few centuries.

Without study, we cannot truly stand for our beliefs. When we don't stand for something, we will fall for anything. Much of what many accept as fact, *vis a vis* Judaism, or Jewish history, is misinformation. Yet we may make our choices, even write checks for causes, based on false data. It has been quipped that most people would rather die than think, and most unfortunately do.

According to R' Meir, when one studies Torah for its own sake, *torah lishma*, the creation of the entire world is worthwhile for him alone, and he brings joy to God (*Pirkei Avot 6:1*). Just as a child must satisfy his hunger day by day, so must a grown man busy himself with the Torah each hour (*Berachot Ch. 9*). A single day devoted to Torah outweighs 1,000 sacrifices (*Shabbat 30a; Menachot 100a*). According to R' Meir, a Gentile who studies the Torah/Bible is as great as the High Priest (*Avodah Zarah 3a*).

In the fable of *The Fish and the Fox*, the latter seeks to entice the former to dry land. Israel cannot live without Torah, as a fish cannot live outside of the ocean (*Berachot*

61b). So, too, a democracy cannot flourish if citizens are not well-informed by their own intellectual pursuits, but instead intravenously receive so-called facts while plugged into entertainment-news channels. We are to love doubtfulness, as doubt leads us to truth and certainty.

...and hate the expression: "And what of it?" (i.e., even of the most unimportant things you should not express yourself thus).

These words were written over 2000 years ago. How often do we hear folks today respond to others with expressions like, 'too much information,' 'so what,' or 'whatever'? Each of these expressions translates to 'I don't care,' or 'I don't have time for you.' Derek Eretz advises us to hate these expressions, because what seems unimportant to us may be quite important to someone else.

In Hebrew, the words for mute (*elem*) and violence (*alimut*) have the same root. When we do not listen to our friends' concerns, when we mute them, we lead them to frustration and potentially to violence. How many times have we heard of a suicide leaving a note stating that no one would listen to him? Active listening is an act of ahavath chesed. Telling someone 'and what of it?' or 'whatever' trivializes his concerns and separates him from us.

Active listening requires the listener to interpret and evaluate what he hears. It is a structured way to listen and respond, with our attention focused on the speaker. We put aside our own frame of reference, suspend judgment, and avoid other internal mental activities in order to fully attend to the speaker.

Although Dr. Thomas Gordon (1918–2002, United States) popularized the term 'active listening,' the ancient sages of Talmudic Judaism taught and practiced it. The ability to listen actively can improve personal relationships by reducing conflict, strengthening cooperation, and fostering understanding.

Do not slander your neighbor, because he who does so has no remedy.

The rabbis note that the universe was created through speech. Thus, Judaism is intensely aware of the power of speech and of the harm that can be done through speech. Of the 43 sins enumerated in the *Al Cheit* confession recited on Yom Kippur, eleven are sins committed through speech. The Talmud tells us that the tongue is an instrument so dangerous that it must be kept hidden from view, behind two protective walls (the mouth and teeth) to prevent its misuse.

Aside from murder and a few other sins, lashon ha ra is one for which it is impossible to make complete teshuvah. The harm caused by speech is worse than the harm done by theft or by cheating someone financially: money lost can be repaid, but the harm done by speech can never be repaired. For this reason, some sources indicate that there is no forgiveness for disparaging speech.

Although this is probably hyperbole, Judaism takes improper speech very seriously. A Chasidic tale vividly illustrates the danger: A man went about the community telling malicious lies about the rabbi. Later, he realized the wrong he had done, and began to feel remorse. He went to the rabbi and begged his forgiveness, saying he would do anything he could to make amends. The rabbi told the man, "Take a feather pillow, cut it open, and scatter the feathers to the winds." The man thought this was a strange request, but the task was simple enough, and he did it gladly. When he returned to report that he had completed it, the rabbi said, "Now, go and gather the feathers. Because you can no more make amends for the damage your words have done than you can collect the feathers."

The person who listens to gossip is worse than the gossiper, because no harm could be done by gossip if no one listened to it. In a spiritual sense, lashon ha ra kills three: the person who speaks it, the person who hears it, and the person about whom it is told (*Arachin 15b*).

Parasha Tazria, Leviticus 12:01–13:59, is entirely devoted to gossip. In this Torah portion we read of various dermatological conditions known as *tsaraat* in Hebrew. *Tsaraat* was mistranslated into Greek and eventually into our English vernacular as 'leprosy.' The chapters describe not only skin eruptions but discolorations on clothing and the walls of homes. These scaly lesions rendered one impure. Only our priests were able to diagnose and treat the maladies. A person afflicted with *tsaraat* was called a *metzora*. Any dermatologist today who has read this portion can tell you that the conditions described were not what we now know as leprosy (Hansen's Disease). Certainly, skin conditions do not spread to our clothes or to the walls of our homes. Both Talmud and Midrash tell us that something else is going on here. Whether we believe that our sages had the answer to this puzzle or simply wish to learn some good life lessons from their explanation, the traditional teachings deserve a retelling. The lessons from them are as fresh today as when they were written.

The Midrash (*Vayikra Rabba 16:02*) states that the word *metzora* comes from *motzi shem ra*, to make a bad name—that is, a slanderer, one who defames with lies. *Rechilus*, or tale bearing, comes from the word regal (foot), as one who bears tales is like a peddler of gossip. We cannot tell Person A that Person B said something bad about him. *Lashon ha ra* is defamatory but true speech about someone. One who indulges in evil talk will be afflicted with *tsaraat*. Judaism teaches that gossip is not a victimless crime. Bad speech destroys marriages, friendships, businesses, congregations, and even lives. The Midrash says that God gave us earlobes to fold over our ears when someone speaks lashon ha ra. The Talmud tells us that our Second Temple was destroyed, and we are in exile, because of it (*Yoma 9b, Gitin 57b*).

One violates fourteen positive mitzvot and seventeen negative mitzvot when one speaks or listens to gossip. For example, do not be a talebearer (*Lev. 19:16*), do not give a false report (*Ex. 23:01*), judge your fellow with righteousness (*Lev. 19:15*), and so forth. We wandered in the desert for forty extra years because we believed the false reports of the spies, who spoke lashon ha ra against the land of Israel.

"Who is the person who desires life [*chofetz chaim*]? He who guards his tongue from evil and his lips from speaking deceit" (*Psalm 34*). Rabbi Israel Kagan wrote a wonderful text called *Guarding the Tongue*. His rules on lashon ha ra, which he begins with the above quote from King David, earned Rabbi Kagan the honorific Chofetz Chaim.

There are six basic rules on how to guard one's tongue. Rabbi Z. Pliskin's text called *Guard Your Tongue* is excellent for an overview of this topic, as is Rabbi Joseph Telushkin's book *Words that Hurt, Words that Heal*.

We cannot say bad things about someone even if it is true, and even if the news is in the media. We cannot make any comment that can cause someone anguish, pain, financial loss, etc., even if it is not derogatory. Any method we use to do these things, other than with our tongues, is forbidden, such as writing, e-mailing, hand gestures, facial expressions, etc. We cannot say mean things, even in kidding. We cannot even badmouth ourselves. One exception: We are obligated to warn a potential bride or groom, or someone going into a business deal, if we know information firsthand that will save them from harm or cheating.

The Midrash (*Devarim Rabbah 5:10*) teaches, "Whoever speaks lashon ha ra causes the Shechinah [God's presence] to depart from this world." In Talmud Arachin 15b, it is written that God says that He and the gossiper cannot dwell together in the same world. King Solomon states, "Six things are hated by God, and the seventh is despised by Him: haughty eyes, a tongue of falsehood, hands which shed innocent bloods...and one who incites quarrels among brothers" (*Prov. 6:16–19*). King Solomon also says, "One who guards his mouth and tongue, guards his soul from tribulations" (*Prov. 21:23*).

In Chofetz Chaim's second lesson he writes that it is forbidden to relate that someone has been remiss in matters of Jewish observance, whether it is a rabbinic law, a Torah commandment, or just custom. It is forbidden to mention an incident in which a law was broken, even in a society where that *halakhah* (Jewish law) is commonly ignored. It is lashon ha ra for us to say Mr. Cohen eats pork, or Mrs. Levine spent money on Shabbat. It is also lashon ha ra for one to badmouth an entire community—to say, for example, that members of Congregation B'nei Korach are not real Jews because they are Reform.

The next time you see someone engage in gossip, watch as he looks around to make sure that no one observes him. He is very concerned that the subject of his defamation cannot hear him. In Talmud Arachin 15b, Rabbi Yochanan says that whoever speaks lashon ha ra denies the existence of God. He quotes Psalm 12:05: "With our tongues we shall prevail, our lips are with us, who is master over us?" A *metzora* has no concern that God is watching him.

The power we wield when we speak goes far beyond what we can perceive. We think we are only exchanging words when, in fact, we can move worlds. Lashon ha ra is so powerfully poisonous that it is taught that God takes the good deeds accumulated by the gossiper and gives them to the subject of the gossip, as well as taking the sins of the subject and giving them to the gossiper. Ben Sira wrote, in the *Apocrypha Ecclesiasticus 19:10*: "Have you heard something? Let it die with you. Be strong. It will not burst you!"

A gossip will not hesitate to speak lashon ha ra about his confidants. Few who denigrate or arbitrarily dislike someone will remain loyal to others. Such individuals are enemy-centered. They are not happy unless they are opposing someone. The *metzora* (our modern bad-mouther) had to warn others that he was 'unclean,' and was required to live outside of the community (*Lev. 13:45–46*). These folks can poison our congregations, sisterhoods, and men's clubs, and prevent civil, decent people, who do not wish to keep their earlobes pulled up, from participating. If we wish our congregations to pursue life, to grow, to be strong, we need to teach the self-made *metzorim* how much damage they cause.

Choose your companions wisely, so that you can pursue life, and not diminish your spirit. Let us do the best we can to *shmirat ha lashon*, guard our mouths, and think kinder thoughts about one another. We are all brothers and sisters, God's children on His earth.

Keep aloof from grumbling, for by grumbling you may come to growl at others, and it will be added to your transgressions.

When we grumble and complain of our lot in life, whether because of temporary setbacks or because we negatively perceive the totality of our experience, we live as ingrates. We view the cup not as half-empty, but as completely empty. We are Godless, and only call upon God to damn Him.

When we are spiritually disconnected, we become disconnected from our fellows. We complain about the people in our lives—our parents, spouses, friends, children, employers, co-workers, employees, teachers, students, the mail carrier, and the waiter. The list becomes endless, because it begins with God, Who is Infinite.

To approach life with the attitude 'what have you done for me lately?' is to stand on a slippery slope. Complaints about others result in hatred, jealousy, or both. Bad relationships ensue. Envy may lead us to steal or otherwise harm one another. Such strife stems from the thought that we are not getting our way, or that we have not been given enough. We may believe we had something that was taken from us, or perhaps we wanted something that we didn't get.

We need to learn to develop a true 'attitude of gratitude.' We do this by thanking God throughout the day for everything—our meals, our friends, our jobs, our health, our families. When a flat tire makes us late and results in an unexpected expense, we can laugh about it, because we recognize that the incident is one inconvenience out of 1000 blessings. Furthermore, we can thank God that we were able to pull over and avoid crashing into a tree.

Learning to pray is not an overnight process; prayer is never fully mastered. Prayer is the way we speak to God and to the spark of God within ourselves. God listens, and there is really no wrong way to talk to God, as long we speak to Him with sincerity.

King David said that we should be so spiritual as to bless God at least 100 times a day (*Menachot 43a*). He meant that we should bless God not only for our meals, but for the singing birds, our first breath in the morning, all of the beauty in the world, and the list goes on. The name Jew, *Yahudee*, means 'grateful.'

The Talmud takes David's idea and makes a list of the ritually-ordained prayers for traditional Jews, of which there are about 20 just for saying grace after three meals—60 blessings right off the bat. Another 40 come from three daily prayer services, and others are said when we wash our hands, awake in the morning, and so forth.

In Jewish spiritual renewal, while it is a grand idea to learn the prayers developed by our sages and set forth in the first book of Talmud (Berachot), the sages teach that one should not learn them by rote. Instead, we should use the prayer book as a starting point from which to pray to God in our own words with true intention (*Berachot 5a*). True spiritual intention is called *kavenah*.

It is not *kavenah* to mumble through a *motzi* (the prayer thanking God for bread) without reflection. It is *kavenah*, and it is Jewish, to thank God from our hearts and souls for the meal we're about to eat, and for the friends and family gathered around us. Tractate Berachot further teaches that it is better to pray in a language we understand than in one we don't. This is not an excuse to drop Hebrew study, but the sages wish to convey that prayer is a personal communication between the individual and God. Kavenah is not found in the words, but in the honesty behind the words.

Praying with true intention makes us feel grateful for all of God's gifts. When we thank God throughout the day for everything, even the littlest things, we recognize how rich we truly are. The times when we don't get what we want will seem insignificant by comparison, and we will be less likely to be upset. Blessings of thanksgiving are called *berachot*, from the root word meaning 'to bend the knee.'

Into the time of the Babylonian exile, Jews prayed on their knees. They continued to do so when the exile was over and some returned to Jerusalem with Ezra. We also read that Solomon dedicated his Temple "kneeling down in the presence of all the multitude of Israel, and lifting up his hands towards Heaven" (*II Chronicles 6:13, I Kings 8:54*).

"I fell upon my knees, and spread out my hands to the Lord my God" (*Ezra 9:5*). "Opening the windows in his upper chamber towards Jerusalem, he knelt down three times a day, and adored, and gave thanks before his God, as he had been accustomed to do before" (*Dan. 6:10*).

You won't find many Jews praying on our knees today. We stopped kneeling when our Christian breakaway brothers continued to do so. We do bend the knee and bow when we stand during certain parts of the synagogue service. We kneel or bow our heads because we are praying to the King of all humanity. Would you have the *chutzpah* to stay seated if the President of the United States walked into the room? Of course not. In a courtroom, as the judge takes the bench, do you not stand when the bailiff orders, "All rise!"? Of course you do. Yet for God, so many people remain seated, denying His existence as their King and their Judge. Such a dearth of reverence does not lend itself to spirituality and a relationship with God. Whether you bend a knee and bow your head, or pray on your knees, choose a posture that you would only show to a supreme ruler with whom you trust your life.

With seven patriarchs covenants were made, and they are: Abraham, Isaac, Jacob, Moses, Aaron, Pinchas, and David.

A covenant is a solemn agreement to engage in, or to refrain from, a specified action. Commonly found in religious contexts, a covenant refers to a sacred agreement between God and human beings.

In the TaNaK there are many covenants. God makes a covenant with Adam and Eve, and all of humanity, after the expulsion from Eden. God also makes one with Cain after Abel's murder. After the Flood, God again makes a covenant with humanity through Noah. As we know, Adam, Eve, Cain, and Noah were not Hebrews, but the seven men listed above were.

Abraham's covenant is about a deed to land, a lot of land. "It was on that occasion that the Lord made a covenant with Abram, saying: 'To your descendants I give this land, from the River of Egypt to the Great River (the Euphrates), the land of the Kenites, the Kenizzites, the Kadmonites, the Hittites, the Perizzites, the Rephaim, the Amorites, the Canaanites, the Girgashites, and the Jebusites'" (*Gen. 15:18–21*).

If we recall ancient and current geography, Abraham and all of his descendants, Hebrew and Islamic alike, have just been granted a parcel of land that runs from the Nile in Egypt to the Euphrates in Iraq. The Hittite's land is what we now call Turkey, Lebanon, and Syria.

Later, in Genesis 17:8, the amount of land is reduced to Canaan. "I will give to you and to your descendants after you the land of your sojourning, all the land of Canaan, for an everlasting possession; and I will be their God." We see, however, during King Solomon's time, the land described in Chapter 15 of Genesis nearly comes under the control of Hebrews. "He [Solomon] ruled over all the kings from the Euphrates to the land of the Philistines, and to the border of Egypt" (*II Chron. 9:26*). We can understand why this covenant was especially important to the rabbis, who lived under Roman oppression after their Temple and Jerusalem were destroyed. They looked to the past for hope, in the form of God and a messiah, that one day the Jews could throw off the yoke of the Roman Empire.

Before Isaac's birth, God gives Isaac's covenant to Abraham: "I will establish my covenant with Isaac, whom Sarah shall bear to you at this time next year" (*Gen. 17:21*). According to the rabbis, this means the covenant will flow through Isaac's line. In the preceding verse God says: "As for Ishmael, I have heard you; behold, I have blessed him and will make him fruitful and multiply him greatly. He shall father twelve princes, and I will make him into a great nation." In the verse before that, God says, "Sarah your wife shall bear you a son, and you shall call his name Isaac. I will establish my covenant with him as an everlasting covenant for his offspring after him" (*ibid. 17:19*). Ishmael is effectively cut out of the Hebraic covenant, long before Sarah decides to banish him and his mother Hagar. Nevertheless, Ishmael and his descendants remain in the Abrahamic covenant, and the same God protects them.

Jacob's covenant appears in Leviticus 26:42: "I will remember my covenant with Jacob and my covenant with

Isaac and my covenant with Abraham, and I will remember the land." Chapter 26 lays out the contract between the Hebraic God and the Hebrews. Verse 42 comes near the end of the chapter. The chapter says, essentially, that if the Hebrews follow God's will, life will go well for them, but if they don't, they are going to be miserable. "I will turn your cities into ruins and lay waste your sanctuaries, and I will take no delight in the pleasing aroma of your offerings. I will lay waste to the land, so that your enemies who live there will be appalled. I will scatter you among the nations and will draw out my sword and pursue you. Your land will be laid waste, and your cities will lie in ruins" (*Lev. 26: 31–33*).

Judaism, unlike Hebraism, does not believe in a God who punishes on this earthly plain. Our actions in this lifetime can cause us misery, but we do it to ourselves. Judaism does believe in a God who judges in *Olam Ha Ba*, the World to Come, but even the most wicked person spends no more than a year in *Gehenna*. There, his soul is re-educated, and he eventually graduates to Heaven. The Talmud Sanhedrin states that all of Israel, all Jews, have a share in the World to Come.

The covenant with Moses comes from Exodus 34:27–28: "Then the Lord said to Moses, 'Write down these words, for in accordance with these words I have made a covenant with you and with Israel.' Moses was there with the Lord forty days and forty nights without eating bread or drinking water. And he wrote on the tablets the words of the covenant—the Ten Commandments." As we see in Ex. 31:16: "Let the children of Israel keep the Sabbath, and celebrate it in their generations. It is an everlasting covenant."

Aaron's covenant follows. From Numbers 18:19: "Whatever is set aside from the holy offerings the Israelites present to the Lord, I give to you and your sons and daughters as your regular share. It is an everlasting covenant of salt before the Lord for both you and your offspring." Salt means salary. (The word salary comes from the Roman word for salt.) Aaron and his sons become the Hebrew Priests.

Pinchas, the son of Eleazar, and one of Aaron's many grandsons, becomes a hero by killing a Hebrew and a foreign woman for having sex. The rabbis in the Talmud, however, are not pleased with Pinchas' vigilante justice. The rabbis have no respect for the priests during the Maccabean period (approximately 165 BCE to the fall of the Temple in 70 CE.) Pinchas receives his reward from the Hebraic God. "Therefore tell him I am making my covenant of peace with him. He and his descendants will have a covenant of a lasting priesthood, because he was zealous for the honor of his God and made atonement for the Israelites" (*Numbers 25: 12–3*).

David, the second King of the Hebrews, the first to unite the twelve tribes as a nation, receives his covenant in Psalm 89:3–4: "You said, 'I have made a covenant with my chosen one, I have sworn to David my servant, I will establish your line forever and make your throne firm through all generations.'" Hence, David's kingship is established, and passed to his son Solomon. Solomon's sons argue and split the nation in two. Many of the rabbis claim Davidic origins, and we know, of course, that the messiah of the Jews will come from the line of David.

Seven patriarchs are resting in glory, and worm and maggot do not affect their earthly remains, and they are: Abraham, Isaac, Jacob, Moses, Aaron, Amram their father, and, according to others, also David, as it is written [ibid. xvi. 9]: "Therefore is rejoiced my heart, and my spirit is glad; also my flesh shall rest in safety."

What does this mean? Everyone becomes food for maggots and worms (*Pirkei Avot 3:1*). If we interpret the above line as hyperbole, what the rabbis are telling us is that the seven men listed were *tzaddiks*, extremely righteous people, who came closer to sainthood than any other Hebrews. Hence, their bodies did not deteriorate.

The troubling part continues, because Judaism, unlike Hebraism, believes in corporeal resurrection during the Messianic Age. Judaism's Olam Ha Ba is one of souls, not of bodies. Why should it matter if their bodies were preserved? After all, when a body is buried according to Jewish tradition, it is not embalmed, so as to turn quickly to dust. It is my opinion that this section of Verse 1:6 may have originated before 70 CE, while Hebraism was still practiced.

We know about six of these men from bible stories we learned in Hebrew school. Why is Amram, the father of Moses, Aaron, and Miriam, listed here? If we include their father, why not include Jesse, the father of David, or Terach, the father of Abraham?

The Midrash Exodus Rabbah 1:17 says that when Pharaoh instructed the midwives to throw male children into the Nile, Amram divorced Yochebed. Although she was three months pregnant with Moses at the time, Amram saw no justification for Israelite men to father children who would then be killed. Miriam, his daughter, chided him for his indifference to his wife's feelings. She persuaded him to recant, and to re-marry Yochebed.

According to the Talmud, Amram promulgated the laws of marriage and divorce amongst the Jews in Egypt. The Talmud also indicates that Amram lived for a very long time, and used his life to ensure that doctrines were preserved through several generations. Despite the legend of his divorce and remarriage, Amram was held to be sinless. Thus, his corpse remained without any sign of decay (*Bava Batra 71a*).

Various Midrashim tell us the bodies of the other six men were also preserved: "I will ransom them from the power of the grave; I will redeem them from death: O death, I will be your plague; O grave, I will be your destruction…" (*Hosea 13:14*). The Christian Bible also hints at this.

None of these men—not even Amram, who was sinless, according to the Midrash—was truly sinless. Each did things that were not in the best interests of others. The Talmud provides Divine excuses for their behavior; nevertheless, they were flawed human beings. Abraham kicked Hagar and Ishmael out of his home. Isaac was *tam*, simple, and ineffectual at raising his sons. Jacob was a con artist. Moses had a temper; he beat a rock for water, and also beat an Egyptian to death. Aaron helped to make the Golden Calf. Pinchas murdered without giving Zimri the benefit of a trial. David had such bloody hands that God would not let him build the Temple. Amram left his wife while she was three months pregnant. Nevertheless, they also did much good. They were *good enough* to make covenants with, and to receive theophanies. When we are dead and buried, we hope that the good we did will be remembered, and will outweigh the bad.

Nine entered the Garden of Eden while they were still alive, and they are: Enoch (Chanoch) the son of Jared, Elijah Messiah, Eliezer the bondsman of Abraham, Hirom the king of Zor, Ebed-melech the Cushi [Jer. xxxviii. 7], and Jabetz the son of R' Yehudah the Prince, Bothiah the daughter of Pharaoh and Serech the daughter of Asher, and, according to others, also R' Yehoshua b. Levi.

Six of those allowed to enter Paradise were neither Hebrew nor Jewish. Two were converts. Three were *ba'alim teshuvah*. "The righteous of all nations, [i.e. religions], have a share in the world to come" (*Sanhedrin 105a*). Although other religions teach that theirs is the only way to salvation, Judaism is pluralistic.

Enoch, whose name means 'initiated,' lived righteously, acquired many disciples, helped others to make *teshuvah*, and brought peace as a spiritual leader. He is considered to have been so pious that the secrets of Heaven were revealed to him.

Elijah called for the repentance of Israel, fought injustice, and was a proponent of God.

Eliezer saved Abraham's life by warning him of Nimrod's ill intentions. He defended the vulnerable in Sodom. He developed the virtues of Abraham, and remained loyal to Torah.

Hirom aided Solomon in building the first Temple, and praised God by doing so. He was a friend to the Hebrews.

Ebed-melech, an Ethiopian slave, appealed to King Zedekiah on behalf of Jeremiah, thus saving Jeremiah's life. This allowed Jeremiah another opportunity to warn the last Hebrew king of Judah to report to Nebuchadnezzar.

Jabetz, a Kenite, converted to Hebraism. He demonstrated faith, honesty, and integrity. He became a Torah scribe and taught Torah.

Bothiah (Bithiah) opposed her father's call for the death of all Hebrew infants. She saved Moses from the Nile, raised him in the palace, and loved him as if he were her own child. She gave up the ways of her father, the Pharoah, and converted to Hebraism.

Serech displayed uncommon ahavath chesed. She gently informed Jacob that his son Joseph was still alive. She helped bring Jacob to Egypt. She guided the Israelites to trust Moses, and assisted Moses in finding Joseph's bones for the Exodus. She taught of God's redemption and saved many lives.

Rabbi Joshua ben Levi's rulings always demonstrated *chesed*, loving kindness. At a time when many rabbis wanted to curse Jews who belonged to the sect of Rabbi Yeshua ben Yosef (now called Christians), he taught of getting along with them. He interceded on behalf of the Hebrews at the proconsul in Caesarea, and saved the inhabitants of a besieged Lydda. He expressed pure love with his comment that the righteous of all nations have a share in the World to Come.

All of these people were righteous. They helped others find spirituality. They made peace. They fought for the rights of the common person. They demonstrated loyalty and humility, and got along well with others. When they were wrong, they made teshuvah. They went beyond the letter of the law, and treated others according to the spirit of the law, with *ahavath chesed*, loving kindness. (*For more information on the lives and works of these individuals, please refer to Appendix A.*)

Throughout both Talmuds and Midrashim, we learn that righteousness is not just a trait one develops by being a pious Jew. Righteousness comes from treating one another properly, regardless of background or status. No one is denied the opportunity to do mitzvot. If a Canaanite slave can do mitzvot, certainly Jewish women, Jewish homosexuals, the physically or mentally challenged, the spouses of Jews, *anusim* (those forced to convert), etc., can be active, equal members of a truly Talmudic rabbinic congregation and society.

Chapter Two

VERSE 1

Let all your ways be for the sake of Heaven. Love Heaven, and fear it. Tremble at, and at the same time, rejoice over all commandments. Sit before the elders, and let your ears be attentive to their words.

Live a life that is good and just. Love what is right, and try to live accordingly. Love, revere, and study our more than 2500 years of rabbinic ethical teachings. Follow them.

Although Judaism teaches we must seek out injustice and help to correct it, Derek Eretz tells us to first root out our own character defects. We must take stock of our lives, and decide we no longer wish to live as stars on Reality TV.

When we live with honesty, integrity, and altruism, we become spiritually connected to the Divine, and are able to hear advice that is universal and timeless.

CHAPTER TWO, VERSE 2

ncline your ears to the words of your comrade. Be not hasty in answering, and consider everything from the right point, and answer to the first question first, and to the last, last; and always confess the truth.

When it is our turn to speak, our sages advise us to let our brains and our souls work before we put our tongues in gear. To "consider everything from the right point" means to focus on the concerns of our friend, and to avoid redirecting the conversation to ourselves. We must do our best to respond to the points made or questions asked in the order presented, thereby to address our friend's most important thoughts first.

The sages counsel us not only to speak the truth, but to confess, *vidui*, the truth. Often we feel we are the only ones dealing with a particular issue. We may suffer from 'terminal uniqueness'. If a friend is going through a divorce, we can share our experiences with divorce to aid him in his time of trouble. We also show him *gam zeh ya'avor*—this too shall pass.

CHAPTER TWO, VERSE 3

Do not discuss in the presence of one who is greater than you in wisdom. If somebody wants to teach you something, do not say that you have heard it already. If you are questioned on the most unimportant matter, and you do not know it, do not be ashamed to say, "I do not know." If somebody taught you something and you did not listen to it, do not be ashamed to say, "Repeat it again"; and say not that you did not listen to it, but that you did not understand it.

The above verse is about observing the proper etiquette while studying. Whether we study Torah the traditional way, one-on-one with a wiser rabbi, or in the relatively new venue of a Jewish theological seminary with 50–100 students per class, or if we are in secular study, the lesson still holds true.

How many of us have been to a synagogue's Torah class, where instead of listening attentively to the rabbi, nearly everyone interrupts to express his opinion? Perhaps a student even quotes a 1000-year-old rabbinic commentary from the footnotes of the Chumash as if it were his own idea. I, too, have been guilty of such behavior. Many years ago, one of my rabbinic teachers told me to take the cotton out of my ears and to place it in my mouth.

Respect for teachers is an important Jewish value—so important that a younger rabbi is forbidden to disagree with his rabbi on a matter of *halakha*, Jewish law, until his teacher dies. When we are blessed to find a teacher who knows more than we do, we are to remain quiet and listen. "Let your home be a meeting place for the wise; dust yourself in the soil of their feet, and drink thirstily of their words" (*Pirkei Avot 1:4*).

Rabbi Hillel (100 B.C.E.) warns us that if we do not constantly advance our spiritual and academic understanding of Judaism, we actually regress (*Pirkei Avot 1:13*).

To admit we are not omniscient liberates and humbles us. Those who think they know everything eventually make fools of themselves. If we refrain from asking questions because we are worried about what the teacher or the other students will think of us, we jeopardize our learning. "A bashful one cannot learn" (*Pirkei Avot 2:5*). As we examine verse 2:3 as a whole, we see that learning begins with humility and ego deflation.

CHAPTER TWO, VERSE 4

Do everything for the sake of the Creator, and talk of your deeds in the same sense. Do not make your merits as a crown to be glorified by it, nor as a hatchet to cleave with it, nor as spade to dig with it.

This verse refers to the study of Scripture.

Do everything for the sake of the Creator, and talk of your deeds in the same sense.

Literally, the phrase *Torah lishma* means to study Torah for its name, or for its sake alone. Torah includes all of our spiritual texts.

"Rabbi Meir said: Anyone who engages in Torah study for its own sake [*lishma*] merits many things....He is called friend and beloved; he loves God, he loves man; he brings joy to God, he brings joy to man....He becomes modest, slow to anger, and forgiving of the wrongs done to him..." (*Pirkei Avot 6:1*).

We don't study Torah for selfish reasons. We study to grow closer to God, and to learn ahavath chesed. Being closer to God brings us closer to others. When we study for God's glory, we do not need to brag about the texts we have studied. King David rejoiced: "If not for Your Torah, my delight, I would have perished in my suffering" (*Ps. 119:92*).

The sages tell us that if a student says he wants to study to become a rabbi, he is disqualified. Furthermore, if he declares he has a Divine calling to study to become a rabbi, he is called *ra*, evil. R' Hillel taught: "One who makes personal use of the crown of Torah shall perish" (*Pirkei Avot 1:13*).

Unfortunately, we have all seen people with tremendous ego who use Scripture for their own gain. Eventually, they disappear. Sometimes they lose face on live television or in the headlines. "Rabban Yochanan...would say: If you have learned much Torah, do not take credit for yourself—it is for this that you have been formed" (*Pirkei Avot 2:8*).

Do not make your merits as a crown to be glorified by it

"Do not make the Torah a crown to magnify yourself with.... Hence, one who benefits selfishly from the words of Torah removes his life from the world" (Pirkei Avot 4:5).

Do not use the Torah as a hatchet to cleave with, nor as a spade to dig with

Based on Deuteronomy 33:4, which says, "The Torah that Moses commanded us is an inheritance of the congregation of Jacob," the rabbis conclude, in Talmud Bavli Sanhedrin 91b, that if someone refuses to teach Torah without payment, he is stealing another's inheritance.

Historically, our rabbis had worldly occupations. They were not beholden to synagogue boards; hence, they could teach true Judaism without fear of losing their livelihoods. The concept of a professional rabbi was not widely accepted until the 1800s, and in many circles is still considered improper. We see few, if any, rabbis on television hawking Torah for their own benefit, *baruch ha shem*. Websites do exist, however, on which we find rabbis offering to pray for us for a fee, or marketing so-called Kabbalah bracelets for an even larger fee. When the economy sours, and rabbis get laid off, we see them fight over what I call the crumbs of Judaism. These crumbs usually consist of fees for officiating at life cycle events.

Our Holy Scriptures are called *kadosh*, the Hebrew word for holy, which means 'to separate.' Although we may use texts such as *Gray's Anatomy*, *Black's Law*, the *Federal Tax Code*, or Van Dyke's *History of Painting* at work, the Scriptures are meant to elevate and separate us from the mundane.

Many sects of Judaism operate rabbinic unions, which are, in actuality, alumni societies. These groups declare that rabbis who haven't attended their programs are inferior to those who have. We are not behaving Jewishly when we treat other rabbis, sects, or congregations as competition, to be hacked at with hatchets or buried with shovels. Without derek eretz, one can't study Torah properly, or even be a rabbi (*Pirkei Avot 3:21*).

To use Torah as a hatchet or a spade can also mean to justify violence with Scripture. Pope Urban II announced, with the Bible in his hand, "Deus Vult" (God wills it), and launched the bloody Crusades. Osama bin Laden held a

Koran in one hand, yelling "Bismillah Arrahman Arraheem" (in the name of Allah, the most gracious, the most merciful), as he ignited a Jihad against the United States. We Jews are guilty, too, of using the Torah as a call for aggression. Prime Minister Rabin was killed by a Jew whose rabbi, quoting Talmud, called Rabin a "rodef," a stalker, against Israel, who "needed killing." A rabbi in southern New Jersey convinced a congregant that the rebbetzin was a rodef against Israel who also deserved to be killed. We must not use the Torah as a license for war.

CHAPTER TWO, VERSE 5

Accept the words of Torah, even when you are in affliction. Do not seek to wrong one who wronged you. Let your accounts always be correct, and your conduct excellent. Keep your promise. Love the Torah, righteousness, rebukes, straightforwardness.

The sages direct us in this verse to approach life with complete trust, faith, and belief in the Divine. Some of my students, even some of my fellow rabbis, admit they are agnostic, atheist, or humanist. Pure Judaism is fine with this, as what matters most is how we behave. Our lives go more smoothly when we follow the above recommendations.

Accept the words of Torah, even when you are in affliction. We can easily say that we love God when our lives go well. To say *Dayan Ha Emet*, to bless God as the True Judge when a loved one dies, takes more courage. We mere mortals will never understand God's ways.

When we accept that we live in God's universe, we believe that *gamzu l'tovah*, all is for the good. Everything works out—in God's time. When we believe the opposite, we become bitter, angry, mean-spirited individuals. We hate God, yet we deny God. We live in conflict with our fellows, on whom we take out our anger.

The commandments were not given to us for God's sake, but for our sake. Being in a spiritual mindset allows us to let go and let God take over. It sets us free. We recognize that the only things over which we have any control are our own thoughts and actions—our will. It is a delusion to think that we can manipulate or control anything else.

Do not seek to wrong one who wronged you.

The sages tell us not only not to wrong someone, but to not *seek* to wrong him.

Have you ever served on an organization's board with cantankerous, ego-driven folks who insist on having their way, who say awful things? Perhaps at night you lie in bed, unable to sleep, running videos in your head of the clever retorts you might have made. Maybe someone has harmed you, and you daydream about ways to get even. Thoughts like these are what the sages mean by "do not seek".

Those who harm others are arrogant and spiritually disconnected. They do not lose sleep thinking of us. Pray for them, as you would for anyone with a terminal illness.

Let your accounts always be correct, and your conduct excellent. Keep your promise.

The Torah commands us to keep accurate scales in business. We cannot own fraudulent weights, or use anything for the purpose of deceiving others. The Hebrew word for accounts, for inventory, is *chesbon*, as in our daily *chesbon ha nefesh*, in which we examine our souls to ensure our actions are correct. We must be principled in all of our affairs. Our personal relationships must be like the holy interactions Martin Buber describes in *I and Thou*. We must not relate to other human beings as if they are vehicles or obstacles to our goals.

Love the Torah

Judaism is more than a religion; it is a way of life. Why honor and remember Shabbat, if we turn the social hour after the service into an opportunity to speak lashon ha ra? By doing so, we negate the prayer to 'keep our tongues from evil,' and we erase all blessings for shalom. We need to love the Torah, for without her, the sages teach, we would have learned modesty, *tzni'ut*, from a cat (*Eruvin 100b*).

Righteousness

The Torah commands us to love righteousness, and to pursue justice. The command is repeated: *"Tzedek, tzedek tirdof"* (*Deut. 16:20*). Why? The Talmud explains that the first *tzedek* teaches us to judge by the letter of the law, and the second reminds us to live by the spirit of the law (*Shnay Luchot HaBrit, Shoftim 101a*).

When Jews stick to the letter of the law and forget the spirit, disaster results. Rabbi Johanan said: "Jerusalem was destroyed only because they gave judgments therein in accordance with Biblical law...they based their judgments strictly upon Biblical law, and did not go beyond the letter of the law" (*Bava Metzia 30b*).

Rebukes

To love rebuke can sometimes be difficult, but when rebuke is motivated by love, and given privately, as commanded, we are fortunate to receive it. To be open, *nevi*, requires humility and ego-deflation. In order to grow spiritually, we must learn to evaluate and accept instruction.

Straightforwardness

Straightforwardness implies more than simple honesty. Often we believe we are honest, when in fact we are lying. We tell half-truths. We attempt to manipulate someone's opinion by describing a situation as if it were better than it actually is. We answer a question with a non-answer. "A man who tells lies merely hides the truth. But a man who tells half-lies has forgotten where he put it" (*Claude Rains, in his role as Dryden in Lawrence of Arabia, 1962*).

"When man seeks truth, help comes from Heaven, but the search must be sincere. When we succeed, we become partners with God, for we have found truth" (*R' A. Kahn*).

> *Loving kindness and truth meet together;*
> *righteousness and peace kiss each other.*
> *Truth shall spring from the earth;*

and righteousness shall look down from Heaven.
Also, the Lord shall give that which is good;
and our land shall yield her produce.

—Psalm 85:11–13

CHAPTER TWO, VERSE 6

Do not run after honor. Do not be proud when rendering a decision. Consider that all you possess today may not be yours tomorrow. Since you cannot be certain that what is in your possession today will be yours tomorrow, what is the use of striving to possess that which belongs to others?

Do not run after honor.

Glory is fleeting; we can't rely on kudos to maintain our self-esteem. If we do, we may become angry or depressed when we are not being praised.

"The pride of your heart has deceived you, you who live in the clefts of the rocks and make your home on the heights, you who say to yourself, 'Who can bring me down to the ground?'" (*Obad. 1:3*).

In my youth, I chased honor quite successfully. Later, through Jewish spiritual renewal, I realized I had been concealing my insecurity behind plaques and framed cert-ificates.

Please understand that humility is not humiliation. When we are truly humble, no one can humiliate us. If we are living a life that is good, just, and honest in God's eyes, we know that recognition is just icing on the cake. "Before his downfall a man's heart is proud, but humility comes before honor" (*Prov. 18:12*).

If we pursue acclaim, we place ourselves in conflict with others who are driven by the same need. It is better to use our time to overcome the *yetzer ha ra*, the ego, and to free ourselves of our defects of character. The Talmud tells us to honor others (*Pirkei Avot 4:1*).

Do not be proud when rendering a decision.

To render a Jewish legal decision, *halakha*, was, for our sages, a challenging task and a significant accomplishment. They were obliged to agree with the decisions of their teachers for as long as those teachers were still alive. Their arguments had to withstand days of debate. Those who succeeded could not have known they would be immortalized in the pages of the Talmud.

In Judaism, we are taught to work hard and well, to do our best. Outcomes, however, are beyond our control. Attempts to engineer outcomes usually result in frustration.

When we do accomplish a worthy goal, we are not to wear our achievement as a crown. We give all of the credit to God, parents, teachers, and friends. We don't just thank them at an acceptance speech; we understand that although the hard work comes from us, every talent we have is a loan from God.

Consider that all you possess today may not be yours tomorrow. Since you cannot be certain that what is in

your possession today will be yours tomorrow, what is the use of striving to possess that which belongs to others?

A Midrash tells us to avoid attachment to our possessions:

> One day King Solomon decided to humble Benaiah ben Yehoyada, his most trusted minister. He said to him, "Benaiah, there is a certain ring that I want you to bring to me. I wish to wear it for Sukkot, which gives you six months to find it."
>
> "If it exists anywhere on Earth, Your Majesty," replied Benaiah, "I will find it and bring it to you, but what makes the ring so special?"
>
> "It has magic powers," answered the king. "If a happy man looks at it, he becomes sad, and if a sad man looks at it, he becomes happy." King Solomon knew that no such ring existed in the world.
>
> Spring and summer passed. Benaiah still had no idea where he could find the ring. On the night before Sukkot, he decided to take a walk in one of the poorest quarters of Jerusalem. He passed a merchant who had begun to set out the day's wares on a shabby carpet.

Benaiah asked, "Have you, by any chance, heard of a magic ring that makes the happy wearer forget his joy, and the broken-hearted wearer forget his sorrows?"

The grandfather took a plain gold ring from his carpet and engraved something on it. When Benaiah read the writing on the ring, his face broke into a wide smile.

That night, the entire city welcomed the holiday of Sukkot with great festivity.

"Well, my friend," said Solomon, "have you found what I sent you after?"

All the ministers laughed and Solomon himself smiled.

To everyone's surprise, Benaiah held up a small gold ring and declared, "Here it is, Your Majesty!"

As soon as Solomon read the inscription, the smile vanished from his face. The old merchant had written three Hebrew letters on the gold band: gimel, zayin, yud, which began the words Gam zeh ya'avor—This too shall pass. At that moment, Solomon realized that his wisdom, fabulous wealth, and tremendous power were fleeting; some day, he would be nothing but dust.

The Talmud teaches that although it's nice to have possessions, a truly wealthy person is one who is happy with what he has (*Pirkei Avot 4:1*). Since we cannot be certain that what we have today will remain ours tomorrow, it is silly to covet or steal another's possessions. Possessions can be gone with the wind at any moment. Besides, the more we own, the more belongings we need to worry about (*ibid. 2:8*). None of us knows what tomorrow may bring.

During the holiday of Sukkot, we learn that we can live for a week in a *sukkah*, a flimsy booth. Through the ceiling we see the sun, moon, clouds, and stars. We find we can still be happy. We are at peace when we rely on God and not on our belongings.

CHAPTER TWO, VERSE 7

Let it be your habit to finish everything in a good manner. Let your tongue be always soft. Be a good merchant, pay well, and strive always to do good. Be afraid of a light sin, for this may bring you to a grave sin. Respect all kinds of men. Do not say, "I will flatter this man, that he may give me food"; "that man, to give me beverages"; "that man, to buy me clothes," for it is better that you should pay your own way than to be obsequious to others.

Let it be your habit to finish everything in a good manner. People today are no different from folks who lived in the Talmudic era; the rabbis' advice to slow down is as relevant now as it was then. When we rush around, trying to beat the clock, we overcomplicate our lives. During the Exodus, God first commanded the Hebrews to establish a calendar. Free people manage their own time, but how many of us are slaves to our schedules? We define a good friend as someone we 'poke' on Facebook. We define our success by the profits we make rather than by the quality of our products. We measure achievement by the number of widgets we sell, instead of by the quality of our relationships with our clients. When we try to do two or three things at once, we substitute mediocrity for excellence. In Verse 2:7, our sages remind us to take our time with whatever we do, and to do it to the best of our ability.

In The 59th Street Bridge Song (1966), the modern psalmists Simon and Garfunkel teach:

> Slow down, you're movin' too fast
> You gotta make the morning last
> Just kickin' down the cobblestones
> Lookin' for fun and feelin' groovy.

Let your tongue be always soft.

The Talmud and Torah often warn us to guard our tongues. Our tongues are more dangerous weapons than spears and arrows. A spear or an arrow can only be thrown a short distance, but evil talk, especially on the Web, can be heard around the globe in milliseconds. "The one who gossips stands in Syria and kills in Rome" (*Talmud Yerushalmi Tractate Peah 1:1*).

Be a good merchant, pay well, and strive always to do good.

The Torah tells us employers are required to pay employees on time: "You shall not oppress your fellow and you shall not rob; the wages of a worker shall not remain with you over night until morning" (*Leviticus 19:13*). Talmudic Jewish business law requires the use of accurate weights and measures, fair pricing, honest labeling, truthful representation of products, and paying one's fair share of taxes. Our business ethics never say *caveat emptor*, let the buyer beware, but *lifne iver*, don't put a stumbling block before the blind.

Three tractates of Talmud, the Bava (Gate) series, are devoted to business ethics. The sages teach that when we arrive at the gates of Heaven, we will not be asked if we kept Shabbat. "When a person is brought before the Heavenly court for judgment, the first question he is asked is whether he was honest in business" (*Shabbat 31a*). We are to develop honest relationships with our clients and employees. What we produce is secondary.

Be afraid of a light sin, for this may bring you to a grave sin.

When we read the headlines of the business section, we see that folks arrested for stealing millions, and even billions, may start out small. One day a man borrows ten dollars from the petty cash drawer, and within time, he has borrowed an eighth of a million dollars for the down payment on his home. He then lies to the mortgage company about his income. When his home becomes upside-down, he illegally borrows against it. He fails to pay utility bills, credit card bills, and school loans. Next, he files for bankruptcy. It all begins with the small sin of stealing ten dollars.

Respect all kinds of men.

To love our neighbor can be difficult, and can be defined in many ways, but to respect everyone, and judge him fairly, is not only great spiritual advice but also good business advice. In Talmudic times, people of different races, cultures, and religions filled the *souk*, Jerusalem's equivalent of the shopping mall. There could be found more diversity than that apparent in our shopping centers today. "Do not scorn any man, and do not discount any thing, for there is no man who has not his hour, and no thing that has not its place" (*ibid 4:3*).

Greet everyone with a smile and a hearty hello. Rabbi Israel Kagan (1838–1933), the Chofetz Chaim, wrote, "When a person does kindness on earth, he awakens kindness above, and the day is crowned with kindness through his actions. Happy is the person who exhibits the proper conduct below, since all depends on his act to awaken the corresponding activity above."

The Talmud tells us that no man, not even a Roman soldier in the marketplace, ever preceded Rabban Yochanan ben Zakkai in extending a greeting of peace (*Berachot 17a*). In other words, Rabban ran to greet everyone, friend or foe. Keep in mind that Rabban lived before, during, and after the 70 CE Roman destruction of the Temple. "Initiate a greeting of peace to every person" (*Pirkei Avot 4:20*). What did our sages mean by every person? If you know that someone bears you ill will, initiate a greeting of peace toward him nevertheless. This will awaken a feeling of love for you within him. Even if he will not humble himself to make peace with you, God will humble him before you so that he will not cause you any harm. An allusion to this is found in Scripture: "But if he does not make peace with you...God shall deliver him into your hand" (*Deut. 20:12–3*).

Don't be discouraged if someone refuses to shake your hand, to wish you shalom, or to return your Shabbat greeting. We don't get attached to outcomes. We do the best we can in Jewish spiritual renewal to live a life of God's will. If we are doing so—and this is a heavy piece of spiritual wisdom—other people's opinions of us are none of our business.

Do not say: "I will flatter this man, that he may give me food"; "that man, to give me beverages"; "that man, to buy me clothes," for it is better that you should pay your own way than to be obsequious to others."
Judaism despises flattery, obsequiousness, and ingratiation; people-pleasing is manipulative. When we attempt to become more attractive or likeable to our target, our hidden intention is to please our selfish egos.

According to social psychologist Edward Jones (d. 1993, United States), methods of ingratiation include *other-enhancement* (unnecessary compliments), *opinion conformity* (adopting others' values), and *self-promotion* (bragging). To this list, researchers recently added *self-deprecation* (putting oneself down to elicit pity), *instrumental dependency* (acting weak for the sake of control), and *name-dropping* (claiming to know famous people.) Another technique, *situation specific behavior*, involves seeking personal information about someone in order to gain his approval.

Each of these techniques of flattery is a form of lashon ha ra or lying or both. Is it worth *developing* our defects of character to attract phony friends, who selfishly need stroking, so that we can attend their parties, eat their food, drink their liquor, and receive gifts? We know in our hearts we are invited not because they like us, but because we flatter them. When we stop the flattery, the invitations stop, too. We can't buy love, affection, or friendship.

If we want to give a *mazel tov* to someone, we can do so honestly, without striving for reward. Flatterers look like friends the way a wolf looks like a dog. King David warns us in Psalm 5:9, "There is nothing reliable in what they say; their inward part is destruction itself; their throat is an open grave; they flatter with their tongue." When we flatter, we are not acting as a friend, but being quite selfish. Proverbs 29:5 teaches, "Whoever flatters his neighbor is spreading a net for his feet." Derek Eretz tells us to engage truthfully with one another.

CHAPTER TWO, VERSE 8

ake care that your teeth shall not shame you, and you shall not be disgraced by your mouth, and not cursed by your tongue, and not put to shame by your lips. Take care that you should not need to bow to someone on account of your own words. If you wish to become attached to your neighbor through bonds of love, always consider what good you are able to do for him. If it be your wish to be kept away from sin, always look to the result of it. If you are craving for merits, consider carefully their details.

Take care that your teeth shall not shame you, and you shall not be disgraced by your mouth, and not cursed by your tongue, and not put to shame by your lips. Take care that you should not need to bow to someone on account of your own words.
This verse is not about the ills of bad dental hygiene, but another admonition from our sages to watch our words carefully. The sages consider lashon ha ra to be among the worst behaviors in a society that wants peace.

When we gossip, we shame, disgrace, and curse our-selves. When we are caught doing lashon ha ra, we feel ashamed and must humble ourselves by begging forgive-ness. "Be very careful with gossip because with it you will embarrass yourself, for one who denigrates is merely projecting his own fault onto someone else. It's natural to take your own faults and point them out in others" (*The Ramchal, from The Ways of the Righteous, The Gate of Lashon Hara*).

The sages ask: "Who is honored?" They answer: "He who honors another" (*Pirkei Avot 4:1*). "Which of you wants a full life? Who would like to live long enough to enjoy good things? Keep your tongue from saying evil things and your lips from speaking deceitful things" (*Ps. 34:12–13*).

If you wish to become attached to your neighbor through bonds of love, always consider what good you are able to do for him.

This is not intended to be a recipe for getting our neighbor to love us, but a prescription for feeling a bond of love for him. Our sages refer to the virtue of altruism. We are to think about what we can do for others, while expecting nothing in return, perhaps not even thanks. When we wake each day and ask God to show us how we can be of maximum service to our fellows and to Him, we cannot feel deprived.

If it be your wish to be kept away from sin, always look to the result of it. If you are craving for merits, consider carefully their details.

Our yetzer ha ra moves quickly and can prevent us from pausing to pray, meditate, and think. We bring harm upon ourselves when we lack restraint. Sometimes the harm comes quickly, but often it comes years later.

When we crave rewards, we are driven by ego. Craving—and the rabbis choose the word carefully—is an addiction, a compulsion, that may lead us to step on the toes of others or to neglect our responsibilities in pursuit of what we believe we want. We need to stop and consider what is involved in obtaining what we seek, and what might occur if we succeed.

If we practice conscious contact with God, we gain awareness of our thoughts, and can anticipate the likely consequences of our behavior.

CHAPTER TWO, VERSE 9

If you have done much good to someone, consider it as if you have done very little. You must not say that you have done good from what belongs to you, because there is One who has given everything to you, and you are obliged to thank Heaven for it. If, however, someone has done you a bit of good, consider it as if he has done you much good. If you have done any wrong to someone, even a little bit, consider it as if it is much wrong. Say: "Woe is me that I was the cause of the wrong." And make amends. If others have done to you much wrong, consider it as nothing.

If there is one verse of Talmud to learn to live by, this is it. The results are life-changing and life-affirming. Neither our sages nor God wish us to allow ourselves to be treated like a *shmateh*, dish rag. Nevertheless, God does not put us here on Earth to live with angst and to commit peccadilloes.

Many years ago, one of my rabbinic teachers asked me: "Avrael, would you rather be happy or right?" He was not talking about a matter of social justice, but about the quality of my day-to-day interactions with co-workers, family, and friends. I used to want—no, I actually *needed*—to be right. Now I prefer to live in shalom.

If you have done much good to someone, consider it as if you have done very little. You must not say that you have done good from what belongs to you, because there is One who has given everything to you, and you are obliged to thank Heaven for it.

From a spiritual Jewish perspective, we exist to be of maximum service to God and our fellows. When we do good for an individual, charity, or institution, even if it is 'much' good, we should think of it as little. Humility and ego deflation require practice, with 3–5 periods of daily prayer and meditation, but can be achieved.

God did not give, but rather has loaned to us, everything we possess. All can be taken away, God forbid, at any moment, and certainly leaves us upon death. We work hard, but the outcome never rests in our hands. Outcomes belong to God.

Although I am well aware of the practical needs of synagogues, I find it ironic that Jewish spirituality opposes the plastering of donors' names over the doorways. Whose name should be above those doors? God's name, inscribed with profound gratitude. When someone thanks us, we are to turn that thanks over to God, and thank that person for allowing us to be of service to him.

If, however, someone has done you a bit of good, consider it as if he has done you much good.

In a society driven by consumerism, we can easily thank those who give a great deal. When someone gives us what we value, we can easily laud him. We must try to show the same appreciation for the cashier and the bagger at our local market. Similar courtesies and acts of kindness are done for us many times each day. We should receive them with the same gratitude we would show for the large favors granted to us.

When we live with an attitude of gratitude, we recognize how much other humans do for us that we previously had taken for granted. We become aware of all that God provides. When we wake in the morning, we thank God for our first breath of the day, and for restoring our souls.

Proper prayer books contain prayers of thanks not only for food, but for running into a long-lost buddy, seeing a rainbow, or crossing paths with a beautiful animal.

If, however, you have done any wrong to someone, even a little bit, consider it as if it is much wrong. Say: 'Woe is me that I was the cause of the wrong.' And make amends.

At home, we can easily hurt another's feelings. Away from home, even acting on our good intentions can harm someone. We are not behaving in a spiritual manner if we dismiss others by telling ourselves that their reactions are their own problem. For the slightest harm we are obligated to apologize, and to make teshuvah.

If others have done to you much wrong, consider it as nothing.

The last verse of Chapter 2 describes how we feel when we live without grudges or angst. Our spiritual task is to grow from *Homo sapiens* to *Homo spiritus*. We must learn to keep the yetzer ha ra in check.

The sages are not saying that if someone crashes into our car and wrecks the rear end, we are to smile, and say: 'Please, would you be kind enough to also crash into the front end?' What they are saying is that while we exchange insurance information, and deal with the auto insurance companies, body shops, and lawyers for the next year, we do so calmly, without malice. We need to learn to let the childish, mean-spirited behavior of others roll off our backs.

Not everyone will treat us respectfully. As quipped by Rabbi Mordecai Kaplan, founder of the Jewish Reconstruction movement, just because you are a vegetarian doesn't mean the bull won't charge at you.

Chapter Three

VERSE 1

eliberate before a word passes your lips, and be thoughtful of how you should act in your worldly affairs. See always that your steps will be rewarded. Justify the judgment that was imposed upon you and free yourself from anger. Judge favorably your neighbor, and see that your verdict will not make him guilty if his guilt is not fully established.

Deliberate before a word passes your lips, and be thoughtful of how you should act in your worldly affairs.

When the ego, the *yetzer ha ra*, is in the driver's seat, we inevitably speak non-Godly words and behave in non-Godly ways. We must learn to walk mindfully with God throughout the day.

To make conscious contact with God is not difficult, but it does take practice. We don't achieve mindfulness in a day or in a week. Learning to walk with God is a lifelong process that is never truly mastered.

The TaNaK is filled with stories of people who walked with God:

> When Abram was 99 years old, the Lord appeared and said to him: "I am Almighty God; walk before Me and be blameless'."
>
> —Genesis 17:1

> And now, Israel, what does the Lord your God require of you, but to fear the Lord your God, to walk in all His ways and to love Him, to serve the Lord your God with all your heart and with all your soul.
>
> —Deuteronomy 10:12

> He stores up sound wisdom for the upright; He is a shield to those who walk uprightly.
>
> —Proverbs 2:7

After we finish our daily morning prayers and meditation, we should spend a few moments reviewing our plans for the day. We know what triggers our anxiety, tension, fear, and resentment. We recognize our character defects, such as ego, jealousy, self-seeking, gossip, dishonesty, selfishness, and self-pity. We ask God to keep us from these defects despite the situations we may encounter.

For example, if we used to get nervous driving on the expressway, if we drove too fast or carelessly, if we viewed other drivers as opponents rather than as fellows, we now know to ask God to keep us calm and connected to Him, to help us proceed carefully, and to treat the other drivers with kindness and courtesy.

Asei ritzono ritzoncho—make His will your will. We humbly ask God to align our will with His. We have learned about the yetzer ha ra and we understand that our hearts and minds can be "deceitful above all things" (*Jeremiah 17:9*) if we are not consciously connected to God. As we go about the day, if ego or other character defects begin to emerge, we immediately ask God to remove them. We will then be able to think before we speak or act.

See always that your steps will be rewarded.

This is simply another way to say "be thoughtful of how you should act in your worldly affairs." There is an undeniable link between walking with God and being open to God's abundant blessings. He wants us to walk in His ways. The reward is a life full of shalom and joy.

When we do not walk with God, we walk with our yetzer ha ra. When we ignore God's benevolence, we only see life's imperfections.

Walking mindfully does not mean walking perfectly. "Surely there is not a righteous man on earth who does good and never sins" (*Eccles. 7:20*). At times, an ego-driven thought will occur unconsciously, or we may be conscious of the thought but choose to ignore it. We may even act on it. We might owe someone teshuvah but have put off making amends. We need to make teshuvah as soon as we realize we have treated someone badly.

Proverbs 24:16 tells us that a person walking mindfully with God will fall seven times a day. This means that we may stumble, but we will not fail. We get up and continue on our path. We remain aware of our thoughts and actions throughout the day, and ask that "God may show us the way in which we should walk and the thing we should do" (*Jeremiah 42:3*).

We ask God to show us "what is right and good in God's eyes" (*Deut. 6:8*). We keep the question uppermost our hearts, minds and souls. God will give us the answers. The closer we are to God, the less apt we are to behave negatively toward others.

Justify the judgment that was imposed upon you and free yourself from anger.

In other words, go with the flow of the universe. Humans tend to get angry for one of two reasons: either we had something that was taken away, or we wanted something, but we didn't get it. Although anger is human, sustained anger is not spiritual. The verse advises us to free ourselves from anger, as anger hurts us and leads to resentment. When things don't go our way, we fix the problem if we can. We focus on the positive: although the car has a flat tire, we thank God that we avoided a crash or serious injury to ourselves or someone else.

Judge favorably your neighbor, and see that your verdict will not make him guilty if his guilt is not fully established.

Although this verse was written for the benefit of rabbis and the laymen called to be judges, I believe it contains a spiritual lesson for all of us. We are to assume the best of everyone. The Talmud teaches us to not judge anyone until we have been in his place (*Hillel, Pirkei Avot 2:4*). Since it is impossible to be in anyone's place, we shouldn't judge at all, but we do err, and we do judge. Our verdict, which is based on our prejudices, makes another guilty in our eyes. How many of us have listened to lashon ha ra about someone we had not yet met, judged him unfavorably before meeting him, and then when we met him, liked him?

The sages teach us not to imagine what someone else is thinking, because most of the time we are barely aware of what we ourselves are thinking. Life is too short. No one knows how much time we have. We are to treat everyone with love and kindness, and make each day a *simcha*. "This is the day the Lord has made; let us rejoice and be glad in it" (*Psalms 118:24*).

CHAPTER THREE, VERSE 2

Be content with your possessions, and adorn yourself with the little you do possess. Do not hate the one who reproves you. Your share will be blessed forever if your eye is always good, and your soul always satisfied.

Be content with your possessions, and adorn yourself with the little you do possess.

The sages ask: "Who is a rich man?" They answer: "He who is happy with what he has" (*Pirkei Avot 4:1*). While Judaism does not oppose the ethical attainment of wealth, from a spiritual viewpoint, we are not to bemoan what we do not have at the moment, but to be grateful for what we do have. Dissatisfaction can lead to bitterness. Bitterness can lead to envy. The Talmud teaches us that jealousy can remove us from the world (*ibid. 4:21*). How much do we really need?

What does 'adorn ourselves' mean? Are we to show off what little we have? No. We are to take comfort and wrap ourselves in what we have, and be content. We are not to live with a cup half empty, nor even with a cup half full, but to live with a cup that overflows with God's benevolence.

Do not hate the one who reproves you.

Reproving means gentle instruction, which is given privately. We actually have a mitzvah in the Torah to reprove our fellows when they are doing something wrong (*Lev.19:17*). It is one of the ways the Torah teaches us to love our fellows. The Talmud goes into detail about when one should reprove. We have to make sure others' ears and hearts are open to learning.

Assuming that we are being reproved for the right reasons, we are to listen, evaluate, and learn from one who reproves us. We are not to ignore him or tell him to mind his own business. When someone takes the time to reprove us, gently, with love, and with our best interests at heart, we must not hate him, as he is giving us information we can use to improve ourselves.

In Judaism, a way of life, the bad behavior of others affects us and the rest of the community. Rabbi Shimon bar Yochai, traditionally considered to be the author of the Zohar, tells the story of a fellow in a small boat who drills a hole beneath his seat. The other passengers yell at him to stop, as he will sink the whole boat if he continues. He responds that he is only drilling under his own seat (*Midrash Rabbah Vayikra 4:6*). All Israel, all humans, are responsible for one another—*Kol Yisroel areivim zeh lazeh* (*Shevuot 39a*).

Your share will be blessed forever if your eye is always good and your soul always satisfied.

What is a 'good eye'? It is an eye that does not covet. The sages teach that the eye is the gateway to jealousy. "The eye and the heart are the two instruments of sin. The eye sees, the heart desires, and the body completes the action" (*Rashi, Bamidbar 25:39*).

When we are content with what we have, we are capable of being happy for others who may have more than we do. We get along better with people. We do not risk a foolish investment to get more. We aren't greedy. Con men who promise us 25% yields, when banks, bonds, and stocks are yielding 80% less, cannot convince us to give them our money. Our share will "be blessed," meaning protected.

Our souls will always be satisfied. We will sleep better, and our days will go more smoothly, when we are not concerned about what we do not have, or with how to get rich quickly. We will know how to live with freedom, contentment, happiness, and joyousness.

CHAPTER THREE, VERSE 3

If you neglect one commandment, you will eventually neglect other commandments. The same is true if you have overlooked the words of the Torah willingly. This will lead you to be overlooked, willingly or unwillingly. If you have taken away others' property, yours will be taken away.

If you neglect one commandment, you will eventually neglect other commandments. The same is true if you have overlooked the words of the Torah willingly.

The sages teach that one sin leads to another sin, while doing one mitzvah gives us the opportunity to do another mitzvah. If, for example, we habitually tell small lies, we will be soon become used to telling big lies. "Once a person becomes accustomed to a certain transgression, it becomes permissible to him" (*Sotah 22a*). It's easy to develop bad habits, but difficult to rid ourselves of them.

When we arrogantly push aside these codes, we may believe we have gained. Perhaps we gossip about a person of whom we are jealous in order to climb a social or professional ladder. Eventually, however, we become known as gossips, and with our ill deeds lose the friends or business. When this occurs, God is not punishing us; we have punished ourselves with our defects of character. With our bad behavior, we put ourselves in the position to be hurt later on. We enter bondage in a *Mitzraim*, Egypt, of our own making.

This will lead you to be overlooked, willingly or unwillingly

We are left alone, spiritually and socially, to rot in the dungeons we construct for ourselves when we ignore the sound advice of Moses and the sages. If we steal, lie, commit adultery, etc., our sins may be overlooked for a while, but eventually they will be examined thoroughly.

If you have taken away others' property, yours will be taken away.

Spiritually, we understand that when we die, we will lose anything we possess. "You can't take it with you," as the adage goes.

On a practical level, we are aware that businessmen who have made their fortunes on the backs of others have children or grandchildren today who are elected officials. When we look at the lives of these folks, we see they are filled with tragedy. *Citizen Kane*, a fictional but believable story, shows how the unethical pursuit of wealth leaves one miserable.

Sooner or later, the money we steal burns a hole in our pocket, through which more money falls and is lost. If we are not spiritually connected, we fail to recognize that we always have enough, and may even squander what we do not yet have.

CHAPTER THREE, VERSE 4

ד he commencement of making vows is the door to foolishness. Frivolity with women is the beginning of adultery. If you have guaranteed a loan for someone, remember that it must be paid by yourself. If you have borrowed money, know that you have borrowed it to be repaid in time. If you have loaned money to somebody, be prepared to have difficulty in collecting it. Remember the time you have to repay, and settle your accounts.

The commencement of making vows is the door to foolishness.

When called to serve as a witness in a trial, Jews are taught to 'affirm' but not to 'swear' (i.e. vow), to tell the truth. The sages recognized that it is virtually impossible for a human being to keep such a vow, because we cannot completely know the truth, *emet*. We only can relate what we saw, heard, or remember. Although we may believe our perceptions or interpretations of events, and report them honestly, they may still be inaccurate.

Furthermore, the Talmud says, two conflicting opinions can both be valid. Some conflicting views cannot even exist without the other. *Eilu v'eilu divrei Elohim Chayim*, "This and also this are the words of the living God" (*Eruvin 13b*). *Eilu v'eilu* emphasizes the incompleteness of any single opinion. The *v'*, which means 'and', is essential, uniting and complementing the two opinions without choosing one or compromising the integrity of either. "Nobody's right if everybody's wrong" (*Stephen Stills, 1966*).

When we promise to do something, we always add, 'if it is God's will.' We may vow to pick someone up tomorrow at 3 PM, and God forbid, find ourselves with a flat tire or worse. Vowing is foolish, as it implies we are in full control of the world about us. We are not, and never will be.

The situation of General Yiftach and his daughter, described in Judges II, is one of the most troubling stories in the TaNaK. Yiftach makes a vow to sacrifice the first thing that comes out of his house if he is victorious in his battle against the Ammonites. He is victorious, and when he comes home, his daughter, who is his only child, runs out dancing with timbrels to greet him. It is she whom he must sacrifice. He does not retract his vow, and the end of the story implies that he does in fact sacrifice her after she spends two months in the hills mourning her virginity with her friends.

All Yiftach had to do was to go to Pinchas, the High Priest, and have his vow annulled through the vehicle of *hatarat nederim*, undoing of vows. The Midrash says that Pinchas was waiting for Yiftach to come to him. Yiftach, the chief political and military leader, was waiting for Pinchas to come to *him*. Each was trying to protect his own honor. As a result, the life of Yiftach's beloved daughter was lost.

Both Yiftach and Pinchas are punished by God. Yiftach dies from a disease that causes his limbs to fall off one by one. He is buried in "the cities of Gilead," a limb here and a limb there. Pinchas could no longer receive *ruach ha kodesh* (the Holy Spirit). Thus, we learn that it is foolish to make vows.

Frivolity with women is the beginning of adultery.
This can be true, just as, for women, flirting with men can lead to adultery. We live in an age with high rates of divorce and adultery, but divorce and adultery also occurred in Biblical and Talmudic times. The Talmud Tractate Sotah is devoted to these issues. The first real case of a suspected adulteress is discussed in Tractate Sanhedrin (Courts).

Judaism teaches us boundaries. Rabbinic Judaism, via the Talmud, is meant to build a fence around Torah. Each of us has an active yetzer ha ra. The yetzer tov speaks to us in a "still small voice." We have to be silent and meditate to hear it. The yetzer ha ra yells at us to come out and play.

When we are frivolous or self-indulgently carefree, our ego is primed to be stroked. The water cooler giggle, the quick touch, and the winking eye can all lead us to that bondage of self, in which our common sense goes out the window, and our hormones go into overdrive. Our ego, our selfish will, the *yetzer ha ra*, takes over, and, well, you know the rest. It is best not to start down that path.

If you have guaranteed a loan for someone, remember that it must be paid by yourself.

The Torah commands Jews to lend, without interest, to a person in true need. Derek Eretz teaches us human nature. We need to know what to expect when we lend, so that when the loan isn't paid back, we do not feel resentment and ill will.

If we co-sign or guarantee someone's loan, we should expect him to default and to have to pay it ourselves. If that doesn't occur, great, but if it does, let it come as no surprise to us, and let us not become angry. In other words, we should not co-sign a loan if we do not have the full funds to repay it, with money that won't be missed.

If you have borrowed money, know that you have borrowed it to be repaid in time.

Conversely, if we borrow, we should do so knowing that we must repay the money, and on time. We must not think, as many did with balloon mortgages, 'Oh, when the balloon comes due, I will have been promoted by then, and my home will have appreciated in value.' If we borrow, we need to have a concrete plan in place to be able to pay it back. "One who borrows and does not pay back is a thief" (*Bava Batra 88a, and Bava Metzia 78a*).

If you have loaned money to somebody, be prepared to have difficulty in collecting it.

We should only lend what we can either afford to lose or have the time to chase. Whenever I have lent money, it was to someone who told me he could not afford medicine or food for his kids. In my mind, I knew the loan was a gift. The Talmud tells us that when we lend, the borrower develops resentment toward the lender. Loans ruin friendships. Hence, we live in an age of banks, credit cards, and credit unions.

Remember the time you have to repay, and settle your accounts.

Although this part of the verse appears redundant, it has a deeper meaning. The Hebrew word for accounts is *chesbonim*. A *chesbon* is an accounting, an inventory, and the *Ivrit* word for the bill in a restaurant. As we have learned, chesbon is also used in the phrase *chesbon ha nefesh*, an inventory of the soul, which includes our character defects, our fears, and a list of those against whom we hold a grudge. We only have a limited amount of time before our defects of character cause harm to us and to others. We must do the mussar steps of transformation, and clear these accounts.

CHAPTER THREE, VERSE 5

The following fifteen customs are ascribed to the sages: He is pleasant in entering, and also when leaving; is prudent in his awe for Heaven; versed in wisdom; wise in his ways, has a good conception, a retentive memory, is clear in his answers, questions to the point, and answers according to the Torah; he learns something new from every chapter taught to him; he learns from the wise; he learns for the purpose of teaching it and performing it. Be as the lower threshold, upon which all persons tread, and still it lasts even when the whole building is demolished.

Most of this verse is self-explanatory. The traits described in Chapter 1, Verse 1 are now put into action. The first two lines in 3:5 relate to humility and courtesy. We are to be pleasant. We smile and greet everyone with sincere *shalom* and leave in the same manner. We don't cause a scene, nor flit around the room like a *prima donna*, trying to make each gathering (service, class, party, even a *shiva*) all about us. We need to be God-conscious in our words and actions.

Customs four through fourteen pertain to learning and teaching. Thirteen and fourteen teach that we learn not only in order to 'talk the talk', but to 'walk the walk.' Remember, please, that *derek* means path, or walk. We never say we know something already. Every time we study a chapter, or go to a lecture, we try to come away with at least one pearl of wisdom. When we teach Torah, we do not dishonor Torah (including Talmud and Midrash) by teaching falsehoods. When our *talmidim* or congregants know all of Torah, Talmud, and the sages' commentaries, then we can share our opinions. Humility allows us to teach others correctly before we share our own thoughts.

A good conception

How we think and form ideas determines our behavior, including style of teaching. As psychologist Dr. Bob Taylor asks, "How could such highly-educated and precisely-trained professionals veer off the path of objectivity?" His answer is simple. We are humans, *Homo sapiens*. We will continue to make poor decisions until we learn to divorce ourselves from ego, meditate for answers, and move toward becoming *Homo spiritus*.

Ideas based in ego represent cognitive bias, resulting in "perceptual distortion, inaccurate judgment, or illogical interpretation." Such biases helped us in primitive times, but wreak havoc in our lives today. The *Semmelweis reflex* is the "predisposition to deny new information that challenges our established views." *Confirmation bias* involves the "inclination to seek out information that supports our own preconceived notions." The *over-confidence effect* results in unwarranted confidence in one's own knowledge. This is a dangerous trait in a rabbi. *Fundamental attribution error* involves the tendency to "attribute other people's behavior to their personalities, and to attribute our own behavior to the situation." When others behave idiotically, we think they have the problem. When we behave even more idiotically, we rationalize and find ways to justify our actions.

Thus, *Derek Eretz Zuta* begins by teaching modesty, humility, and ego deflation. "Having a good conception" means doing away with ego, arrogance, and preconceived notions, so that we can learn and teach properly. Rabbis, parents, anyone in a profession or social situation—in fact all of us—need to develop this trait.

Be as the lower threshold, upon which all persons tread, and still it lasts even when the whole building is demolished.

We are to remain as humble as a building's lower threshold. We shouldn't take ourselves, our accomplishments, recognition, or possessions too seriously. Everything ends, leaving us with our inner spiritual selves. The building gets demolished, but the lower threshold remains.

Due to the economy, many of the people I work with have literally lost their homes on or near the ocean front, their cars, their memberships in country clubs, even their synagogue memberships. With these losses, they have also lost their pseudo-friends. They are left with only the lower threshold. They are learning, for the first time in their lives, to live spiritually. Jewish spiritual renewal doesn't require a vow of poverty—quite the opposite—but leads us to understand that our toys are far less important than our relationships with family, true friends, and the Divine.

Chapter Four

Scholars always are agreeable in society, but not so ordinary people. He who occupies himself only with study of the Scripture pursues the right course, yet the sages do not think so; with Mishnayot, it is a course to be rewarded; but he who occupies himself with the study of the Talmud pursues a course of which there is no better. Still, it is advisable that one shall occupy himself with the study of Mishnayot more than with that of the Talmud.

By promoting the study of Mishna and Talmud over the study of only the TaNaK, the rabbis reaffirm Talmudic Judaism over Temple-bound, priest-based, Torah-only Hebraism. We see this theme often repeated in the Talmud, e.g., in the forward to Pirkei Avot. We also find occasional references to rabbis versus ordinary people, i.e., 'am ha eretz.' Verse 4:1 reminds us that rabbis must maintain higher standards of behavior than the hoi polloi.

In keeping with the quip 'two Jews, three opinions,' the verse presents seemingly contradictory points of view. The Hebraic position is that it's enough to study only the TaNaK, but the rabbis disagree. The result would be, to offer an analogy in today's terms, the difference between the high number of executions carried out annually in the State of Texas instead of only one execution in 62 years in Israel. Without the Talmud, we would still be painting blood on our doorposts on Pesach, and imposing the death penalty for 'carrying' on Shabbat. The verse tells us it's great to study the Mishna (the Oral Law), but even better to study the Talmud, including the Gemara (rabbinic commentary and rulings on the Mishna.) If we study only the Mishna, we will misunderstand the intentions of the rabbis. The text then says it's better to study Mishna and not just the Talmud, meaning it is better to study the Mishna in addition to the Gemara. The Mishna comes from the earlier rabbis, hence is closer to the teachings from Sinai; the Gemara is by more recent rabbis. The Talmud tells us: "Rabbi Zeira said in the name of Rava bar Zimna 'If the earlier Sages were the sons of angels, then we are the sons of men; but if the earlier Sages were the sons of men, then we are donkeys'" (*Bavli Shabbat 112b*). To summarize, the best course of study is to learn the TaNaK, and then to continue with the Talmud. When one learns only a bit of TaNaK, usually for one's *bar* or *bat mitzvah*, but does not learn Talmud, one has not learned Judaism, and tends to not learn the Talmudic concepts of forgiveness, character development, and living in shalom.

CHAPTER FOUR, VERSE 2

Do not exact pay for thy teaching. Moreover, take no compensation whatever for it, for the Omnipotent has given His teaching to you gratuitously; for the one who asks for reward destroys the whole world (because there are many who cannot afford to pay and will remain ignorant.) And do not say: "I have no money to live on, and therefore I must take reward for my teaching." Remember all money is the Lord's, as it is written [Haggai, ii. 8]: "Mine is the silver, and mine is the gold, says the Lord of hosts" (and He will supply you with money).

Verse 4:2 clearly states that rabbis and Jewish school-teachers should not charge to teach the TaNaK or Talmud, nor take any compensation, such as a free meal. Financial need is no excuse. Rabbis in Talmudic times and later worked as doctors, wine merchants, olive growers, sandal makers, carpenters, etc. Many of our rabbis, such as Judah ha Nasi, were very wealthy. Others, like Hanina ben Dosa, who had only carob beans to eat for Shabbat (*Ta'anit 24b*), were impecunious.

The reason for the prohibition against accepting payment is twofold. Because the Torah is an "inheritance to the children of Jacob" (*Bavli Sanhedrin 91b*) one who charges to teach it is stealing another's inheritance. More importantly, a rabbi paid by a lay board of *am ha eretz* will sermonize about what the congregants want to hear instead of what they should hear. The day he finally teaches what he should teach, the lay board will dismiss him.

Over time, in the Diaspora, the concept of the professional full-time congregational rabbi developed. Itinerant rabbis, *melameds*, roamed the towns of Europe looking for students to teach. Melamedim were mentioned in the TaNaK in Psalm 109:99 and Proverbs 5:13, and were regulated in the Talmudic period as teachers of children (*Bava Batra 21a*). Nowadays, most rabbis cannot work for free, and hence do charge for their teaching services, ignoring this verse of *Derek Eretz Zuta*.

CHAPTER FOUR, VERSE 3

If you have done charity, be assured that you will be favored with money; and if it has been your good lot to acquire money, do charity with it so long as it is in your power. Give it to those who need it in this world, in order that you may get the World to Come; for if you do not use it for charitable purposes, it will disappear suddenly, as it is written [Prov. xxiii. 5]: "When you merely let your eyes fly over it, it is no more."

Charity, from the Latin *caritas*, is defined as selfless love. The best translation to Hebrew is *ahavath chesed*, loving kindness. It would be wonderful if we helped others out of selflessness. The rabbis, knowing most humans hearts, ask us to give to others for what are actually selfish reasons. *Tzedakah*, defined as righteousness, is a Hebrew word often used in place of charity in English. In a sense, Judaism believes in wealth redistribution, but with some promise of gain.

I would prefer to show you our texts that explain that everything we have is a loan from God, that we gain nothing without God's aid. Since everything is a loan, the loans are called occasionally when we need to help others.

The Talmud teaches us that if two beggars have one coin a piece, each beggar should give the other his coin. This spiritual lesson helps us in times of good as well as in times of not-so-good. We can live with more, and we can live with less. We do our best, and do not get attached to results. Results are always in the realm of God.

But let us return to the verse. If we give away money, it will eventually flow back to us. When we understand that the money we have is a loan from God, and that parting with some of it is not going to harm us, we loosen the tight grip on our wallets.

When our hands relax and open, we are able to receive more blessings from God. It's a spiritual truism. When a salesman goes out believing he has to make 'x' amount of sales, his pressure tactics and his angst are felt by others and no sales are made. When he relaxes, without this pressure, he comes across calmly, promotes his product wisely, and sales are made.

The verse then tells us that if we have gained financially, to give some of the money as tzedakah. This seems to be a universal impulse; when one sees game show contestants or lottery players win, they usually, when asked, pledge to help others.

Next, the verse tells us that if we use our money to help those in this world, we get the benefit of entrance into Olam Ha Ba, the World to Come. Indeed we see this in our Yom Kippur liturgy that tzedakah and chesed atone for our sins. As we have learned, they may help make us right with sins done to God, but for sins done to another human, we must make ourselves right with him or her face-to-face.

The end of the verse warns that if we do not use some of our money for tzedakah it will be taken from us. The Talmud elsewhere refers to tzedakah as a 'salt-preservative' for our wealth.

Rabbi Nakdimon ben Guryon was one of the three richest men in Jerusalem and helped support the Jews there during the Roman occupation of Vespasian. Yet we learn he lost everything. His daughter was found picking barley seeds from the dung of Arabs' donkeys because R' Nakdimon reneged on her dowry of one million gold dinars as he became impecunious (*Ketubot 66b*).

She tells Rabbi Yochanan that charity is the salt, the preserver, of one's wealth. She explains that her father, when he walked from the Temple to his house and back, asked his servants to lay silk carpets along the streets for him to walk on. As an act of tzedakah, R' Nakdimon would then have his servants give the carpets to the poor.

The Gemara chides R' Nakdimon for his act of self-glorification, and says that furthermore, although he was very generous, for a man of his wealth he could have given much more.

Upon hearing this story, R' Yochanan ben Zakkai bursts into tears, and says, "Happy are you, Israel. As long as you perform the will of God, no nation or people can rule over you. But when you fail to perform the will of God, you are delivered into the hands of a humiliating nation; and not only the hands of a humiliating nation, but also into the hands of the beasts of the humiliating nation."

While it is a *mitzvah*, a commandment, to give tzedakah, it is better to give altruistically, and with ahavath chesed.

CHAPTER FOUR, VERSE 4

Do not complain of being less wise than another, for you have not served (the sages) as much as he did. Neither shall you complain that the other one is rich and you are not, for it is not every man who is favored with two tables (of this and the World to Come). Do not complain that another one is beautiful and you are ugly, for at the time of death a man becomes a carcass; moreover, a carcass of any animal may be sold or presented to somebody, while no one cares even to look at a human carcass. Do not say: "That man is righteous, while I am not"; for both of you will have to account. Do not say: "That man is powerful, while I am weak"; for there is no power aside from the Torah, as it is written [Ps. Ciii. 20]: "Bless the Lord, because His angels, mighty in strength, execute His word, and listen to His voice." Bear always in mind the following: Know where you came from, where you are going, and before Whom you will have to render an account, and do not turn your eyes on money which is not yours; for they close the gates of Heaven against prayer. Let your ears not listen to vain talk, for they are most likely to get burned. Do not slander, for the mouth will be first on the day of judgment to give account. Be not possessed of slander or other bad things, or of robbery, for all the members of your body will testify against you on the day of judgment. Let your feet not rush you to evil-doing, because it is likely that the Angel of Death will get there sooner, and wait for you. Be not afraid of the court of justice on earth, where only witnesses may be bought, but fear the Court above, because you are certain that there will be witnesses who will testify against you. And not only this, but your own deeds proclaim your accusation from time to time."

The verse responds to common *kvetches*, complaints, to make us think. If someone knows more than we do, and perhaps has a better-paying occupation as a result, chances are that he spent more time studying. The rabbis could have said those who work harder make more money, but they didn't, because they knew that hard work does not guarantee wealth. They remind us that although someone may be wealthy in this world, he may not be in Olam Ha Ba, the World to Come. The Talmud describes this world as an "upside-down world," full of unfairness, which is corrected in the Jewish version of Heaven (*Bava Batra 10b*).

We should not worry about physical beauty, because in the end, we all become worthless, ugly corpses. Although a dead animal has some uses, a dead human does not.

We shouldn't look upon another and say he is more righteous than we are. No one is 100% righteous. Proverbs 24:16 tells us that a righteous person falls, sins, or misses the mark seven times a day. Appearances can be deceiving. Furthermore, no is stopping us from being as righteous as we wish to be.

We are not to be jealous of those who appear to be powerful, because with Torah, i.e. God, all of us are powerful. We are to be humble, and to remember we come from nothing, as Pirkei Avot 3:1 says, "a putrid drop" from our fathers, and that we will go to "the place of dust, worms, and maggots." Everyone stands before God on the day of his death. We might play the big shot, the *macher*, on this plane of existence, but in God's eyes, to do so is meaningless.

We should not envy another's wealth. If we do, the quality of our thoughts and behavior may deteriorate until we are unable to concentrate and our prayers become blocked.

Gossip "kills three," one of whom is the listener (*Arachin 15a*). We are to avoid vain talk, even if we must leave the room. We are not to slander or gossip because our mouths will be judged by the mouth of God. In addition, when we gossip and slander we put our low self-esteem and jealousy on display.

Running to sin, pursuing sin, is a sure way for us to die spiritually, if not corporeally. We should fear the Heavenly court more than any human court. Human courts need witnesses, but we may have kept our misdeeds a secret. In the Heavenly court God is a witness, and He sees everything.

Finally, the verse tells us to make an accounting of our misdeeds, a *chesbon ha nefesh*, and to admit to our sins through *vidui*, confession. Vidui is a completely Jewish concept, as is a deathbed confession.

Practicing humility and gratitude enables us to avoid jealousy and resentment, destructive emotions that can lead to slander or stealing. We are to cultivate an 'attitude of gratitude' toward life.

CHAPTER FOUR, VERSE 5

I f you have performed all My commandments with joy, My attendants will come to meet you, and even I Myself will say to you: "Let your coming be in peace." Your eyes that never looked at property not belonging to you shall have light in darkness, as it is written [Is. lviii. 10]: "Then shall shine forth in the darkness your light, and your obscurity be as the noonday." Your ears that have not listened to vain talk shall hear of peace in the World to Come, as it is written [ibid. xxx. 21]: "And your ears shall hear the world behind you, saying, 'This is the way, walk in it, when you turn to the right, and when you turn to the left.'" Your mouth that has not slandered will be coveted by those who were used to slander. Your mouth that has studied the Torah will be a blessing to those who wish to be blessed. Your hands that have kept away from robbery, what can those who do injustice do to you? Your hands that you have not withdrawn from doing charity, what can mighty men do to you? Your feet that have not carried you to sin, what can the Angel of Death do to you? All that is said above is a warning to you, and you may do as you please, but do not say that you were not warned.

This verse is unusual in the Talmud, in that here God speaks directly to us rather than through Moses or the Prophets. God's attendants are angels. We are told not only to fulfill the commandments, but to do so with joy. Where will the angels and God Himself greet us? They will meet us at the gates of Heaven.

The Talmud tells us that all Jews, as well as all righteous non-Jews, go to Heaven. Those few who are so perfect that they have joyfully done every positive commandment and avoided every negative commandment go straight to Heaven. The rest of us take a detour, for no more than 12 months, to *Gehinnom*, where our souls are purified and we are re-educated.

When we covet, we focus obsessively on what we do not have, yet believe we deserve. We cannot recognize God's blessings. When we understand we are surrounded by God's abundance, we can thank Him for every breath we are given. We know what is important in life, and what is vain. We develop that third eye of enlightenment and spiritual awakening. When we give altruistically, we meet many human 'angels,' and make friends who welcome us. We feel better about ourselves, and we welcome each new day.

God promises that if we don't listen to vain talk now, we will hear only peaceful talk in the Hereafter. If we avoid gossip, gossipers, slanderers, and liars in this life, we will live more happily. As the verse quotes Isaiah, we will do the right thing, whether our journey takes us to the right or to the left. We won't be diverted from the path by people who rationalize their bad behaviors and want us to walk with them.

The mouths of those who don't slander will be envied by those who do slander. Why? Lashon ha ra is one of Judaism's worst character defects. It is akin to murder, what we today call 'character assassination.' Gossipers may believe they have friends, and temporarily they do, because there are those who love to hear gossip as much as there are those who love to tell gossip. Eventually, however, these people turn on each other. When the slanderer hits bottom, he will wish he had the mouth of one who never spoke lashon ha ra.

If we study Torah, we will we be a blessing to those who want Torah. The verse doesn't say that by studying Torah we will be a blessing to all. The sad truth is that when we become God-centered and spiritually awakened, we have fewer friends. Hanging out at the bar on St. Paddy's Day doesn't cut it for us any longer. Listening to gossip at the Oneg Shabbat is a turn-off for us. For those who want what we have, blessed new friendships are forged.

If we don't steal, we are protected from criminals. If we give tzedakah to the poor, we are immune from those who think they are mighty. If we never sin, all the Angel of Death can do to us is shuffle us off to Olam Ha Ba.

Some time ago, in the Roma Termini train station, a pick-pocket stole my wallet. I lost about 300 Euros, which is roughly equivalent to $400 U.S. dollars. I've never been a thief. I didn't feel the loss. Getting a new driver's license required phone calls and paper work, but emotionally, I did not feel robbed. I still felt protected. The lost money, intended for food and taxis, was returned to me in the form of 'the kindness of strangers' (angels) over the next few weeks, people who gave us rides and invited us into their homes and for Sukkot meals.

Those who abuse their power and position, be they *shul* board members or government politicians, are thwarted by tzedakah, acts of righteousness and justice. When we learn to give, learn to do without, and learn to be humble, no one with this pseudo-power (as compared to the power of the Omnipotent One) can truly hurt us.

The verse and chapter end with God speaking to us as a parent to a child: "All that is said above is a warning to you, and you may do as you please, but do not say that you were not warned."

Free will, *bechira*, is a fundamental concept within Judaism. As the Rambam points out (*Mishneh Torah Hilchot Teshuvah 8:1–5*), without the concept of *bechira*, the nature and purpose of Torah falters. Only because of the human being's free will can we be held responsible for our actions, and thus receive reward and punishment. Furthermore, it is only because of *bechira* that the concept of a *mitzvah* can exist, for how could God command if we did not have the ability to listen and follow the command?

Free choice is nevertheless a concept that is difficult to understand. If we truly believe God exists and that He gave us the mitzvot, is that like the 'freedom' we have when someone holds a gun to our head and tells us what to do? Is the choice meaningful? The last part of this verse is reminiscent of the *tochecha* (the warning in Lev. 26:3–46; Deut.28:1–69), and raises the question, that when faced with such repercussions, especially the negative ones for violations, how could a person choose to transgress?

We Jews are not to accept anything on blind faith. We will always doubt, because we have ego, our *yetzer ha ra*. In these moments we will not be perfect. As Proverbs says, a righteous person falls seven times a day. Doubt in Jewish jurisprudence is a solid defense against punishment. For this reason, two witnesses who see a crime 'about to occur,' must warn (*hatra'ah*) the sinner, quoting chapter and verse. If no two witnesses have done this, there is no conviction.

As Rabbi Hecht writes: "We have the alternative to listen to God and receive reward. We have an equal alternative, given fully that we accept the existence of God and know the punishment for transgressing, not to listen. There is a strong drive to simply not wish to listen to God." It is this drive to ignore God that Derek Eretz addresses.

Chapter Five

scholar must not eat while standing, nor lick his fingers, nor yawn in the presence of others.

In a verse reminiscent of Emily Post, the Talmud establishes rules for scholars (i.e. rabbis) that didn't apply to the *am ha eretz*, the common folk. We have all seen enough movies about ancient times to know how people used to behave when they ate. The rabbis expected better from each other.

Remember that for Judaism, the dining table replaces the Holy Sacrificial Altar of the Temple (*Berachot 55a*). How we behave while eating is important, especially when we recognize that everything we eat is a gift from God. We must not eat on the run, so to speak. We need to settle ourselves to prepare to give thanks.

To not lick our fingers implies more than concern for hygiene or etiquette. We must learn to be satisfied with what we have. The Torah tells us to eat, be satiated, and bless...*V'ochalto v'sovoto u'veirachto* (*Deut. 8:10*). To lick our fingers implies that we have not received enough.

At a Jewish table, one washes one's hands both before and after one eats. One also blesses God with prayers after the meal.

Yawning is an uncontrollable, reflexive action. We have all yawned in front of others and apologized for doing so. The verse tells us to be interested in the conversation of those we are dining with.

CHAPTER FIVE, VERSE 2

Talk little, laugh little, sleep little, indulge little in pleasure, say little "yes" and little "no."

Pirkei Avot 1:15 teaches us to say little and do much. The more we say, the more we are likely to offend. The same is true of laughter. There is a time and place for jovial behavior, but unless we are visiting with the *dybbuk* of Lenny Bruce it is best to keep our laughter under control. The rabbis disapproved of sloth. They knew that for most people, idle time becomes the yetzer ha ra's workshop. To oversleep or spend one's day in bed was not a middah they wanted to foster.

Jewish meals and holiday dinners begin with wine. Passover Seders include four full cups of wine per person (*Pesachim 10:1*). At Purim, Rabbi Rava says one is commanded to become so intoxicated that one cannot tell the difference between *'Barukh Mordekhai, Arur Haman,'* Blessed be Mordechai, and Cursed be Haman (*Megillah 7b*). The rabbis were not opposed to pleasure; they want us to live joyously. They ask us not to indulge, not to overdo, because they want us to learn personal boundaries and limits.

Immediately following Rava's opinion comes a story to illustrate the point. Rabbah and R' Zeira meet for Purim Seudah (the feast on the afternoon of Purim). They get drunk, and Rabbah cuts R' Zeira's throat (literally, Rabbah butchers him). The next day, Rabbah prays on R' Zeira's behalf, and he is brought back to life. A year later, Rabbah asks, "Would you like to have Purim Seudah with me again this year?" R' Zeira replies, "One cannot count on a miracle every time" (*Megillah 7b*).

The Talmud teaches us to let our righteous yes be a yes, and our righteous no be a no (*Bava Batra 49b*). In Verse 5:2, because they are concerned about the pitfalls of making vows, they instruct us to limit our yeses and noes. They remind us that our best intentions to keep a promise can be thwarted by unforeseen events or circumstances. It is advisable to add to a promise the phrase, "God willing."

CHAPTER FIVE, VERSE 3

One has always to know with whom he is sitting, near whom he is standing, with whom he is eating, with whom he is conversing, for whom he signs contracts and notes of debt.

What does it mean to know about everyone with whom we have any social or business relationship? Certainly this 'know' in the Talmud is not the same as 'to know' in the Biblical sense. We are not to judge others, but we are to watch, listen, and discern the *middot*, the character traits, of those with whom we do business or with whom we associate casually.

No doubt we can all agree that we must know about the people with whom we enter into financial agreements. This is especially true of our business partners and borrowers. Ask any business attorney, and he or she will tell you that the break-up of a business is worse than a divorce. We have all heard of the apparently charming, nice gentlemen who hoodwinked their clients. We need to learn that being charming or pleasant does not make one just, honest, or righteous.

We must choose our friends and acquaintances wisely in order to avoid harm, even from people with whom we casually sit, stand, eat, or converse. We are not meant to be snobbish or alone, but there are folks we can trust with the intimate details of our lives and our money, and others with whom we are best off talking about the weather. "Distance yourself from a bad neighbor; do not cleave to a wicked person" (*Pirkei Avot 1:7*).

The spiritual lesson of the verse is to discern the level of spirituality of those with whom we come into contact. If we discover someone is lacking while we are sitting, standing, eating or conversing with him, it may or may not be a good time to try to help increase the Divine spark within that person.

CHAPTER FIVE, VERSE 4

By four things the scholar is recognized: his pocket, his goblet, his anger, and his dress; and, some say, even his talk.

Those who know we are rabbis will judge us. We must not, as many clergy do, flaunt our money. People are as cynical today as they were in Hebraic Temple times, and most will assume we have acquired our money unethically. When the Priests entered the Temple to collect tithes, they wore clothing without pockets, so no one could accuse them of misappropriating funds (*Shekelim 3:2*).

Except for on Purim, rabbis cannot get drunk. We cannot make fools of ourselves. We need to dress appropriately, and to be careful with our words. We cannot engage in gossip and slander. We need to practice what we teach.

We should be mindful of the concept *ma'arit ayin*, what looks good to the eye. If we behave badly, we allow the misinformed to think that our poor behavior is permissible, and by so doing put a stumbling block before the blind. We must take care to set a proper example. Behavior that is correct for rabbis is correct for everyone.

"Better one who is slow to anger than one with might, one who rules his spirit than the captor of a city" (*Proverbs 16:32*). We are all human, and we may have days when something brings us to anger. As Pirkei Avot 5:11 teaches, "There are four types of temperaments. One who is easily angered and easily appeased—his virtue cancels his flaw. One whom it is difficult to anger and difficult to appease— his flaw cancels his virtue. One whom it is difficult to anger and is easily appeased is a righteous person. One who is easily angered and is difficult to appease is wicked." Note that even the righteous person, who is difficult to anger, still gets angry at some point. We must learn how to be quickly appeased, and to make amends.

Here is the story, mentioned in the first chapter, about Rabbi Hillel (ca. 100 BCE) and anger:

> *It once happened that two men made a wager with each other, saying, "He who goes and makes Hillel angry shall receive four hundred zuz."*
>
> *Said one, "I will go and incense him."*
>
> *That day was the Sabbath eve, and Hillel was washing his head.*
>
> *He went, passed by the door of his house, and called out, "Is Hillel here, is Hillel here?" [Note he did not use the title 'Rabbi'.]*
>
> *Thereupon Hillel robed and went out to him, saying, "My son, what do you require?"*

"I have a question to ask," said he.

"Ask, my son," he prompted.

Thereupon he asked: "Why are the heads of the Babylonians round?" [R' Hillel was a Babylonian.]

"My son, you have asked a great question," replied he: "Because they have no skillful midwives."

He departed, tarried a while, returned, and called out, "Is Hillel here; is Hillel here?"

He robed and went out to him, saying, "My son, what do you require?"

"I have a question to ask," said he.

"Ask, my son," he prompted.

Thereupon he asked: "Why are the eyes of the Palmyreans bleared?"

"My son, you have asked a great question," replied he; "Because they live in sandy places."

He departed, tarried a while, returned, and called out, "Is Hillel here; is Hillel here?"

He robed and went out to him, saying, "My son, what do you require?"

"I have a question to ask," said he.

"Ask, my son," he prompted.

He asked, "Why are the feet of the Africans wide?"

"My son, you have asked a great question," said he; "Because they live in watery marshes."

"I have many questions to ask," said he, "but fear that you may become angry."

Thereupon he robed, sat before him and said, "Ask all the questions you have to ask."

"Are you the Hillel who is called the nasi [head Rabbi] of Israel?"

"Yes," he replied.

"If that is you," he retorted, "may there not be many like you in Israel!"

"Why, my son?" queried Hillel.

"Because I have lost four hundred zuz through you," complained he.

"Be careful of your moods," he answered. "I would rather you lose 400 zuz, and lose another 400 zuz myself, than lose my temper."

—Talmud Bavli Tractate Shabbat 31a

CHAPTER FIVE, VERSE 5

The beauty of the Law is knowledge; the beauty of knowledge is modesty; the beauty of modesty is the fear of Heaven; the beauty of the fear of Heaven is noble performance; the beauty of noble performance is secrecy (i.e., not publicly, for the purpose of being praised).

Verse 5:5 defines beauty as *the beautiful result of.* The beautiful result that we wish to gain from studying Torah and Talmud is wisdom. Judaism makes a distinction between wisdom, understanding, and knowledge (*chochmah, binah* and *da'at*).

Chochmah, conceptual wisdom, means to acquire a formulation of facts. For example, we can be taught that it is a mitzvah to love our fellows. If asked if it is a mitzvah to love our fellows, we can learn to say yes. When we can explain important corollaries to loving our fellows, such as avoiding gossip, we have gained *binah,* understanding. This, too, is only on a conceptual level. When we have the wisdom and the understanding, and are able to apply it in our daily lives, we have gained *da'at,* knowledge. At this level, it has become as natural as breathing for us to behave in a way that demonstrates our love for our fellows. We have combined wisdom and understanding into true knowledge. We have then truly gained the spiritual awareness that loving our fellows means living with happiness, joy, and freedom.

Studying Torah and Talmud at the basic level should yield the *chochmah* of the Torah and Talmud. We can learn the ethical behavior required to love one's fellow, but until we truly have *da'at*, we can still allow ourselves to selfishly walk past someone who needs aid.

As we work into the *da'at* stage of knowledge, we begin to become modest and humble; we recognize how little we truly comprehend. What we know trumps the intellect and reaches our very soul. As we awaken spiritually, we develop true love and awe for God, *Adon Olam*.

Because we love God, and His goodness, kindness, grace, and mercy, without a second thought we can live our lives doing not only the ritual mitzvot, but also and especially those mitzvot which are life-changing and life-affirming for others.

These mitzvot are done as privately as can be, without striving to get our names in synagogue bulletins. When we pray each day for our names to be like dust, we do not seek the *kavod*, the honors, others may seek, because we have the *da'at* that all honor belongs to God. We know we are here on earth to be of maximum service to our fellows. We need thanks for performing good deeds no more than we require applause for breathing. We understand that this is what life is, and it is beautiful.

Chapter Six

Four things are derogatory to scholars: to walk alone in the dark (and arouse suspicion); to be perfumed; to be the last in entering a prayer-house, and to hold much discourse at a confederacy of dunces.

Traits considered desirable for rabbis and scholars are desirable for everyone. The sages list four actions to avoid, but do not explain why. The reasons are found in other parts of Talmud. To walk alone in the dark on a city street may invite theft or assault, but the text says, "and arouse suspicion." Why?

Human nature is the same today as it was 2500 years ago. We are not permitted to speak lashon ha ra, but we do. If a rabbi was seen outside at night alone, some might have assumed he was *bikur cholem* (visiting the sick), but others might have spread rumors that the rabbi was up to no good. We need to keep in mind the Talmudic concept of *ma'arit ayin*—what looks good to the eye.

Judaism advocates sexual restraint outside of a committed relationship. If a rabbi was in the company of women or men who were so heavily perfumed that the aroma spread to his clothing, others might have drawn untoward inferences about his sexual behavior.

The Talmud teaches that we should run to synagogue, but depart slowly. Lateness might demonstrate that a rabbi valued another activity more than prayer or study, which could harm his reputation and effectiveness as a teacher or on a beth din.

The rabbis know that speech may be taken out of context. They advise us to say little, but do much. They repeatedly warn against idle talk, especially if it means engaging with those who wish to argue with us. They advise us not to argue with those who do not believe in Talmudic Rabbinic Judaism (for them, the Sadducees). They advise us to avoid idle talk with unschooled women. Educated women were allowed to enter the academies and to give their opinions. The rabbis do not intend for us to ignore the *am ha eretz*, people of the land, common folk, or the uneducated. They simply don't want us to waste our time trying to reach those who are too thick or too set in their ways to understand, because at best, we will anger the closed-minded, and deprive others who do wish to learn.

As Bertrand Russell said, "Most people would rather die than think; in fact, they do so." This adage is useful to remember when trying to explain to someone that his *minhag*, tradition, may be binding on his community, but is not real halakhah. Few will understand. A learned rabbi, in Tractate Sanhedrin, "is first likened by the Jewish dunce to a vase of gold; if he converses with him, he is looked upon as a vase of silver; and if he accepts a service from him, he is regarded as a vase of earth."

CHAPTER SIX, VERSE 2

hen entering, the greater shall be first; when leaving, the smaller shall be first. When ascending steps, the greater shall be first; when descending, the smaller shall be the first. At a public meeting, the greater shall have the preference. When entering a prison, the smaller shall do so first. For saying benedictions, the greater is first. The one entering the house must always greet first the one who is in the house. One must not lean at meals (as was the custom in the Orient [Babylon]) when a greater man than he is at the table. One shall not drink in public unless he turns away his face from the bystanders.

Verse 2 is reminiscent of Emily Post, but its purpose is to instill humility by teaching us to treat our elders and teachers with respect.

When entering, the greater shall be first; when leaving, the smaller shall be first.

When we enter a room we show *kavod*, honor, by allowing an elder, rabbi, or teacher to enter first and to leave last. If we precede such a person, we demonstrate bad manners and arrogance. Disrespect toward rabbis leads to a lack of respect for their teachings.

When ascending steps, the greater shall be first; when descending, the smaller shall be the first.

We see the same pattern for stairs as for entering rooms. We show kavod to a superior by allowing him or her to ascend first. Descending stairs is considered to be a less important act, hence the 'smaller' goes first.

At a public meeting, the greater shall have the preference.

How often do we see people with low self-esteem attempt to take over meetings or to make long statements when they should be asking short questions? It is proper decorum to give all honor and preference to the 'greater' person in the assembly.

For saying benedictions, the greater is first.

When dining, we allow the scholar or rabbi to make the *berachot*, blessings. In my home, my guests are given this honor. Tractate Berachot discusses the etiquette of blessings at length, as a means to show chesed and kavod to others.

The one entering the house must always greet first the one who is in the house.

How often do we see guests congregating in the vestibule to chat with one another, instead of greeting their host? We are to thank and bless the host before we hobnob with our fellow guests.

One must not lean at meals (as was the custom in the Orient) when a greater man than he is at the table.

When dining with a superior, we demonstrate respect by sitting upright and attentively. Our posture conveys that we are ready to receive some pearls of wisdom. Leaning on the table implies that we are equals, and suggests a lack of humility. The Talmud tells us that a boor cannot fear sin, which means that someone who leans at a table while dining cannot effectively learn Torah. Ironically, the word 'boor' comes from the German word *gebur*, a peasant farmer.

One shall not drink in public unless he turns away his face from the bystanders.

Judaism does not oppose the use of alcohol. Jewish holy day meals, including Shabbat, begin with drinking wine and thanking God for it. The Passover Seder mandates four cups of wine for each adult during the service. Public drunkenness, however, is frowned upon, with the exception that on Purim we are commanded to become so drunk that we cannot distinguish between 'Blessed is Mordechai' and 'Cursed is

Haman.' Nevertheless, the Talmud offers the cautionary tale of the rabbi who becomes violently drunk and nearly kills his friend. The following year, his friend decides not to push his luck, and declines the invitation to join him for Purim. For the sake of ma'arit ayin, if we are drinking in a bar, we should be discreet. We don't want anyone to see us have one small drink and assume that we have been in the bar for hours consuming cases of liquor.

We wish to avoid giving people the opportunity to badmouth us. More importantly, we do not want to give the impression that we are *chillul ha shem*, hollowing out God's holy name. If those who know that we are Jews or rabbis see us behave improperly, they may make negative assumptions about all Jews, Judaism, and God Himself.

CHAPTER SIX, VERSE 3

The first step to sin is in one's thoughts, the second is scorn, the third is haughtiness, the fourth is cruelty, the fifth is idleness, the sixth is baseless hatred, and the seventh is an evil eye; and these were meant by Solomon [Prov. xxvi. 25]: "For there are seven abominations in his heart."

The above character defects make an excellent checklist when we review the day with a chesbon ha nefesh katan. We complete an inventory of our souls before we go to sleep, to make sure that we are on the right track for spiritual growth, and to determine whether we owe anyone *teshuvah*, amends. In our morning prayers, we also ask God to keep us from these defects throughout the day. Let's review them one at a time.

Our thoughts:

In previous chapters, we discussed the need to remain God-conscious throughout the day, and to be mindful of our thoughts. When one thought jumps wildly after another, we need to calm our minds so that we can focus and be rational. When a silly idea comes up—for example, 'So-

and-so doesn't like me'—we need to catch it and replace it with a rational thought right away. If we don't, we will find ourselves thinking of ways to get even with 'So-and-so.' Soon we will be speaking lashon ha ra against him, or worse.

The spiritual truth is that what someone thinks of us is none of our business. If we are living a spiritual life, our only concern is to be right with God. We need not harm another. God forbid, if we do, we acknowledge (to ourselves and to God) that we owe him teshuvah. If we make teshuvah and the other person still wants to hold a grudge, the sin becomes his, and reveals his spiritual deficiencies.

Scorn:

To scorn someone means to believe he is worthless, despicable, and undeserving of respect. How we judge and treat others is eventually how we are judged and treated. If someone rubs us the wrong way, the Talmud says it is because we see in him something that reminds us of our own defects. Scorn can make us want to harm others, even in ways as silly as black-balling them from a club, or speaking *motzi shem ra* (making a bad name) about them.

Haughtiness:

Haughtiness is an exaggerated sense of one's own import-ance, and manifests in excessive or unjustified claims. Haughtiness goes beyond arrogance into the territory of the delusional. For one whose self-esteem is so low, and whose spirit is so disconnected, all the good God has granted has become invisible to him. He tries to make up for his low self-esteem with lies. He exaggerates, and augments his resume with fabrications. Eventually, he comes to believe the stories he tells about himself. We have seen this in the case of medics who return from military service and call themselves doctors, or when an MSW puts himself on the same level as a PhD in psychology, or when a prayer leader begins to call himself a rabbi.

Cruelty:

Cruelty can be defined as indifference to suffering, or pleasure in inflicting it. Cruelty is a form of perversion. Sadism can be related to this form of behavior. Volumes have been written on the topic. No amount of Torah study, prayer, or rabbinic nagging can correct the truly cruel. Only intense psychotherapy, medication, and in-patient treatment can keep a cruel person from harming another.

Idleness:

I have witnessed firsthand what happens when retired folks have too much time on their hands. Synagogues, churches, community groups, and board rooms turn into wrestling arenas. It is not a pretty sight. Idleness is the yetzer ha ra's petri dish. When we dwell on ourselves too much, we become prisoners of our own *Mitzraim*, our own narrowness. The best cure is to actively help others, and to do so anonymously. Let someone else be president of the local symphony board. You can set up the chairs for the concerts.

Baseless Hatred:

The Talmud teaches that *sinat chinam*, baseless hatred, was one of the primary causes of the destruction of Jerusalem and the Temple in 70 CE. The sages were not speaking of the Romans' hatred of Jews. They were talking about Jews who hated other Jews for no reason: cliques, lashon ha ra, opposing factions, and rabbis who disrespected one another.

I agree with the sages that sinat chinam, in addition to lashon ha ra, keeps good potential Jews away from synagogues, and allows bullies and others with massive egos to run rampant. The rabbis of the Talmud say that the *Shechinah*, God's Holy Presence, did not exist in Ezra's Temple in Jerusalem. The Talmud tells us that God and an arrogant, hateful, or gossipy person cannot abide in the same Universe. By *kal v'chomar*, an *a fortiori* deduction, God and such people cannot dwell in a synagogue together.

The Evil Eye:

The *ayin ha ra*, or evil eye, is not folklore superstition in Judaism. In Pirkei Avot, Chapter 2, Rabbi Eliezer says an evil eye is worse than a bad friend, a bad neighbor, or an evil heart. Judaism believes that a 'good eye' designates an attitude of good will and kindness toward others. One with this attitude will rejoice when his fellow man prospers; he wishes everyone well. An evil eye denotes the opposite attitude. A man with an evil eye will not only feel no joy, but may actually experience distress when others prosper, and relief when others suffer. A person of this character represents a great danger to our moral purity.

Worse than jealousy or coveting, an evil eye shows a terrible disconnect from one's fellows and the Divine. One with an evil eye does not believe that God helps to provide his basic needs, and wishes harm on those he thinks are doing better than he is. Such a perspective will certainly lead to untoward actions. "Anger is cruel and fury overwhelming, but who can stand before jealousy?" (*Prov. 27:4*)

King Solomon defines the sociopath: "Though his speech is charming, do not believe him, for seven abominations fill his heart" (*Prov. 26:25*). The rabbis end Chapter Six by telling us Solomon is referring to the above seven character defects. Although we are to love everyone, there are those we need to avoid. As the Talmud says, "Stay away from an evil neighbor."

Chapter Seven

There are seven things that characterize a boor, and seven that characterize a wise man. A wise man does not speak before one who is greater than he in wisdom or age. He does not interrupt his fellow's words. He does not rush to answer. His questions are on the subject and his answers to the point. He responds to first things first and to latter things later. Concerning what he did not hear, he says, "I did not hear." He concedes to the truth. With the boor, the reverse of all these is the case.

Verse 7:1 is an exact copy of Pirkei Avot 5:7. From this information we can date the two tractates of Derek Eretz. Rabba Ben BagBag, quoted in a verse after Pirkei's 5:7, is an early Tanna, a rabbi from the Mishnaic Age (10–220 CE). Assuming that Derek Eretz quotes Pirkei Avot, and not the other way around, we can deduce that Derek Eretz was written in the late Tanna period, or a bit later. (For more information about the periods of Talmudic development, please refer to Appendix B.)

Again, the rabbis want us to learn good manners and the proper way to relate to others. They distinguish between learned individuals and those without learning. The list they provide in 7:1 is self-explanatory.

CHAPTER SEVEN, VERSE 2

A scholar must be careful in his eating, drinking, washing, anointing, in wearing sandals, in his walking, dressing, in the use of his voice, in the act of spitting, and also with all his good deeds.

'Anointing' refers to the use of oil and fragrant perfumes. One of the 39 *melachot* (forms of work forbidden on Shabbat) is perfuming one's clothing. One is also forbidden to anoint one's skin or hair on fast days, e.g. Yom Kippur. The verse cautions against excessive anointing, a practice reserved for kings. We are to keep ourselves humble.

One is forbidden to clean one's shoes on Shabbat, and must clean them beforehand. The sages are concerned that one's sandals be presentable at all times, and that one dress properly.

Spitting should be done into one's handkerchief, or away from others. Those of us who rode the subways in the 1950s and 1960s may remember people spitting at their feet (and ours), and the 'Do Not Spit' signs. The sages want us to behave properly in public, and certainly to refrain from causing offense.

CHAPTER SEVEN, VERSE 3

As a bride, who so long as she is in her father's house pursues privacy and modesty, and when she is given away in marriage announces publicly, saying: "All those who can come to testify against me, let them come and do so," so a scholar must pursue privacy in his deeds but publicity in his ways; namely, he must run after truth but not after falsehood, after honesty but not after robbery, after modesty but not after haughtiness, after peace but not after war, after the advice of the old but not after that of the young. He should rather follow a lion than a woman.

A woman's chaste behavior and virginity were the prized possessions of her father, which awarded him a higher bride price. For as long as an unmarried daughter lived in the home of her father, her behavior was monitored and guarded. When her wedding day came, she could announce that she was chaste and challenge anyone to speak against her.

We see vestiges of this practice in some traditional weddings. The officiant announces that if anyone has a reason to oppose the marriage, he should speak now. Although we rarely hear of anyone interrupting a wedding ceremony today, a century ago it was not uncommon for an observer to claim a bride was not a virgin.

According to our strict rules of lashon ha ra, one of the two times when we are permitted to speak negatively about someone is if we have firsthand knowledge that a bride or groom has a sordid past.

We should pursue privacy in our deeds but publicity in our ways.

One interpretation is that we need to let private matters remain private, but not be afraid to let ourselves be public examples for proper behavior. Another interpretation is that we are to do good deeds as anonymously as we can, but teach correct behavior publicly.

In Talmudic times, people looked up to rabbis. There is a story in the Talmud about rabbinic students who followed rabbis into the privy and bath house to see how they used the toilet and bathed (*Berachot 62a*). Another tale describes a student who hid under his teacher's bed in order to learn the proper way to have marital relations (*ibid*). From this, we learn that rabbis are always on display, as are we.

We must run after truth but not after falsehood.

We aren't given the option here. We must pursue truth, *emet*. We are to run from falsehoods. We are to speak out for truth and against lies. The Talmud does not say to do this only when questionable circumstances come to our attention. The sages tell us we are to seek out and rectify these situations.

We must run after honesty but not after robbery.

We are obligated to pursue justice. The Torah repeats the word for justice, *tzedakah*, twice, to emphasize this point: "Justice, justice shall you pursue" (*Deut. 16:20*).

"To do righteousness and justice is more acceptable to the Lord than sacrifice" (*Proverbs 21:3*). A Midrash recounts God's statement to David that his justice and righteousness are more beloved than the Temple. We are commanded to be rigorously honest in all our interactions.

We should run after modesty but not after haughtiness.

Humility is a virtue often encouraged in the Talmud. Micah 6:8 tells us to "walk humbly with God." The Torah describes the humility of Moses (*Num. 12:3*). We learn that God cannot abide in the same world with one who is arrogant (*Sotah 4b*). "Everyone that is proud in heart is an abomination to the Lord!" (*Proverbs 16:5*). Through the process of Jewish spiritual renewal, we learn to ignore the yetzer ha ra, which is driven by ego and arrogance. As we practice listening to our yetzer tov, we learn humility.

We are to run after peace but not after war.

Wouldn't it be wonderful if all of humanity did this? "Hillel would say: Be of the disciples of Aaron—a lover of peace, a pursuer of peace, one who loves the creatures and draws them close to Torah" (*Pirkei Avot 1:12*). To make peace is more difficult than to make war. To be resentful and argumentative is easier than to be agreeable. Our yetzer ha ra wants to scream, 'My way or the highway.' It takes conscious and sustained effort to quell the ego and its petty desires, and to practice the art of peace-making and compromise. "Who is strong? He who converts an enemy into a friend" (*Avot of Rabbi Nathan*).

Talmud Bavli Tractate Berachot 12a tells a story of Rabbi Meir and his wife Beruriah. Meir has a vicious enemy who stalks him as he walks to the Beit HaMidrash. He prays for his enemy's demise, but his wife stops him. She says, "Don't pray for his death, pray that he change his ways." One of God's holy names is Shalom.

We are to seek after the advice of the old but not after that of the young.

Many of my *talmidim*, students, are younger than I am, and I have learned much from them. The rabbis in the Talmud record similar experiences. Rabbi Chanina remarks, "I have learned much from my teachers, more from my colleagues, and the most from my students" (*Ta'anit 7a*). The rabbis do not intend to advocate age discrimination, but advise us to seek advice from the learned and experienced—from those whose opinions count.

He shall rather follow a lion than a woman.

There are a number of possible interpretations for this line. One is that when a man follows a lion, instead of allowing a lion to follow him, he puts himself in a relatively safe position. If the lion turns to attack, he can defend himself with a spear, or a bow and arrows. When a man follows a woman and watches her movements, his yetzer ha ra leads him to seek "after the lusts of [his] own heart and [his] own eyes, after which [he goes] a whoring," (*Num. 15:39*). The lesson is to avoid physical and spiritual harm.

In the Talmud, learned rabbis are called 'lions.' Although many women in the TaNaK and Talmud are regarded as bright, brave, and influential (e.g. Deborah the Warrior Judge, Beruriah the wife of Rabbi Meir, and the nurse of Rabbi Judah ha Nasi), scholars were advised not to follow women or listen to them. Pirkei Avot 4:20 reads: "Be the tail of lions rather than the head of foxes."

> *It is better to be in the company of those greater than us in Torah. Better to be the lowly, humble student of lions rather than a great scholar among the foxes. We naturally adapt ourselves to our environment. If we associate with scholars, we will both learn from their ways and be motivated towards greater growth. If we associate with the unlearned, we will stagnate, with little incentive to realize our own potential. There are few who are so self-motivated as to require no outside stimulus for spiritual growth. Only through having our own role models and recognizing who we ourselves can be will we be impelled and inspired to follow the path of the lions before us.*
>
> —*R' Rosenfeld*

If we drop the misogyny, and interpret 'lion' as 'top Talmud scholar,' and 'woman' as 'a less educated person,' the sages are telling us to choose carefully with whom to study, and to pick the best teacher.

CHAPTER SEVEN, VERSE 4

ho respects the sages? He who gives food, drink, dress, shoes; goes out to meet and accompanies when leaving, without distinction between rabbi or disciple. And who shows them disrespect? He who occupies the seat of his master, even during his absence, or substitutes him (without permission) in lecturing, or contradicts him.

Verses 1–3 describe ideal behavior toward everyone. In Verse 4, we learn how to treat our rabbis.

In our modern era, instead of taking shoes and clothing to our rabbis, we can donate usable items to Good Will or another organization that distributes them to the needy.

The rabbis ask us to be good companions. It would be nice if we went out to greet our guests, and escorted them when they are ready to leave. Note that the verse mentions both rabbis and students. In the preceding verses we learned that students give preference to their rabbis when entering and leaving. Here, lay people show respect to any rabbi or any rabbinic student.

Although today we can interpret the text to mean that we should treat everyone with respect, we always honor the position and the title of Rabbi, regardless of the sect of Judaism to which the rabbi belongs.

Often a rabbinic student goes on to surpass his or her teacher in study and teaching, so we can't assume a student should be treated as inferior to a rabbi. As we learn in Pirkei Avot 6:3, one who teaches us just one verse or letter of Torah deserves our respect.

Accordingly, we must treat our gardeners with the same respect we show to our doctors. "Who is wise? One who can learn from anyone" (*Pirkei Avot 4:1*). Anyone can be our 'rabbi;' anyone can teach us something.

And who shows them disrespect? He who occupies the seat of his master, even during his absence, or substitutes him (without permission) in lecturing, or contradicts him.

How often do we encounter board members of synagogues who believe they can run a service or teach better than a rabbi? How many times have we heard of lay leaders who call themselves spiritual leaders, or even Ravs, Rebs, or Rabbis? They may perform life-cycle events and play the part very well, but they are acting. They may become so delusional that they believe their own press. They deceive the public into thinking that anyone with knowledge of Hebrew prayers can be a rabbi. While the Torah calls us a "nation of Priests," (*Ex.19:6*), the Talmud never calls us a nation of rabbis.

Who are we to dissect a rabbi's sermon and chastise him or her about it at the Oneg Shabbat, or when we bump into the rabbi while grocery shopping? Taking these examples farther, how often do we hear of an employee who takes over the job of an absent co-worker? He may do this to be a good 'team player,' but also to advance his own position by undermining the person who is absent. Disrespect for our fellows increases the risk of retaliation.

Chapter Eight

Chapter Eight repeats what is stated in other parts of *Derek Eretz Zuta*. During the European Renaissance, the Talmudic publishers deleted it, and it is lost to us today.

Chapter Nine

VERSE 1

REliezer the Kapar said: Keep aloof from anger, for by being angry at others you will add to your transgression. Love your admonisher, for by doing so, you will add wisdom to your ability; and rather shun the one who honors you, that your wisdom be not lessened. Love the prayer-house, in order that you shall be rewarded daily; and the house of learning, in order that your children shall come to study. Love the poor, in order that your children shall not come to poverty.

Whether we desire a toy or world peace, anger occurs in humans of all ages for one of two reasons: either we want something and cannot get it, or we had something and it was taken from us. Anger can motivate us to rationally assess the correct way to right a wrong, but if we live with chronic anger, we commit acts that are bad for others and for our own souls. Revenge may bring momentary relief, but at what cost?

A common misquote of Talmud is 'When a person gets angry, it is as if he is worshipping an idol.' The passage referred to, Talmud Bavli Tractate Shabbat 105b, actually says, "He who rips his clothing or throws something in his anger, it is as if he worships idols." The rabbis teach the not-so-subtle distinction between he who gets angry, and he who completely loses himself in his anger. Although it is never correct to lose control, controlled anger may have its place. For those of us who are not tzaddiks, 'controlled anger' may be an oxymoron. We may think we have our anger under control, but our yetzer ha ra lies to us. We rationalize. We must ask God to remove our anger.

> *The angry person is overcome by all forms of hell.*
>
> —*Nedarim 22a*

> *...the angry person considers God unimportant...the angry person forgets wisdom and increases in stupidity.*
>
> —*Nedarim 22b*

> *Remove anger from your heart.*
>
> —*Ecclesiastes 11:10*

> *A person must train himself to be gentle.*
>
> —*Ta'anit 4a*

> *Anger in a home is like rottenness in fruit.*
>
> —*Sotah 3b*

When someone admonishes us, assuming he does so honestly, we have found a fantastic teacher. Ideally we make a daily chesbon ha nefesh, but at times we may forget to look at ourselves, or we may rationalize. If someone takes the time to show us our shortcomings, we should listen and love him for it. Conversely, those who always tell us how wonderful we are only feed our egos and our yetzer ha ra. We should never take good press too seriously, as we will tend to sit on our laurels and fail to increase in wisdom. Rabbi Hillel taught that one who doesn't increase his wisdom, regresses spiritually (*Pirkei Avot 1:13*).

True prayer, called *tephila* in Hebrew, means self-judging. It is not 'dovening' at break-neck speed in a rush to finish and leave the prayer-house. Thrice daily prayer includes meditation, during which we sit quietly and listen to God's instructions for us. God, the still small voice in each of us, speaks to us constantly. We need to learn to calm our minds and listen. When we judge ourselves and listen to God's will for us, we are less likely to err, and more likely to succeed.

When we study, and our children see us study, they will grow to love study as well. It's no coincidence that a generation of immigrant Jews who grew up studying Torah and Talmud produced a generation of doctors and lawyers. The purpose of Torah study is to learn *ahavath chesed*, loving kindness, and *derek eretz*, the proper behavior towards others. Children raised without this instruction are like children raised near water who don't know how to swim. A father's obligation includes teaching his children Torah, an occupation, and how to swim (*Kiddushin 29a*).

In the United States, Jewish education is waning in Jewish homes, but it is now mandatory in South Korea. Yes, South Korea requires its students to learn Talmud. The Korean version of Talmud is a translation of Rabbi Marvin Tokayer's compilation of stories from the TaNaK and the Talmud for the Japanese audience. To the Koreans, these are children's tales, each a wise or ethical lesson. It is odd, nevertheless, that South Korean school children can quote Rabbis Papa, Abaye and Rava, while most Jewish kids in the United States cannot.

"The parent who teaches his son, it is as if he had taught his son, his son's son, and so on to the end of generations" (*Kiddushin 30a*). When we do not teach our children, we deprive future generations and harm Judaism.

Love the poor, in order that your children shall not come to poverty.

There are so many laws in the Torah and Talmud about taking care of the poor that it would be impossible to include them all in this book. The Talmud calls helping the poor 'salt,' meaning a preservative, for our own wealth. Charity means selfless love. *Tzedakah*, righteous giving, is a Hebrew word often used in place of charity, but the best translation of charity is *ahavath chesed*, loving kindness.

We gain nothing without God's aid. Everything is a loan from God. Sometimes the loans are called and we need to help others. The Talmud teaches that if two beggars each have one coin, one should give the other his coin. When we gain the spiritual awareness that our money is a loan from God, we understand that parting with some of it will not harm us. When we open our hands to give, we become able to receive more of God's blessings. If we do not use some of our money for tzedakah, it will be taken from us.

By loving and helping the poor, we help our own children. The Talmud tells the story of a father who did not help as much as he could have, and what happened to his daughter as a result. Rabbi Nakdimon ben Guryon was one of the three richest men in Jerusalem. He lost everything, and was forced to renege on his daughter's dowry of one million gold dinars. She was found picking barley seeds from the dung of Arabs' donkeys (*Ketubot 66b*).

His daughter tells Rabbi Yochanan that charity is the salt, the preserver, of one's wealth. She explains to a shocked R'Yochanan that her father, when he walked from the Temple to the his house and back, asked his servants to lay silk carpets on the streets for him to walk on. He would then give the carpets to the poor.

R'Yochanan ben Zakkai bursts into tears and says, "Happy are you, Israel. As long as you perform the will of God, no nation or people can rule over you. But when you fail to perform the will of God, you are delivered into the hands of a humiliating nation, and not only the hands of a humiliating nation, but also into the hands of the beasts of the humiliating nation." The Gemara chides R'Nakdimon for his self-glorification and ego. Although he was generous, a man of his wealth could have given much more (*Ketubot 66b*).

It is a *mitzvah*, a commandment, to give tzedakah, but it is better to give altruistically, with ahavath chesed. When we love the poor, our children learn chesed, and the gift becomes a salt for their eventual inheritance.

Love modesty, that you may enjoy longevity; love the pious, in order that you may be saved from the Black Angel. Be careful in the reading of Shema, and prayer in general, in order to be saved from Gehenna. Your house shall be wide open, so that you shall never lack food. Be careful that the doors of your house are not closed when you take your meals, so that you shall not be punished with poverty.

What is modesty, and how does it contribute to longevity? There is a cute but wise observation in the Talmud: "If the Torah had not been given, we would have learned *tzni'ut* [modesty] from a cat" (*Eruvin 100b*). Traditional Judaism places emphasis on the way one dresses or relates to the opposite sex, but in the study of derek eretz, modesty means humility.

Moses is referred to as "exceedingly humble, more than any man in the world" (*Num. 12:3*). The Talmud states that humility is a desirable character trait for the Jewish people (*Yevamot 79a*). Humility is a sign of Godly strength and purpose, not weakness. "God opposes the proud but gives grace to the humble" (*Proverbs 3:34*). The rabbis teach that the man who thinks he can live without others is mistaken; the one who thinks others can't live without him is even more deluded.

Humility is a desirable trait because it creates in us the capacity to truly love God and others. When we understand that we are connected with a transcendent unity, we can experience egolessness. Ego separates us from God and our fellows. If we resent someone, we probably recognize in him our own defects of character. We prefer to shun him or to hold a grudge against him than to work on ridding ourselves of those defects.

An over-the-top ego distances from our fellows and limits our spiritual awareness. The resulting chronic stress can take years off of our lives, which is why the sages teach that modesty ensures longevity.

Love the pious, in order that you may be saved from the Black Angel.

The Black Angel is not an outside force, but our *yetzer ha ra*, our inclination to disregard what we know is right. The sages tell us that even God has a yetzer ha ra, which they define as Satan (i.e. Ha Satan, or 'the Adversary').

When we love and spend time with spiritual people, we learn their ways. Rather than just reading about Derek Eretz, we see them practice it. We can easily read about ignoring the wrongs that are done to us, but it is difficult to learn how to actually do so. When we see a spiritual person living derek eretz, we learn by example. Spending time with spiritual folk who live what they teach inspires us to maintain spiritual fitness.

Be careful in the reading of Shema, and prayer in general, in order to be saved from Gehenna.

When the Talmud discusses the Shema in Tractate Berachot, the rabbis are not only referring to the line "Hear O Israel, the Lord our God, the Lord is One," but to all that follows, which is known as the *V'Ahavtah*.

To understand and believe the first sentence puts life in its proper perspective. The rest is a checklist. Do we really love God and our fellows...at home, on the road, at work, and so forth? To question ourselves when we pray is called *tephila*, which means to self-judge.

As King David says in Psalm 16:07: "I bless God who is my counselor, but in the night, my inmost self instructs me." The tractate of Berachot begins with the Shema, which we use to judge ourselves, as follows:

Deuteronomy 6:4–9

Sh'ma Yis'ra'eil Adonai Eloheinu Adonai echad.
Hear, Israel, the Lord is our God, the Lord is One.
[In an undertone:]

Barukh sheim k'vod malkhuto l'olam va'ed.
Blessed be the Name of His glorious kingdom
forever and ever.

*V'ahav'ta eit Adonai Elohekha b'khol l'vav'kha uv'khol
naf'sh'kha uv'khol m'odekha.*
And you shall love the Lord your God with all your heart
and with all your soul and with all your might.

*V'hayu had'varim ha'eileh asher anokhi m'tzav'kha
hayom al l'vavekha.*
And these words that I command you today
shall be in your heart.

V'shinan'tam l'vanekha v'dibar'ta bam
And you shall teach them diligently to your children,
and you shall speak of them.

*B'shiv't'kha b'veitekha uv'lekh't'kha vaderekh
uv'shakh'b'kha uv'kumekha*
When you sit at home, and when you walk along the way,
and when you lie down and when you rise up.

Uk'shar'tam l'ot al yadekha v'hayu l'totafot bein einekha.
And you shall bind them as a sign on your hand, and they
shall be for frontlets between your eyes.

Ukh'tav'tam al m'zuzot beitekha uvish'arekha.
And you shall write them on the doorposts of your house
and on your gates.

Deuteronomy 11:13–21
V'hayah im shamo'a tish'm'u el mitz'votai
And it shall come to pass if you surely listen
to the commandments

Asher anokhi m'tzaveh et'khem hayom
That I command you today

L'ahavah et Adonai Eloheikhem ul'av'do b'khol
l'vav'khem uv'khol naf'sh'khem
To love the Lord your God and to serve him
with all your heart and all your soul,

V'natati m'tar ar'tz'khem b'ito yoreh umal'kosh
V'asaf'ta d'ganekha v'tirosh'kha v'yitz'harekha.
That I will give rain to your land, the early
and the late rains,
That you may gather in your grain,
your wine and your oil.

V'natati eisev b'sad'kha liv'hem'tekha v'akhal'ta v'sava'ta.
And I will give grass in your fields for your cattle
and you will eat and you will be satisfied.

Hisham'ru lakhem pen yif'teh l'vav'khem
V'sar'tem va'avad'tem Elohim acheirim
v'hish'tachavitem lahem
Beware, lest your heart be deceived
And you turn and serve other gods and worship them.

V'charah af Adonai bakhem v'atzar et hashamayim
v'lo yih'yeh matar
V'ha'adamah lo titein et y'vulah

And anger of the Lord will blaze against you, and He will
close the heavens and there will not be rain,
And the earth will not give you its fullness,

Va'avad'tem m'heirah mei'al ha'aretz hatovah asher
Adonai notein lakhem.
And you will perish quickly from the good land
that the Lord gives you.

V'sam'tem et d'varai eileh al l'vav'khem v'al naf'sh'khem
Uk'shar'tem otam l'ot al yed'khem v'hayu l'totafot bein
eineikhem.
So you shall put these, My words, on your heart
and on your soul;
And you shall bind them for signs on your hands,
and they shall be for frontlets between your eyes.

V'limad'tem otam et b'neikhem l'dabeir bam
And you shall teach them to your children,
and you shall speak of them

B'shiv't'kha b'veitekha uv'lekh't'kha vaderekh
uv'shakh'b'kha uv'kumekha.

When you sit at home, and when you walk along the way,
and when you lie down and when you rise up.

Ukh'tav'tam al m'zuzot beitekha uvish'arekha.
And you shall write them on the doorposts of your house
and on your gates.

L'ma'an yirbu y'maychem vi-y'may v'naychem
al ha-adamah.
Asher nishba Adonai la-avotaychem latayt lahem
ki-y'may ha-shamayim al ha-aretz.

In order to prolong your days and the days of your children
on the land
That the Lord promised your fathers that He would
give them, as long as the days that the heavens are
over the earth.

Numbers 15:37–41

Vayo'mer Adonai el mosheh lei'mor
And the Lord spoke to Moses, saying...
Dabeir el b'nei Yis'ra'eil v'amar'ta aleihem
Speak to the children of Israel and say to them

V'asu lahem tzitzit al kan'fei vig'deihem l'dorotam
V'nat'nu al tzitzit hakanaf p'til t'kheilet.
They should make themselves tzitzit [fringes] on the corners
of their clothing throughout their generations,
And give the tzitzit of each corner a thread of blue.

V'hayah lakhem l'tzitzit ur'item oto uz'khar'tem
et kol mitz'vot Adonai
Va'asitem otam v'lo taturu acharei l'vav'khem
v'acharei eineikhem
Asher atem zonim achareihem.
And they shall be tzitzit for you, and when you look at
them you will remember all of the Lord's commandments
And do them, and not follow after your heart and after
your eyes, which lead you astray.

L'ma'an tiz'k'ru va'asitem et kol mitz'votai viyitem
k'doshim lei'loheikhem

In order to remember and do all My commandments, and be holy for your God.

Ani Adonai Eloheikhem
Asher hotzei'ti et'khem mei'eretz Mitz'rayim
lih'yot lakhhem leilohim
Ani Adonai Eloheikhem

I am the Lord your God who led you from the land of Egypt to be a God to you.
I am the Lord, your God.

Ask yourself, are you really doing the *mitzvot*, the duties of the heart? Do you love God with all your heart, with all of your soul and with all your might? Do you sincerely try to do what is right and just while at home, at work, and on the street? Do you let your eyes go astray and worship other gods, such as the god of money, the god of lust, or the god of ego? Do you try to keep God in your awareness throughout the day? Do your actions make you a good teacher to others?

This is how to say the prayer with *kavenah*, true spiritual intention. To say it aloud with fellow congregants as if it were a mantra or a Jewish pledge of allegiance is not kavenah. Maimonides (*The Guide for the Perplexed, Part 3, Chapter 51*) expresses the point directly: "Do not pray moving your lips with your face to the wall (as if you are engaged deeply in prayer) and all the while you are thinking of your business transactions....Do not think you have achieved anything [by doing these things]."

My best prayers are not communal, but said at home, in quiet, where God can hear me and I can hear Him. You can say your *tephila* prayers silently if you wish. Psalm 65:2 says: "To You, silence is praise." Each morning, consider the day ahead. If you know, for example, that you have a company party to attend and the sin of gossip is on your *chesbon ha nefesh gadol*, ask yourself how well you have been avoiding this defect. Ask God to help you avoid this defect when you attend the party. We have a prayer specifically for this sin "May God guard my tongue from evil and my lips from speaking guile" (*Berachot 16b–17a, Psalm 34:14*).

If ego and showing off are character defects of yours, ask God to "let your name be like dust to everyone." The less you concern yourself with prestige, the less you will let selfishness interfere with your service to God and your fellows, or to daily spiritual growth and self-improvement. You will be able to ignore barbs, snubs, and insults from others, as they will mean nothing to you.

Remember that prayer is a lifelong process. You will find that the practice evolves over time. As you learn the prayers, you will find some that you like and stay with them. Others, you may not like as much and choose to not say them. This is fine, so long as you are saying your prayers with kavenah. Choose prayers that you like from our prayer books, or from the TaNaK, especially Psalms, or even other spiritual texts.

Continually self-judging and striving to do better keep us from a life that is hell, *Gehenna*, on Earth.

Your house shall be wide open, so that you shall never lack food. Be careful that the doors of your house are not closed when you take your meals, so that you shall not be punished with poverty.

At Passover, we go to the door of our homes at the beginning of the Seder, and say in Aramaic, "Let those who are hungry come and eat." Many think this is just what Jews say once a year at a Seder. The Talmud Bavli Tractate Ta'anit 20b teaches that Rabbi Huna would open his door and announce, "Whoever is needy, let him come and eat." He announced this every day. (This is the same Rabbi Huna who says, in Tractate Kiddushin, "One should not walk six feet without a kippah on his head.")

"A man saw not his fellow, neither rose any from his place for three days" (the Plague of Darkness, *Exodus 10:23*). No greater darkness exists in which 'a man saw not his fellow'—in which a person becomes oblivious to the needs of his fellow man. When that happens, his personal development is stymied—'neither rose any from his place.' This was taught by Rabbi Yitzchak Meir of Ger (1789–1866).

Our doors should always be open, never closed to those in need. Neither should our hearts and wallets be closed. When we become so jaded that we ignore the plight of others, and call those who care 'socialists' or 'wealth redistributors,' we harm our own souls and our own wealth, despite foolishly believing that we are protecting them.

CHAPTER NINE, VERSE 3

Be careful about the honor of your wife.

"Live happily with the woman you love through all the meaningless days of life that God has given you under the sun. The wife God gives you is your reward for all your earthly toil." So teaches King Solomon in Ecclesiastes 9:9. A happy marriage is one of the highest goals of Judaism.

In the Torah, women have the status of chattel. They belong to their husbands, fathers, or in the absence of a father, to their brothers. Many laws in Hebraism protected women. A man was required to love all of his wives equally. A woman had the freedom to choose whether to marry her brother-in-law if her husband died and left her childless. Daughters could inherit. In Judaism, more laws were enacted to give women honor, status, and rights.

Judaism does not consider sex to be sinful or obscene. We do not think of sex as an impure act that we must tolerate in order to have children. The rabbis admit that the desire for sex comes from our yetzer ha ra, but we can tame desire. The rabbis tell the story that they petitioned God to do away with the yetzer ha ra, and when God granted their request, no one went to work, no one built homes, and no children were born. The rabbis then asked God to return the yetzer ha ra to humanity.

Judaism wants us to control our sexuality. When sex involves love as well as desire between a husband and wife, sex is a mitzvah. Sex in Judaism is not just for procreation. It helps to create a loving bond between the wife and husband, who are equals in a marriage. Certain types of contraception are allowed in Judaism.

The Hebrew word for sex, dat, literally means 'to know.' A relationship is not Judaic if it is based on sex without a co-joining of hearts and minds. The need for physical compatibility is also important in Judaism. In the days of arranged marriages, the couple met before the wedding. If either party found the other sexually unattractive, the wedding was called off.

The Talmud lists times to have sex and times not to have sex. Selfish sex without regard for the partner's pleasure is disallowed. Sex should be a joyous time for both. Long before the recent marital rape laws, Judaism forbade a man to force his wife to have sex. Sex can't be used abusively, whether through force or denial. One can't have sex if inebriated, or when fighting.

Unlike Hebraism, Judaism makes sex the wife's right and not the man's right. A husband is obligated to give his wife pleasurable sex regularly. He must watch for signs that his wife wants sex, and offer before she has to ask. The

Talmud calls a wife's right to sex *onah*. It is one of her three basic rights, in addition to clothing and food. A man cannot reduce his wife's onah. The Talmud goes into detail about the quality and frequency of sex that the husband must give to his wife. This is spelled out in the *ketubah*, marriage contract.

A husband may not go away on a voyage for a long time, as to do so would deprive his wife of sexual intercourse. In Judaism, if a husband, even after having children, refuses to have sex, a woman can divorce him. In Hebraism, only a man could institute a *get*, bill of divorcement. Nor does Judaism allow a woman to withhold sex from her husband, even though we have mentioned it is her right and not his. If she withholds sex from her husband, he may divorce her, and she loses the settlement enumerated in her ketubah.

Sex is not just vaginal-penile penetration in Judaism. The Talmud states, "a man may do whatever he pleases with his wife," if both are agreeable. The Talmud encourages foreplay to arouse the woman. It specifically forbids a man from using a 'morning erection' without first having his wife's permission and arousing her.

There are numerous other ways in which a man can honor his wife beyond the bedroom.

> We find that God...adorns the bride, as it is written, "And the Lord God built...". Rabbi Yochanan said, "He built Eve [interpreting the word binyan as b'naeh, *with beauty*] and

adorned her with jewels and showed her to Adam." Said Rabbi Abahu, "Perhaps you will say that He showed her to him from some carob tree or bush? But no, after He adorned her with 24 kinds of jewelry, only then did He show her to him. For it says, 'And He brought her to the Adam.'"

—Midrash Rabbah Ecclesiastes 7:7

Rita Rudner quipped, "I think men who have a pierced ear are better prepared for marriage. They've experienced pain, and bought jewelry."

The Code of Jewish Law, Orach Chaim 529, reads: "Men are instructed to buy our wives new clothes and jewelry before every Jewish holiday, each husband according to his financial means." Men are happy when we "drink wine and eat meat." Women, however, would rather "wear diamonds."

The Talmud tells us that a man's livelihood depends on acquiring jewels for his wife. According to Bava Metzia 59a, Rebbe said in the name of Rabbi Chelbo, "A person should always be careful about the honor of his wife, for blessing is found in a person's home only due to his wife, as the verse states, 'And He did good to Abram for her sake.'"

Obviously we are to refrain from speaking lashon ha ra about our wives. We know to honor them by treating them with dignity, love, respect, and sensitivity. But jewels? Really? Yes, because when God provided manna for us every day in B'Midbar, according to Talmud Bavli Tractate Yoma 75a, God also provided women with jewelry! Trying to be just, kind, merciful, and forgiving is hard enough, but buying gems? And at maybe even at retail?!

On the same *daf*, Rava says to his town's people, "Honor your wives, in order that you will become rich." Ravi explains in Shabbat 62a, "There are three things that bring a man to poverty...and one is when his wife curses him." Rava adds, "When she curses him about jewelry, because he can afford it and does not provide her."

> When a man buys his wife fine clothes and jewelry, he should have in mind that he is beautifying the Divine Presence, represented in this world by none other than his wife.
>
> —Shaar Ha-Otiot, Maamar 7

> Every man must see himself as standing between two women—the Shechinah [Divine Presence] above, providing him with all his needs, and the Shechinah below, i.e. his wife, to whom he provides in turn.
>
> —Rabbi Moshe Cordovero

Men are a channel from God to their wives and children. God provides for us according to how we provide for our families. "A man should eat and drink less than his means, clothe himself according to his means, and honor his wife and children beyond his means. For they depend upon him, and he depends on the One that spoke and the world came into being" (*Chullin 84b*).

A Jewish marriage is not a business deal, as it was in Hebraism. If a marriage is based on 'you give this and I give that,' it is not a spiritual union. Rabbi Don Yitzchak Abarbanel said, "Love turns one person into two and two into one." Our souls need to fuse as one.

To show love, one buys something that has no purpose at all, which the sages tell us is jewelry. God provides for all of our earthly needs, but we need God for spiritual reasons also. We need a relationship with God that goes beyond the physical into the metaphysical. The prophets and Midrash describe the Jews' relationship with God as a marriage. God is the groom, the Israelites are the bride, and the Torah is the Ketubah.

CHAPTER NINE, VERSE 4

Be glad of your chastisement, for this probably saves you from Gehenna.

We are told to love one who reproves us in Chapter Three of Derek Eretz Zuta. Reproving means gentle instruction, done privately. Chastisement is a bit stronger.

Assuming that someone is chastising us for the right reasons, we are to listen, evaluate and learn. We are not to ignore him, or tell him to mind his own business. In Judaism, a way of life, others' behavior affects us and the community. Rabbi Shimon bar Yochai, traditionally cited as the author of the Zohar, tells of a fellow in a small boat who drills a hole under his seat. The other passengers yell at him to stop, because he will sink the whole boat. He responds that he is only drilling under his own seat (*Midrash Rabbah Vayikra 4:6*). *Kol Yisroel areivim zeh lazeh*—all Israel, all of humanity, are responsible for one another (*Shevuot 39a*).

CHAPTER NINE, VERSE 5

Be joyful at your table when the hungry derive benefit from it, in order that you may enjoy longevity and have a share in the World to Come. Be also joyful when giving charity from your house, in order that you may pacify the Angel of Death, as it is written [Prov. xxi. 14]: "A gift in secret pacifies anger, and a bribe in the bosom, strong fury." If you have troubled your feet for the poor or for the sake of a merit, the following passages may be applied to you [Deut. xxviii . 6]: "Blessed shall you be when you come in, and blessed shall you be when you come out."

Although today a bribe has negative connotations, King Solomon wrote Proverbs at a time when Hebrews lived in places where one person held a great deal of power. Money could keep this power from killing them. The Hebrews still believed in a God who smites, thus in the above verse the metaphor of a "bribe in the bosom" compares charity given in secret, to a bribe to an official, who would place the money in the ancient equivalent of the pocket of his sports jacket. Proverbs is telling us that a charitable gift made in secret can overcome God's anger, just as a hidden bribe to an official could stop his anger against the Hebrews. In our Yom Kippur services, we are forgiven for sins against God through *tzedakkah v'chesed*, charity and kind acts. We make amends to God by being kind to His children in need, and keep His wrath from us. Derek Eretz uses the verse from Proverbs as a way to say charity will keep us alive in a spiritual sense.

The rabbis discuss what we are obligated to provide for someone living in poverty. They cite the verse that instructs us to provide the pauper, "...sufficient for his needs which he is lacking" (Deut. 15:8). Ketubot 67b explains how to give charity. "You are obligated to provide the poor person 'sufficient for his needs,' but you are not obligated to make him rich. When the verse in the Torah adds, 'which he is lacking,' this implies even a horse to ride upon and a servant to run before him." The Gemara explains that if we provide a servant for someone who is used to luxuries but has fallen on hard times, we are not making him rich. To be rich is to go beyond the fulfillment of our needs, to have no concerns. Even if our feet hurt from running to do mitzvot of chesed for those in need, we receive joy, longevity, Heaven, a painless death, and Divine blessings whether in or out of our homes.

CHAPTER NINE, VERSE 6

I f you keep your mouth from slander, you will spend all the days of life in peace. One who is audacious towards one who is greater than he will finally be punished with a plague.

The 'plague' mentioned here is the state of living in chronic discord, brought about by insolence toward our rabbis, teachers, parents, employers, and, frankly, anyone. If we want peace, we need to treat our social superiors and all others with respect.

Careless, caustic speech leads to resentment, hostility, jealousy, discontent, suspicion, and alienation. Our words impact the perceptions and beliefs of others, and thus can have life-altering consequences, for good or ill. When we practice the rules of proper speech, *shmirat ha lashon*, literally 'guarding our tongue,' our intent is to avoid causing harm.

By mindfully seeking to avoid causing pain, we learn to observe the best in others, and to appreciate the many blessings in our lives. *Lashon tov*, good speech, elevates those around us and deepens our connection with the Divine. It enables us to see God's image in everyone. "And I have placed My words in your mouth...to implant the heavens and to set a base for the earth..." (*Is. 51:16*).

> *When Ha Shem rewards the wicked in this world for whatever good they have done [reserving their punishment for the World to Come], He grants them wealth, property, longevity, honor, and other benefits—but He does not grant them tranquility, as is it written, 'There is no peace,' says my God, 'for the wicked.'*
> —Sefer Ma'alot HaMiddot, Is. 57:21

Peace is given to the righteous: "And the deed of righteousness will be [rewarded with] peace" (*ibid. 32:17*).

CHAPTER NINE, VERSE 7

If you run to do honor to a sage, you will be rewarded with enviable children; and for running to do honor to the poor, you will be rewarded with sons of learning and a law-abiding record in Israel. If you see a sage die, do not turn away from him until after burial, that you, too, may receive respect and attention when it is your time to die.

Not only should we honor scholars, we should also honor the poor. More often than not, we do mitzvot when the opportunity presents itself. Just as we are to actively pursue justice and peace, we should seek out individuals to honor, rather than wait for a rabbi or a poor person to cross our paths.

When someone dies, we are to stay with the body. We never leave a body unattended before burial. Although some of our rabbis were rich, like Judah ha Nasi, others, such as Chanina ben Dosa, were so poor they only could afford to eat carobs (*Ta'anit 24b*). Chanina's wife concealed their poverty by burning wood in the fireplace to create the appearance that she was baking. One day a neighbor spied on her. When she opened the oven, a miracle occurred—she found loaves of challah bread inside. The poor and the sages are intertwined in this verse because we can never truly know if our sages are poor, or if our poor are indeed sages.

CHAPTER NINE, VERSE 8

hen you see your neighbor has become poor and his power is on the decline, do not refuse to help him, as it is written [Eccl. viii. 5]: "Whoever keeps the commandment will experience no evil." If you have loaned him something when he was in need, the following passage will be fulfilled on you [Is. lviii. 9]: "When you call, the Lord will answer."

We are obligated to help our fellows as their livelihood declines, rather than wait until they have hit rock bottom. We are not to close our hands to the poor. By doing so, we not only deprive them of help, we dishonor them. We can give, or we can lend without interest, but we must help.

"If there is a poor man with you, one of your brothers, in any of your towns in your land which the Lord your God is giving you, you shall not harden your heart, nor close your hand from your poor brother" (*Deut. 15:7*). "If you lend money to one of my people among you who is needy, do not be like a moneylender; charge him no interest" (*Exodus 22:25*).

CHAPTER NINE, VERSE 9

If you lower yourself, the Lord will lift you up; but if you assume superiority over your fellow men, the Lord will lower you.

If we are humble, in God's time, doors will open for us. If we act superior and obnoxious, others will put us in our place. As we pray each morning, "Let my soul be like dust to everyone." If we push to sit at the head of the table, or to be chair of the board, someone else will do his best to kick us off. If we sit humbly at the end of the table, and don't seek office, people will ask us to move to the head, or to hold a position.

CHAPTER NINE, VERSE 10

If others quarrel with you, whether in a house of learning or at an ordinary meeting place, do not leave until peace is restored, and they shall praise you in your absence as Pinchas b. Elazar. Great is peace, that even when it reigns among idolaters nothing can be done to them, as it is written [Hosea, iv. 17]: "Ephraim is bound (bound together) to idols; let him alone." But if they quarrel among themselves, it is said of them [ibid. x. 2]: "Their heart is divided; now shall they bear their guilt." Hence that house in which there is strife will be destroyed, and the sages say that even a prayer-house in which there is strife will be demolished.

The Torah tells us not to be like Korach, a quarrelsome man. Because the sages understand human nature, they know that we will quarrel. When we do, whether in a synagogue or a business meeting, we should make sure that the quarrel is put to rest and peace is restored before we leave. The sages know that anger can lead to untoward behavior. They know that holding a grudge tears us apart. On a spiritual level, every unkind act masks the Divine sparks of light that an act of chesed would unhusk. On a psychological level, unresolved quarrels cause us to lose sleep, to replay and rewrite the situation in our heads.

When we look back on our lives, was the ill will generated by any fight worth what we thought at the time was so important? Ninety-nine percent of the things we argue about with others are, "Meaningless! Meaningless! Utterly meaningless! Everything is meaningless" (*King Solomon, Eccl: 1:2*).

Pinchas is rewarded in the Torah for killing a Hebrew who fornicates with a Midianite woman. His descendants become the Kohanim Gadol, the head priests. The Talmud does not speak very kindly of him, however. The sages attempt to justify his actions by explaining that Moses taught him, "He who has sexual relations with a heathen may be attacked by zealous people" (*Sanhedrin 82a*). They also allow the couple to defend themselves. If the zealots are killed, the couple is deemed not guilty of murder.

In Judaism, peace is more important than worship or belief in God. God would prefer for us to ignore Him, even to worship idols, than to be at odds with one another. The sages tell us that homes and synagogues filled with strife will be destroyed. This isn't a Divine punishment, but is simply what happens when people in any group treat each other poorly. It is ironic that most break-away congregations have the word 'Shalom' in their names. It has been quipped that all that is necessary to start a new synagogue is a quarrel, resentment, and a mezuzah.

CHAPTER NINE, VERSE 11

The same is it with two chiefs of the court who live in one town and quarrel with each other. They will finally die. Abba Saul said: Strife between courts is a destruction of the world.

In Talmudic times, the Jewish courts made decisions on halakhah, in addition to decisions on legal cases involving monetary disputes. Within the same town, halakhah and *minhag*, custom, had to be consistent. Tractate Sanhedrin tries to resolve the different opinions of rabbinic judges, in order to bring about one 'law' for all. When two rabbis disagreed, especially if they were deceased and could no longer be consulted, the current rabbis looked for evidence that they actually did agree.

In contemporary Judaism, the use of a three-man court is rare, aside from those existing in Orthodox communities. We can apply the statement to situations in which two rabbis in the same town, or from two congregations in the same town, argue and don't get along. Derek Eretz tells us such friction destroys the world, or at least the town's Jewish community. The holiday of Lag B'Omer reminds us of a plague that struck 24,000 rabbis, circa 100 CE, because they argued with and failed to respect one another. Shalom in the Jewish community is more important than debating who is a Jew, or whether institutional ordination is better than traditional one-on-one semikah.

CHAPTER NINE, VERSE 12

Abba Issi b. Yohanan said in the name of Samuel the Little: This world resembles the eyeball of a man. The white is the ocean that surrounds the whole land; the black is the world; the circle in the black is Jerusalem, and the image (the pupil) in the circle is the Temple, which will be rebuilt in the near future. Amen.

An honest reading of the TaNaK shows us that Jerusalem was not a city of pure shalom, nor was the Temple a place of pure shalom. Humans resided and worked in both, and humans are not saints. Kings fought kings, princes fought princes, priests fought rabbis and also fought each other.

Tractate Kiddushin 70b states, "If you see a Kohan who is arrogant, be assured that his lineage is genuine." Hoshea 4:04 says, "Your nation is argumentative like a Kohan." Tractate Bava Batra 160b observes, "Kohanim are bad-tempered." The Maharal says that Kohanim think the "fire of holiness" is in them and their blood "boils." The Talmud reports that Kohanim would kill each other in the Temple courtyard while they argued over who would perform the Temple sacrifice. Certain services yielded better cuts of sacrificed meats.

In the first Babylonian Diaspora, second Roman Diaspora, during the periods in between in an occupied Judea, and in Judea under the anti-rabbinic rule of the Hashmonean Hebraists, the rabbis conceptualized Jerusalem and the Temple as the center of the universe. Jerusalem was the center of God's eye, and a place where, if all the laws were followed, everyone would live in peace.

The Temple held seventy sacrifices every Sukkot, one for each of the known nations (*Sukkot 55b*). The Talmud says if Rome had understood that the priests were asking God to protect them and the rest of the world, the Romans would not have destroyed the Temple. The Zion to which the priests refer, and to which they wish to go, is the Messianic Jerusalem—a city, a nation, and a world in shalom. The Messianic Temple (the third in Jerusalem, and the fifth in the history of Hebraism including the Leontopolis and Elephantine Temples) is one devoid of animal sacrifices. The only grain sacrifices left are those for *gomal*, thanks given to God for restoring us from an illness, or for allowing us to return safely from a voyage.

Chapter Ten

THE CHAPTER ON PEACE

The rabbis were so impressed with Chapter Ten, so dedicated to its message, that some of them wanted to make it a tractate of Talmud by itself (*Rabbi Leopold Zunz, aka Reb Yom Tov, b. 1794*). It is rarely referred to as Chapter Ten, but rather as "the Chapter on Peace."

Rabbi Joshua ben Levi, oft-quoted in this chapter, is the hero of almost all of the paradise legends in the Talmud. He travels as Elijah's companion when Elijah wanders the earth (*Midrash Pesikta 36a*). He meets Elijah before the gates of paradise (*Sanhedrin 98a*). While still alive, he is permitted to visit Paradise and the netherworld. He sends a description of what he sees there to Rabban Gamaliel (*Seder ha-Dorot*) via the submissive Angel of Death. The original accounts are in the *Zohar*, which captures the essence in fragmentary documents (*Zohar Beresheit, 38a–39b, 41a, and Zohar Lecha 81a, b*). One of these accounts is credited to Enoch. Midrash Konen is probably the first compilation of and elaboration on these fragments. Many of the legends about Joshua have been collected in separate small works entitled *Ma'aseh de-Rabbi Yehoshua' ben Levi* and *Masseket Gan Eden we-Gehinnom*.

Why did Rabbi Joshua ben Levi merit to enter Paradise while he was still alive, as stated in *Derek Eretz Zuta* 1:6? He based his rulings on *ahavath chesed*, loving-kindness, and peace. At a time when many rabbis cursed Jews who belonged to the sect of Rabbi Yeshua ben Yosef (now called Christians), he taught of getting along with them. He believed that the righteous of all nations (religions) have a share in the World to Come.

CHAPTER TEN, VERSE 1

RJoshua b. Levi said: Great is peace, for it is as the leaven to dough. If the Holy One had not given peace to the world, sword and beast would devour up the whole world, as it is written [Lev. xxvi. 6]: "And I will give peace in the land."

Without peace in the land, one literally cannot plant grain from which to make bread. Nor can we make bread without leaven. Bread is our sustenance. It is not by happenstance that synonyms for income are both 'bread' and 'dough.' Without peace, we cannot live effectively with others. When we are not at peace with others, we are torn up inside. We feel as though wild beasts and swords are destroying our souls.

CHAPTER TEN, VERSE 2

It is written [Eccl. i. 4]: "One generation passes away, and another generation comes, but the earth endures forever." King Solomon meant to say: Although one generation passes away and another one comes, one kingdom disappears and another one appears; and although evil decrees one after another are enacted against Israel, still they endure forever. The Lord does not abandon them, and they are never abandoned. They are never annihilated, neither do they decrease, as it is written [Mal. iii. 6]: "For I the Lord have not changed: and you sons of Jacob, you have not ceased to be" (i.e., as I have never changed and will never change, so you sons of Jacob have never ceased and will never cease to be). But [Deut. iv. 4]: "You who remained faithful to the Lord your God are alive, every one of you, this day."

Although the passage does not contain the word 'peace,' it is meant as a balm to the Jewish people during times of hardship. Verse 2 assures us that *Am Israel*, the people of Israel, will survive. Each of us eventually dies, and some die too soon, as martyrs, but a new generation arises. The phrase "one kingdom disappears and another kingdom appears" can be viewed in two ways.

Israel was a small tribe under our Patriarchs. We lost our freedom in Egypt. We sprouted a new nation under Moses and Joshua, and continued as such until the end of Solomon's kingship. Two Jewish states, Israel and Judea, emerged side-by-side. Israel eventually perished, and Judea went into Babylonian captivity. Some people stayed in the Persian Empire, while others returned to establish a Jewish community in Judea under Persian control. We lived under Greek rule, and regained statehood in the Maccabee's war. Next, we lived under Roman rule, with a small period of independence under Bar Kochba. Ultimately, we lost our homeland and lived under the rule of our host nations. They were sometimes kind, sometimes brutal, and at other times deadly. In the verse, and as history has borne out, the Jews live on.

Another way to read the verse is that other kingdoms come and go, but Jews continue. Canaanites, Philistines, Pharaoh's Egyptians, Moabites, Midianites, Amaleks, Assyrians, Babylonians, Persians, Alexandrian Greeks, Imperial Romans, Constantinians, Ottomans, and even the Third Reich (may their names be blotted out) are not flying flags at the United Nations, but Israel is.

Evil decrees are levied against the Jewish people, yet we survive. Pharaoh tried to kill our first-born males; the Persian Haman tried to wipe out all the Jews; the Greeks tried to keep us from study, as did the Romans who forbade *semikah*, rabbinic ordination. We were banned, expelled, persecuted, rounded into ghettos, and killed almost everywhere we settled. Yet no evil decree could destroy us. "*Ootzoo etza v'toofar, dabroo davar v'lo yakoom, key imanu El*"—"Form your plot, it shall fail. Lay your plan, it shall not prevail, for God is with us" (*Is. 8:10*).

The verse ends with Talmudic Judaism's (not Hebraism's) fundamental belief that those who have died will be bodily resurrected during Messianic times. Hence, Judaism's population never decreases, but can only increase.

CHAPTER TEN, VERSE 3

RJoshua said: Great is peace, for at the time Israel arose and said [Exod. xxiv. 7]: "All that the Lord has spoken will we do and hear," the Holy One was pleased to give to them His Torah and blessed them with peace, as it is written [Ps. xxix. 11]: "The Lord will bless his people with peace."

We learn in the Talmud and Midrash that, although the Torah says the Hebrews intended to accept and obey the laws of Torah unconditionally ('will do'), and later study them ('will hear'), God held Mount Sinai over their heads and threatened to drop it on them if they didn't accept it (*Shabbat 88a*). Even so, when we live according to the spiritual and ethical lessons of the Torah, we enjoy peace: "Its ways are ways of pleasantness, and all its paths are peace" (*Prov. 3:17*).

Most of us can only control our thoughts, speech, and actions if we keep our *yetzer ha ra*, our selfish ego and will, at bay. We can control nothing else. If we think we can, we are delusional. Others also have free will.

God tells Israel, "My children, I have created the Evil Inclination, and I have created the Torah as an antidote against it. I wrote in

My Torah: 'If you do good, you will be more powerful. If you do not do good, sin awaits crouching at the door; it desires to control you, but you can overpower it'" (Gen. 4:7). "*As long as you are engrossed in the Torah and doing its mitzvot, you will not be controlled by the Evil Inclination. This is why the Torah says: 'If you do good, you will be more powerful'. But when you are not engrossed in the Torah, you will be under the control of the Evil Inclination, as the verse continues, 'If you do not do good, sin awaits crouching at the door.' Not only that,*" God says, "*but the Evil Inclination will spend all its time and energies trying to make you sin, which is why the verse says 'it desires to control you.'…If you want to, you can overpower the Evil Inclination, as it says, '…it desires to control you, but you can overpower it.'*

—Kiddushin 30b

If we wish to live in peace, we must negate our selfish will and align it with God's will. Integration, *shlema*, and wholeness, *shalom*, come from understanding that this is our true purpose in life. We achieve inner peace, peace in the home, and peace in the community by understanding that living according to Torah means that all of our *derekim*, paths, are towards peace.

CHAPTER TEN, VERSE 4

Hezekiah said: Great is peace, for at every commandment in the Torah it is written "if," as, for instance, Exod. xxiii. 4, "If you meet," etc., which means, if such a thing occurs to you, you must do the commandment; but concerning peace, it is different, there it is written [Ps. xxxiv. 15]: "Seek peace, and pursue it," which means, seek peace at the place where you are, and if you do not find it, seek it in other places.

Hezekiah was one of Judea's better kings. He witnessed the Assyrian destruction of Israel and the beginning of the Babylonian siege of Judea and Jerusalem. The Talmud credits him with overseeing the compilation of the biblical books Isaiah, Proverbs, Song of Songs, and Ecclesiastes (*Bava Batra 15a*).

Most of our mitzvot are time-bound or situational. If it is Shabbat, we do or refrain from doing certain things. If it is Purim, we read the Megillah Esther, and perform other rituals. If we are in business, we must have honest scales. If we see our enemy's donkey struggle with the burden it carries, we are to help it upright. The pursuit of peace and justice are not time-bound. In places without them, we work to establish a peaceful and just environment. We are to be like the disciples of Aaron—to love peace, to pursue peace, and to bring people closer to Torah and one another (*Pirkei Avot 1:12*).

CHAPTER TEN, VERSE 5

Great is peace: about all the journeys of Israel it is written, "And they removed...and... encamped," which means they removed in strife and encamped in strife, but when they came to Sinai there was no more strife, and they encamped in peace, as it is written [Exod. xix. 2]: "And Israel encamped opposite the Mount" (i.e., all Israel were united). The Holy One, blessed is He, then said: "Because Israel hates discord and loves peace, and all are united, this is a favorable time to give them my Torah."

The pursuit of peace is the most important aspect of Talmudic Judaism. Without peace, life is devoid of joy, freedom, or happiness. God does not give Israel the Torah until they are at peace with one another.

When we have *makloket*, strife, within a synagogue, between synagogues, among rabbis or different sects of Judaism, or between individual Jews, God weeps. His Holy Torah leaves our hands, as we become undeserving. "If Israel will accept the Torah, the universe will continue to exist. If not, I will return the world to the empty void it was at first" (*Shabbat 88a*).

The global population is six billion. 99.75% are not Jewish. There are approximately 15 million Jews on Earth. Jews make up just 0.25% of the population of the world. We are an endangered species. As a rabbi, I have seen Jews paste 'Save the Whales' bumperstickers on their cars, but treat their fellow Jews horridly. At Yom ha Shoah or Israel Independence Day events, Jews wail over dead Jews they have never met, then snub other Jews at the receptions that follow. Every time we label a sect, and compartmentalize the Jews within it, the statistic of 0.25% becomes smaller. When we say 10% of Jews are 'Orthodox,' we've created a sub-species, if you'll allow me to stay with my metaphor, of 0.025% of the globe's population.

The Midrash tells us that God created the Torah, and the idea of Jews, two thousand years before He created the universe (*Beresheit Rabbah 8*). He didn't think of us as Pharisees, Sadducees, Essenes, Zealots, Reform, Orthodox, Belzers, Satmars, Chabadniks, Mitnagdim, Humanists, Conservatives, Reconstructionists, Renewalists, Litvaks, Galitzianers, Ashkenazis, Sephardim, or Karaites. Every time we define, group, sub-divide, and re-group ourselves, the statistical reality is that we reduce our own significance.

In the eyes of the Creator, we are all connected as One People. God cries out to us through His Prophet Malachi 2:10, "Do we not all have one Father? Has not one God created us? Why do we deal treacherously, each against his brother, so as to profane the covenant of our fathers?"

No matter how much material wealth one has, he who puts his petty will above what is good and just in the eyes of God is morally bankrupt. When egos collide, shalom is destroyed. A morally bankrupt society is doomed to fail. Judaism is the first ethical monotheistic religion. Love of God without love for our fellows is like a restaurant with a menu but no food. $J = ME^2$: Judaism equals Monotheism times Ethics Squared.

CHAPTER TEN, VERSE 6

Adonijah the son of David was killed because he was quarrelsome, and it is permitted to support the accusation of a quarrelsome man, as Nathan the prophet did when Bath-Sheba accused Adonijah [I Kings, i. 14]: "I myself will come in after you, and confirm your words."

Adonijah is the fourth son of King David. When David is dying, Adonijah proclaims himself King. Bathsheba and the prophet Nathan tell David to name his younger son King. Adonijah flees, but Solomon offers pardon if he behaves. Adonijah then tries a *coup d'etat*; he attempts to marry one of King David's widows. Bathsheba pleads for his life, but Solomon has him executed.

The point of this verse, with some of the Talmud's occasional hyperbole, is that he who causes strife is worthy of death, even if he is a prince. When we 'commoners' cause or engage in strife, we experience a living death. The field of medicine has shown that chronic discord can be fatal.

CHAPTER TEN, VERSE 7

nd Rabbi said: All manner of lying is prohibited, unless it is to make peace between neighbors.

In the Talmud, whenever we see the name 'Rabbi' by itself, the sages are speaking of Rabbi Judah ha Nasi, the head of the Rabbinic academy (d. ca. 200 CE). He was the redactor of the Mishna and the first to set it in writing.

As kids we learned the prohibition against lying, one of the Ten Utterances (i.e. Ten Commandments). Dishonesty and deception are serious crimes in Jewish law. The Torah explicitly demands that one should "distance himself from a false matter. Thou shall not lie one to another" (*Lev. 19:11*). Rabbi Shimon ben Gamliel proclaims, "The world endures on three things: justice, truth, and peace" (*Pirkei Avot 1:18*).

There are, however, situations in which Jewish law permits or even requires that one engage in deception. One may lie for the sake of peace. In the TaNaK, Talmud, and Midrash, there are instances in which lying is permitted: to save someone's honor, to prevent death or injury, to safeguard property, or to preserve humility.

Rabbi was delivering a lecture and the strong odor of garlic caused a disturbance. Rabbi said: "Let the person who has eaten the garlic, please leave." Rabbi Chiya arose and left; then all the disciples arose and left. It turned out that Rabbi Chiya had not eaten garlic, but left in order not to shame the true perpetrator.
—Sanhedrin 11a

Some Talmudic passages address the issue of permissible lying. Following are three verses from Talmud Bavli:

Rabbi Ille'a said in the name of Rabbi Elazar son of Rabbi Shimon: It is permitted for a person to deviate from the truth in the interest of peace, as it says (Genesis 50:16–17): "Your father [Jacob] commanded before his death, saying: So shall you say to Joseph, 'O Please forgive the offense of your brothers and their sin for they have treated you so wickedly.'"

Rabbi Nathan said it is a commandment to deviate from the truth in the interest of peace, as it says (I Samuel 16:2): "And Samuel said, 'How can I go? If Saul hears of it, he will kill me.'"

At the Academy of Rabbi Yishmael it was taught: Great is the cause of peace, seeing that for its sake, even the Holy One, blessed be He, changed the truth, for at first it is written (Genesis 18:12), "My lord [husband Abraham] is old," while afterward it is written (18:13), "And I am old."

A white lie is allowed for the sake of peace. Rabbi Nathan believed that it is a *mitzvah*, a commandment, to lie if doing so will bring peace. In Pirkei Avot 1:12 we are told to be like Aaron—to love and pursue peace.

> When two people had a dispute, Aaron, the High Priest, went and sat near one of them and said to him: "My son, see what your friend is doing? He is beating his heart and tearing his clothing saying: "Woe is me. How can I lift up my eyes and look at my friend? I am ashamed of myself since I was the one who offended him." Aaron would sit with him until he removed the hatred from his heart. Aaron would then go and sit next to the other and say to him: "My son, see what your friend is doing? He is beating his heart and tearing his clothing saying: "Woe is me. How can I lift up my eyes and look at my friend? I am ashamed of myself since I was the one who offended him." Aaron would sit with him until he removed the hatred from his heart. When the two met, they would hug and kiss each other.
> —Talmud Bavli Avot D'Rabbi Nathan 12:3

Bar Kappara said: Great is Peace, as among the angels there is no animosity, no jealousy, no hatred, no commanding, no quarreling, because the Holy One, blessed is He, has made peace among them, as it is written [Job, xxv. 2]: "Dominion and awe are with Him: He establishes order in the heights of Heaven." Dominion is the angel Michael and Awe is Gabriel, one of whom is of fire and the other of water, and still they do not oppose each other, for the Holy One, blessed is He, has made peace between them.

Shimon bar Kappara was a student of Rabbi. He was a talented poet and storyteller, and it is said that at the wedding feast of Simeon, the son of Rabbi, he kept the guests captivated with fables until their food got cold.

The verse tells us that there is peace in Heaven among God and his angels. Gabriel means 'God's strength' (gavor), and Michael means 'Who (mi) is like (cho) El (God).' They have opposing tasks (awe and dominion) and personalities (fire and water), yet they co-exist peacefully.

For this reason, many of our prayers—Kaddish, Berachot ha Mazon, and the Amidah—end with: *Oseh shalom bim'romav, Hu ya'aseh shalom aleynu v'al kol Yisrael v'mru Amein.* "He who makes peace in High Places, He will make peace for us and for all Israel, and let us say Amen" (*Job 25:2*). Angels do not have free will. They are tasked by God. Humans do have free will, and we ask God to help us live as peacefully together as do the angels.

CHAPTER TEN, VERSE 9

RJoshua said: Great is peace, in that the covenant of the priests was made with peace, as it is written [Numb. xxv. 12]: "I give to him my covenant of peace."

Because the rabbis had difficulty with Pinchas' actions, we may be surprised to find a reference to him in a verse about peace. God gives the covenant of the priesthood from Aaron to his grandson Pinchas, with a blessing for shalom. As we are called a "kingdom of priests" (*Ex. 19:16*), we too must do our best to keep our daily speech, thoughts, and actions peaceful.

CHAPTER TEN, VERSE 10

The name of the Holy One, blessed ie He, is also "peace" (Shalom), as it is written [Judges, vi. 24]: "And called it Adonai-shalom."

The Hebrew Judge Gideon, after an encounter with an angel, prepares an altar for a sacrifice. He is about to go into battle with the Midianites and Amalekites. He calls his altar "God is Peace." This comes a few verses before he blows his famous trumpet (shofar). Hence, one of God's names is Peace.

Acting without peace is blasphemy or desecration, *chillul ha Shem,* a hollowing out of His name. "You shall not profane My holy name" (*Lev: 22:32*).

CHAPTER TEN, VERSE 11

RJose the Galilean said: The name of the Messiah is also "peace" (Shalom), as it is written [Is. ix. 5]: "The prince of peace."

Rabbi Jose was a contemporary of Rabbi Akiva, circa 130 CE, and disagreed with him and other rabbis on a few stances of Jewish law. He taught that poultry may be cooked with milk and eaten (*Chullin 113a*), as was done in his own native town in the Galilee (*ibid. 116a*).

The concept of a Messiah is not Hebraic. Nor are Olam ha Ba and bodily resurrection. These are Jewish rabbinic concepts. The rabbis discuss these ideas at length in the last chapter of Tractate Sanhedrin.

According to Isaiah 2:4, during the Messianic Age, humans will no longer have a yetzer ha ra. War, hate, persecution, and poverty will no longer exist. Everyone, humans and animals, will live in total peace and well-being.

There is a story, in Talmud Tractate Sanhedrin 98a, in which we find Rabbi Joshua ben Levi meditating near the tomb of Rabbi Shimon bar Yochai, in Meron, Galilee. The prophet Elijah visits him. "When will the Messiah come?" asks Joshua. "Ask him," the prophet replies. "The Messiah is at the gates of Rome, sitting among the poor, the sick, and the wretched. Like them, he changes the bindings of his wounds, but does so one wound at a time, in order to be ready at a moment's notice." Joshua travels to Rome to meet the Messiah. He greets him with the words, "Peace be upon you, Master and Teacher." The Messiah replies, "Peace be upon you, O son of Levi." Joshua asks, "When you will be coming?" and is told "Today." Joshua returns to Elijah, who asks what the Messiah said. "'Peace be upon you, O son of Levi'," Joshua answers. Elijah explains that this means Joshua and his father will have a place in the World to Come. Joshua says the Messiah did not speak the truth, because he promised to come today, but did not. Elijah replies, "This is what he said to you: Today, if you will hear his voice," a reference to Psalm 95:7. The coming of the Messiah is conditional, and the condition remains unfulfilled.

If we as individuals and as a society love, work for, and pursue peace, we can attain it. If we do not love and pursue peace, we will not have peace. If we are not doing our best, and not listening to God's voice of love and peace, we are not spiritually deserving of the Messianic Age.

The Talmud, in Tractate Shabbat 118b, offers a test. It says that if all Jews could put aside our differences and observe one Shabbat, the Messianic Age would come. In reality, if all Jews agreed to do so, without fighting about what time to light candles or about whether the gefilte fish should have added sugar, we would already be in the Messianic Age. If the Messiah's name is "Prince of Peace," let us now learn to love peace.

CHAPTER TEN, VERSE 12

aid R' Joshua: Israel is also called "peace," as it is written [Zech. viii. 12]: "For the seed shall be undisturbed, the vine shall give its fruit," which is to be interpreted thus: "The vine will give its fruit to the seed of peace" (Israel).

The Prophet Zechariah speaks of the prophecy of the return to Judea and Jerusalem from captivity in Babylon. His prophecy began in the second year of Darius, king of Persia (520 BCE), about sixteen years after the return of the first group of Hebrews from Babylonian exile. From then on, the names of the land of Israel, and the Children of Israel, its people, are "peace." We use *shalom* for hello and goodbye.

How many of us have received a letter, email, or synagogue bulletin signed '*b'Shalom*'? According to Talmud Tractate Moed Katan 29b, Rabbi Levi bar Chaisa said that when one parts with the deceased, he should not say, "*Lech l'Shalom*"—"Go towards peace, peacefully"—but rather, "*Lech b'Shalom*"—"Go in peace." Conversely, when one parts with his friend, he should not say to him, "*Lech b'Shalom*", but rather, "*Lech l'Shalom.*" Rav Naftali Kohen of Frankfort explains:

> *A living person must always seek to grow spiritually and avoid stagnating on the same spiritual level. A dead person, in contrast, can no longer grow and achieve; he remains at whatever spiritual level he attained in his lifetime. For this reason, the blessing given to a living person is, "Go towards peace" ("L'Shalom")—towards a greater level of spiritual wholeness ("Shalom" from the word "Shalem," whole). In contrast, the blessing given to the deceased is, "Go in peace" ("B'Shalom"), since his soul leaves this world at the level of spiritual accomplishment that he achieved in his lifetime.*

Peace allows us to grow toward Jewish spiritual renewal and to become whole and integrated. When we are whole, in *shlema*, we need not lose our serenity.

CHAPTER TEN, VERSE 13

R Jose the Galilean said: When the Messiah comes to Israel, he will begin with peace, as it is written [Is. lii. 7]: "How beautiful upon the mountains are the feet of the messenger of good tidings, that publishes peace, that announces tidings of happiness, that publishes salvation, that says to Zion, your God reigns."

There is a Jewish belief that the time before the Messiah comes will be hell on earth. Some parts of the Talmud explain how he will come. He will not arrive on the Sabbath, because that would require people to violate the Sabbath to welcome him (*Pesachim 13a*). The prophet Elijah, who ushers in the Messianic Age, will arrive no later in the week than Thursday, leaving room for the Messiah to arrive by Friday. Elijah will announce the arrival of the Messiah from Mount Carmel in Haifa, Israel (*Talmud Yerushalmi Pesachim 3:6*). The sages believe the Messiah will arrive on the eve of Passover, the first redemption, which serves as a model of the final redemption (*Mekilta de-Rabbi Ishmael, Pischa 14*).

In the footsteps of the Messiah, arrogance will increase; prices will rise; grapes will be abundant but wine will be costly; the government will turn into heresy; and there will be no reproach. The meeting place of scholars will become a whorehouse; the Galilee will be destroyed; the highland will lie desolate; the border people will wander from city to city and none will show them compassion; the wisdom of authors will be putrid; sin fearing people will be detested; truth will be missing; young men will humiliate the elderly; the elderly will stand while the young sit; sons will revile their fathers; daughters will strike their mothers, brides will strike their mothers in law; and a man's enemies will take over his house. The face of the generation is like the face of a dog! Sons have no shame in front of their fathers; and on whom can one depend? Only upon our Father in Heaven.

—Talmud Bavli Tractate Sotah 9:15

The sages write of God's war against Gog and Magog. A rabbinic statement written during Emperor Hadrian's pogroms (132–35 CE), offers the frightening assessment that the Messiah will arrive in a period when Torah learning disappears, poverty increases, religious despair deepens, and Jews collaborate with their enemies:

The son of David will not arrive until informers are everywhere. Another view: Until there are few students left. Another view: Until the last coin is gone from the pocket. Another view: Until the people despair of redemption...as if there is no support or help for Israel.

—Talmud Bavli Tractate Sanhedrin 97a

For the Messiah to be effective, he must bring peace. If he does not, being human, he will not survive the world as described above. The verse describes how low humanity can sink without peace, without justice, and without daily prayer to God to keep the *yetzer ha ra*, the inclination to do wrong, at bay.

CHAPTER TEN, VERSE 14

We also said: Great is peace, because even wars are waged for the sake of peace, as it is written [Deut. xx. 10]: "When you come near a city to make war against it, then summon it with the word of peace."

The Torah teaches that before we go to war, we must offer a just peace plan. This is not a plan to subjugate another people. The peace plan we offer must be fair and result in true accord. We cannot cut down another people's fruit-bearing trees, nor can we attack on all four sides. One side must be left open for our enemies to escape. Even when we make war, the object is to eventually live in peace with those we fight.

In the Middle Ages, Rabbi Judah ha Levi wrote a book about the Khazar king who wanted to choose a religion for his people. He summoned a rabbi, an imam, and a priest to teach him about their religions. To the rabbi he asked: "You have many wonderful laws of kindness and peace, even to the point of making war peacefully. But you are a landless people. When you get back your land, will you be able to abide by your own laws?" And the rabbi answered "You have found our Achilles' heel."

Our rabbis were so opposed to war and so much in favor of peace that they put a new twist on the Torah commandment to blot out the name of Amalek. In Hebraic terms, the commandment meant to kill the Amalekites. When King Saul spared the Amalek king and some prized cattle, the Judge Samuel was ordered by the Hebraic God to finish the task. Saul lost his crown, which led to the establishment of the Davidic dynasty.

Our rabbis, knowing that Haman was an Agagite, a descendent of Amalek, instructed Jews to blot out his name with noisemakers, not swords, on Purim. They taught that Jews should spend our time ridding ourselves of the Amalek inside of us, the yetzer ha ra, before we try to rid the world of those who live according to the dictates of their yetzer ha ra.

The Torah (*Deut. 21:10*) reads, "*Kee saytzay la milchomo al oyvecho*"—"When you go out to war against your enemies." Hebrew has both singular and plural forms for 'you.' Usage depends on how many persons are being addressed. In this verse, Moses speaks to the Hebrew people as a whole. He should address them in the plural, *saytzu*, 'you [collectively] go out,' but instead the Torah employs the singular form *saytzay*, as if Moses were speaking to one person. The sages explain that the use of the singular means that the central battle in life is an individual's war against the number one enemy, the yetzer ha ra within.

The yetzer ha ra strives to keep each person's Jewish spirituality down by keeping his ego alive. The yetzer ha ra encourages the individual do his own will. Character defects and negative behavior remove us from God, the ability to do mitzvot, to experience inner peace, and to live harmoniously with others. Again, peace, both inner and outer, is the primary goal of Judaism.

CHAPTER TEN, VERSE 15

RJoshua said: In the future the Holy One, blessed is He, will uphold the righteous with peace, as it is written [Is. xxvi. 3]: "The confiding mind will You keep in perfect peace; because he trusts in You."

The Talmud Bavli Bava Batra 10b teaches that this world is an 'upside down place' in which righteous people may have little wealth and much grief, while dishonest people may acquire large homes and appear to live in comfort. The sages promise that God corrects injustice in the World to Come.

The verse says, "in the future" for this reason, and also because we grow spiritually when we confide in God as our loving parent through daily prayer, meditation, and an accounting of our actions (*chesbon ha nefesh*). The more spiritual we are, the more skilled we become at getting along with others. Getting along with others helps us to earn a living and to be peaceful.

When we trust, believe in, and have complete faith in God, we know true inner peace. Pirkei Avot 3:6 teaches that when we pick up the yoke of God, all other human and societal yokes fall from our shoulders. That is peace.

Again he said: Great is peace, because it accompanies the living as well as the dead— the living, as it is written [Ex. iv. 18]: "And Jethro said to Moses, go to peace"; the dead, as it is written [Gen. xv. 15]: "But you shall come to your fathers in peace."

As discussed in Derek Eretz 10:12, we wish the living to go 'to' peace. We want to grow spiritually toward peace. For those who are deceased, growth stops; hence, it is sufficient to wish them to go 'in' peace.

At funerals we often hear people say, "He is finally at peace." By such an expression, we admit that we know peace is desirable. Judaism believes that peace is attainable in life. If we put our petty wills and yetzer ha ra aside, we can have peace right now. We can all 'get back to the Garden,' before we die, as did the nine people who went to heaven while they were still alive (Derek Eretz Zutah 1:6).

"Shalom is the only pipeline through which blessing comes down to earth from Heaven" (Midrash Bamidbar Rabbah). Our defects and resentments keep us from true shalom. One of God's names is Shalom. The Torah's "ways are sweet and all of its paths are peace" (*Proverbs 3:17*). We must rid ourselves of defects and resentments. We must continue to do so daily. If we allow ourselves to stay attached to our defects, we will be at war with others, with ourselves, and with the universe.

"Great is peace between husband and wife" (*Chullin 141a*). Rabbi Shimon Ben Gamliel says, "A person who brings peace into his house is considered by God as if he brought peace on the entire Jewish people" (*Avot of Rabbi Nathan 28:3*). Everyone understands what it is like to live without *shalom bayit*, peace at home. None of us can leave such a home and go to work and be as kind and gentle as we would like to be.

This is why the study of the Tractates of Derek Eretz Zuta and Rabbah are so important. We must never lose sight of the fact that God created all of us to be happy. He wants us to live in shalom. We have the power to 'get back to the Garden' every day of our lives, if only we choose to do so.

CHAPTER TEN, VERSE 17

RYehoshua of Sachnin said in the name of R' Levi: Great is peace, in that all the benedictions and prayers conclude with "peace." The reading of Shema we conclude with "peace," "and spread the tent of Your peace"; the blessing of the priests concludes with peace, "and give you peace"; and the eighteen benedictions conclude: "Blessed are You, Master of peace."

Rabbi Yehoshua of Sachnin was a highly venerated rabbi and healer of the 3rd century CE. His grave, known in Arabic as Nabi as-Sideiq, has been a focus of pilgrimage since the Middle Ages. The tomb is located near a 3000-year-old Phoenician fortress, and is visited by Jews, Muslims, and Christians. Sachnin is in the Galilee, between Acre and Safed, and is one of the few towns in Israel with an Arab majority.

If we attend synagogue services, we are accustomed to hearing the word 'shalom.' We pray for shalom. How many of us generate discord or strife, *makloket*, as we enjoy coffee and cake after the service? Our prayers are for naught if we cannot follow through with action. How can we expect

God to grant us peace if we do not try to embody peace in everything we say and do?

The *Shema* (Hear O Israel), also known as the *V'Ahavtah* (You shall love), ends with a call for shalom. The *Amidah*, the *Shemoneh Esrei* (18 Blessings), referred to by the sages in Tractate Berachot as simply The Prayer (*ha Tephila*), ends with a section of prayers for peace. Our blessings after meals conclude with wishes for peace. So does the *Kaddish*, which appears multiple times in our traditional service, and is also used for remembrance of the deceased and at funerals. The last word of the entire Talmud is 'Shalom' (*Uktsin 3:12*).

Before the tribal leaders bring their offerings, Moses teaches Aaron and his sons how to bless the children of Israel (*Numbers 6:24–6:26*).

The first of the three priestly *berachot* is, "May God bless you and safeguard you" (*Numbers 6:24*). To wish God's blessings upon someone is to acknowledge that all blessings come from the Almighty. Only God can assure success, abundance, and good health. We insert this prayer into our *Shemoneh Esrei* every day. When we pray that God will bless and keep someone, we accept God's Oneness and greatness.

In Deuteronomy 28:1–14, God promises successful crops and businesses, healthy flocks, and increased possessions. The Mishna teaches, in Pirkei Avot 3:15, that where there is no flour, there is no Torah. When we prosper, we have more time for Torah study, and more wealth to share with others. Why does the priest also ask God to safeguard us? Material possessions bring the risk of robbery, jealousy, and bodily harm. The Midrash teaches that the best way to show our thanks to God for His generosity and to ensure continued blessings is to use what we have to help others.

God wants us to be prosperous. He wants us to be wealthy! Not to impress our friends, not because those who die with the most toys win, but so that we will have the means and the time to do His work. As the adage goes, 'Nobody ever asked a poor man for a job.' Wealth is needed to employ others, and to enable them to sustain themselves and prosper, so that they, too, are better able to do God's work.

"May God illuminate His countenance for you and be gracious to you" (*Numbers 6:25*). Physical gifts are important, but they are not everything. Although survival depends upon being able to meet physical needs, we need much more. The second priestly blessing is a spiritual one, based on the inspiration and hope that come from Torah. In Proverbs 6:23 we read, "The commandments are a lamp and the Torah is a light."

The word 'countenance' literally translates as 'face' in Hebrew. We are taught that only Moses saw God 'face to face.' We understand this as metaphor because God is incorporeal. The blessing expresses the hope that we will comprehend the wisdom of the Torah, appreciate God's gift of creation, and recognize God's purpose for us in His universe. According to Rabbi Raphael Hirsch, such awareness is akin to knowing how to read facial expressions.

Torah study helps us learn to read God's 'face.' The 'light' of Torah is the ability to appreciate God's gifts, and to know what to do with them.

The Midrash Sifre states that we wish for God to let our fellows look upon us with grace. "A person can have a host of personal attributes, but unless his fellows appreciate and understand him, his relationship with them will not be positive." The quality of being liked by others is called grace. The Or ha Chaim (Rabbi Chaim ben Attar, 18th-century Italy) says that the prayer asks that other nations will like and understand us. The Rambam says that Israel, or we as individuals, should find favor in God's eyes.

"May God lift His face to you and establish peace for you" (Numbers 6:26). The third of the priestly blessings is a wish for God's compassion, forgiveness, and shalom. Rashi says that the blessing asks God to suppress His anger against us even if we have sinned. We cannot look at another while angry with him. We pray that God will look directly at us, not turn His back to us.

In Talmud Bavli Tractate Rosh Hashanah 17b, the proselyte Bloria asks how God can show mercy to someone who is undeserving. The Kohan Yose answers that God mercifully forgives sins committed against Him. Sins committed against other people are not forgiven until we make amends with those we have harmed.

Judaism and Christianity diverge significantly on this point. In Judaism, we are born into God's grace and maintain it through repentance to God and to those we have hurt.

Grace must be continually earned. The Midrash teaches that the gates to repentance, our Jewish spiritual renewal, are always open. Christianity says we are born into a state of sin, and only the acceptance of Jesus can bring us into grace, which we keep regardless of our actions, for as long as we still believe.

In the last words of the entire Talmud (*Bavli Tractate Uktsin 3:12*), Rabbi Shimon ben Chalefta says, "God could find no container that would hold Israel's blessings as well as peace." He quotes Psalm 29:11, with which we conclude our Blessing after the Meal: "God will give might to His people. God will bless His people with peace."

The Or ha Chaim wrote that peace is not just harmony among people. Peace is the "balance between the needs of the body and the needs of the soul." Universally, peace is the balance between the infinite Holy elements and the earthbound human, mundane elements. *Shalom* (wholeness, integration, serenity) is so important, that without it, we cannot fully enjoy life's blessings.

Said R' Joshua b. Levi: The Holy One, blessed is He, said to Israel, You have caused me to destroy My house and to exile My children. Now pray for peace and I will forgive you, as it is written [Ps. cxxii. 6]: "Pray for the peace of Jerusalem." Therefore he who loves peace, runs after peace, offers peace, and answers peace, the Holy One, blessed is He, will make him inherit the life of this world and the life of the World to Come, as it is written [Ps. xxxvii. 11]: "But the meek shall inherit the land, and shall delight themselves because of the abundance of peace."

So ends *Talmud Bavli Tractate Derek Eretz Zuta*. R' Joshua tells Israel that God said they caused Him to destroy the Temple and to exile them. This refers to the Roman sacking of Jerusalem in 70 CE, and the eventual Diaspora which began in 135 CE.

When we read between the lines, we understand that the sages do not mean to say that God is punishing us. We cause our own suffering with bad behavior. Our wills and egos clash with the wills and egos of others. The result is *makloket*, strife. The Talmud tells us repeatedly that when bad things happen, we are to look inside of ourselves for the reason, not outside (*Berachot 5a*).

Jerusalem was destroyed because of *sinat chinam*, baseless hatred among Jews (*Yoma 9b*). The rabbis give the example of a party snub as the proximate cause. Bar Kamtza (which literally means 'son of a small thing' and therefore is smaller than small) receives an invitation to a party. When he arrives, the host tells him the invitation was meant for Kamtza, not for him. All dressed up with nowhere to go, Bar Kamtza is embarrassed. The host gruffly tells him to leave. He begs to stay for his honor's sake, and even offers to pay for his own meal. The host refuses his request. He offers to pay for half the cost of the party. The host again tells him no. He offers to pay for the whole party. The host rejects his offer. Meanwhile, rabbis witness this exchange as it unfolds, and they 'stand idly by.'

Later, as a gesture toward peace, the Roman governor sends an unblemished calf to the Temple for the Hebraic sacrifice. Somehow, Bar Kamtza is assigned the task of bringing the calf. He cuts a marking into the calf, which renders it blemished. The priests receive the calf, see the blemish, and reject the Roman's peace offering. A rabbi argues that the Roman's peace offering is more important than a rule in the Torah. The priests stick to their rules, and the Romans find out. Bar Kamtza tells them that the Jews at the party were planning a rebellion. The Romans decide to break through the walls and gates (*Gittin 55a–56b*).

The Temple, Jerusalem, and a number of towns in Judea were all destroyed. Destruction occurred not by Divine decree, but because people hated one another, and failed to live by the spirit of the law (*Bava Metzia 30b*).

Rabbi Joshua teaches that if we pray for peace, but more importantly, love peace, run after peace, offer peace, and answer with peace, we will have peace! In the Torah, the Hebrew word *anav*, often poorly translated as 'meek', means subdued, gentle, saintly, and humble. To be *anav* means to truly live in God's world, and to know the difference between what we can and cannot control. It means our skin is like Teflon instead of like Velcro. We know what to let go of, and recognize the few things for which we need to fight. We understand that although we should make our best efforts, outcomes are not in our domain. God gives us what we need, so we don't have to covet or envy. We can be happy about the success of others. "Now the man Moses was very meek, above all the men which were upon the face of the earth" (*Num. 12:3*). Meek, in the Talmudic sense, means spiritually connected. When we are spiritually connected, we are serene, and live in an 'abundance of peace.'

> The whole of Torah is for the purpose
> of promoting peace.
>
> —*Gittin 59b*

Shalom ha gadol—Peace is the greatest of virtues.

—*Shabbat 10a*

Hadran alach Derek Eretz Zuta—we will return to you, Derek Eretz Zuta. In modern Israeli Hebrew, the word *hadran* means 'encore'. In Biblical Hebrew, it means, 'we will return.' With these words, we express the hope that we will study this text again.

When we reach the end of a volume of the Talmud, a *hadran* prayer is printed, with a special kaddish, *Kaddish D'itchadita*, in honor of the completion of that volume. Judaism considers this to be an important achievement and a milestone worth celebrating. It is time now for a *siyum*, completion, and a *seudat mitzvah* feast.

Thank you for honoring me with the study of my commentary on Tractate *Derek Eretz Zuta*. I look forward to continuing with *Derek Eretz Rabbah*. As Rabbi Hillel asked, may each of us love peace, pursue peace, love and bring others close to Torah.

Conclusion

"If you believe that you can damage, then believe that you can fix. If you believe that you can harm, then believe that you can heal" (*Rebbe Nachman of Breslov, 1772–1810, Ukraine*).

Jewish spiritual renewal is an ongoing process of growth and study in which, with practice, we become better at prayer and meditation, and increasingly aware of God's presence in our lives. As long as we are doing our *chesbon ha nefesh katon*, the daily accounting of our soul, we continue to progress. If we slip, we ask ourselves what might be the cause, and get back on track with God's help.

In *The Path of the Just*, Rabbi Moshe Chaim Luzatto, AKA the Ramchal, writes:

> "...man is the center of a great balance. For if he is pulled after the world and is drawn further from his Creator, he is damaged, and he damages the world with him. And if he rules over himself and unites himself with his Creator, and uses the world only to aid him in the service of his Creator, he is uplifted and

the world itself is uplifted with him. For all creatures are greatly uplifted when they serve the Whole Man, who is sanctified with the holiness of the Blessed One."

The struggle to triumph over the *yetzer ha ra*, the evil inclination, is ongoing. It takes work to remain acutely self-aware, to avoid reflexive, unthinking action. It takes effort to turn our focus away from our own concerns and to direct our energies toward helping and uplifting others. Traditional Judaism says we can't win this inner battle without God's help—we are simply not strong enough. There is a reason why Jacob broke his hip wrestling with the angel.

We may define 'God' as the best within ourselves. We can learn to trust and honor our capacity to experience the numinous, to be amazed by the beauty and intricacy of the natural world, to be awed by the phenomenon of life, to be vulnerable with another human being. If we believe in God, we might say that the Holy Spark within us has been given by God as a doorway to God. We can practice awareness of our mortality and of the knowledge that we can truly own nothing. We are temporary creations of the Eternal. The more we empty ourselves of ego, the more room there is to allow the creative energy of the universe to flow through us. When we practice 'how can I help?' instead of 'what's in it for me?' we gain a sense of spiritual expansion.

In *Tales of the Chasidim*, Martin Buber recounts the story of the Chaim of Zanz, who sought in his youth to morally reform his entire country. At 30, he'd not been successful, and thinking he'd taken on too much, decided to try only to reform his province. By the time he was 40, he still had not succeeded. He then chose to limit the scope of his work to reforming his own town. At the age of 50, he found that he'd not even been able to morally reform the town. Finally, he concluded that he could not reform others until he had taken the time to repair his own soul.

Happy studying, and we will meet again in Talmud Bavli Tractate Derek Eretz Rabbah.

Shalom uvracha,
Rabbi Dr. Arthur Segal

Appendix A

We learn in Talmud Bavli Tractate Sanhedrin 105a, that "the righteous of all nations [i.e. religions] have a share in the World to Come," which reminds us of Judaism's pluralistic view of other religions. *Derek Eretz Zuta*, in Chapter One, tells us that "Nine entered the Garden of Eden when they were still alive, and they are: Enoch (Chanoch) the son of Jared, Elijah, Messiah, Eliezer the bondsman of Abraham, Hirom the king of Zor, Ebed-melech the Cushi and Jabetz the son of R' Yehudah the Prince, Bothiah the daughter of Pharaoh and Serech the daughter of Ascher, and, according to others, also R' Yehoshua b. Levi."

Enoch

We learn of Enoch (Chanoch) the son of Jared, in Genesis 5:18–24:

> *Jared lived one hundred and sixty-two years, and begot Enoch. After he begot Enoch, Jared lived eight hundred years, and had sons and daughters. So all the days of Jared were nine hundred and sixty-two years; and he died. Enoch lived sixty-five years, and begot Methuselah. After he begot Methuselah, Enoch walked with God three hundred years, and had sons and daughters. So all the days*

*of Enoch were three hundred and sixty-five
years. And Enoch walked with God; and he
was not, for God took him.*

Enoch is one of the central figures of Jewish mysticism during the first millennium BCE, notably in *The Book of Enoch.* He avoids the mortal death ascribed to Adam's other descendants.

In classical Rabbinic literature, there are divergent opinions of Enoch. During the separation of Christianity from Judaism, the Jewish view of Enoch was that he was the only pious man of his time and was taken by God before he could be corrupted. Following the separation of Christianity and Judaism, the prevailing view of Enoch was that expressed in *Targum Pseudo-Jonathan.* It describes Enoch as a pious man taken to Heaven, and recipient of the title *Safra Rabbah* (Great Scribe).

According to Rashi, from Midrash Genesis Rabbah, "Enoch was a righteous man, but he could easily be swayed to return to do evil. Therefore, the Holy One, blessed is He, hastened and took him away and caused him to die before his time. For this reason, Scripture changed the wording in the account of his demise and wrote, 'and he was no longer in the world to complete his years.' "

Among the minor Midrashim, esoteric attributes of Enoch are expanded upon. In the *Sefer Hekalot,* Rabbi Ishmael visits the 7th Heaven. There, he encounters Enoch, who claims that in his lifetime Earth had been corrupted by the demons Shammazai and Azazel. Enoch tells Rabbi Ishmael that he was taken to Heaven to prove that God is not cruel. Similar traditions are recorded in *Ecclesiasticus*.

Later elaborations of this interpretation treat Enoch as a pious ascetic who preaches repentance when called to dwell with others. Enoch gathers (despite the small human population) such a vast number of disciples that he is proclaimed king. Under his guidance, peace reigns on Earth, until Enoch is summoned to Heaven to rule over the sons of God. In a story that parallels that of Elijah, he ascends to Heaven on a horse while a crowd of onlookers begs him to stay.

Three extensive apocryphal works are attributed to Enoch. The first, known simply as *The Book of Enoch*, is in the Ethiopian Bible, usually dated between the third century BCE and the first century CE. *The Second Book of Enoch* is in the Old Slavonic Bible, usually dated to the first century CE. *The Third Book of Enoch*, a Kabbalistic Rabbinic text in Hebrew, is usually dated to the fifth century CE.

These books recount Enoch's ascension to Heaven, where he is appointed guardian of the celestial treasures, chief of the archangels, and the immediate attendant to God's throne. He is subsequently taught all secrets and mysteries and, with the angels at his back, fulfills of his own accord the decrees that issue from the mouth of God. Enoch is seen as the inventor of writing, and as a teacher of astronomy and arithmetic. All three books interpret his name to mean 'initiated.'

Much esoteric literature identifies Enoch as the Metatron, the angel who communicates God's word. Enoch is viewed in this literature, and in the ancient Kabbalah of Jewish mysticism, as the one who communicates God's revelation to Moses, in particular the Book of Jubilees.

Elijah

Elijah, whose name (*El-i Yahu*) means "Yah is my God," was a prophet in Israel in the 9th century BCE. He appears in the TaNaK, Talmud, and even in texts of other religions. In the Book of Malachi, Elijah's return is prophesied "before the coming of the great and terrible day of the Lord," which makes him a harbinger of the Messiah. He appears in numerous stories and references in the Haggadah and in rabbinic literature, including the Babylonian Talmud.

By the 9th century BCE, the Kingdom of Israel, once united under King Solomon, split to become the northern Kingdom of Israel and the southern Kingdom of Judah. Judah retained the historic seat of government and the Hebrew Temple in Jerusalem. Omri, the king of Israel, continued policies dating from the reign of Jeroboam which were contrary to the laws of Moses. These policies were intended to divert religious focus from Jerusalem. Omri encouraged the building of local temple altars for sacrifices, appointed priests from outside the family of the Levites, and allowed or even encouraged temples dedicated to the Canaanite god, Baal. Omri achieved domestic security with a marriage alliance between his son Ahab and Princess

Jezebel, a priestess of Baal and the daughter of the king of Sidon in Phoenicia. Omri's compromises brought security and economic prosperity to Israel for a time, but alienated the Hebrew prophets, who were interested in a strict Deuteronomic interpretation of Mosaic Law.

As King, Ahab exacerbated these tensions. He allowed the worship of a foreign god within the palace. He built a temple for Baal and allowed Jezebel to bring an entourage of priests and prophets of Baal and Asherah into the country.

It is in this context that Elijah is introduced in I Kings 17:1 as "Elijah the Tishbite." He warns Ahab that, because he and his queen have "done evil in the sight of the Lord," a drought is coming that will be so severe, not even dew will fall.

Elijah appears on the scene with no fanfare. Nothing is known of his origins. He may have acquired the name 'Yah is God' because of his challenge to Baal worship. Elijah's challenge to Ahab is characteristic of his behavior in other episodes in the TaNaK. He is bold and direct.

Baal was the local nature deity responsible for rain, thunder, lightning, and dew. Elijah not only challenges Baal on behalf of the God of Israel, he challenges Jezebel, her priests, Ahab, and the people of Israel.

Following Elijah's confrontation with Ahab, God tells him to flee from Israel to a hiding place by the brook Cherith, east of the Jordan, where he will be fed by ravens. When the brook dries up, God sends him to a widow in the Phoenician town of Zarephatho. When Elijah finds her and asks to be fed, she says that she does not have sufficient food to keep herself and her son alive. Elijah tells her that God will not allow her supply of flour or oil to run out. "Don't be afraid... this is what the Lord, the God of Israel, says: 'The jar of flour will not be used up and the jug of oil will not run dry until the day the Lord gives rain on the land," a statement which illustrates that the demand of the covenant is not given without the promise of the covenant. The widow gives him the last of their food, and Elijah's promise miraculously comes true. By an act of faith the woman receives the promised blessing. God gives her 'manna' from Heaven even while He withholds food from his unfaithful people in the Promised Land.

Later, the widow's son dies, and the widow cries, "Did you come to remind me of my sin and kill my son?" Moved by a faith like that of Abraham, Elijah prays to God to restore her son, so that the veracity and trustworthiness of God's word might be demonstrated. I Kings 17:22 relates that God "heard the voice of Elijah; and the soul of the child came into him again, and he revived." The revival of the widow's son is the first instance of raising the dead recorded in Scripture. A non-Israelite widow is granted the best covenant blessing in the person of her son, the only hope for a widow in ancient society. The widow cries, "...the word of the Lord from your mouth is the truth." She makes a confession that the Israelites fail to make.

After more than three years of drought and famine, God tells Elijah to return to Ahab and announce the end of the drought: not occasioned by repentance in Israel, but by the command of the Lord, who has determined to reveal Himself again to His people. While on his way, Elijah meets Obadiah, the head of Ahab's household. Obadiah has hidden a hundred prophets of the God of Israel from Ahab and Jezebel, who wish to kill them. Elijah sends Obadiah ahead of him to inform Ahab that he is returning to Israel.

When Ahab confronts Elijah, he refers to him as the "troubler of Israel." Elijah retorts that Ahab has troubled Israel by allowing the worship of false gods. Elijah berates Ahab and the people of Israel for their acquiescence to Baal worship. "How long will you go limping with two different opinions? If the Lord is God, follow him; but if Baal, then follow him" (*I Kings 18:21*). The people are silent. The Hebrew for 'go limping' or 'waver' is the same as that used for 'danced' in Verse 26, in which the prophets of Baal frantically dance. Elijah speaks with sharp irony: Israel's religious ambivalence is a wild and futile dance.

Elijah proposes a test of the powers of Baal and the God of Israel. The people of Israel, 450 prophets of Baal, and 400 prophets of Asherah are summoned to Mount Carmel, part of modern Haifa. Two altars are built, one for Baal and one for the God of Israel. Wood is laid on the altars. Two oxen are slaughtered and cut into pieces; the pieces are laid on the wood. Elijah invites the priests of Baal to pray for fire to light the sacrifice. They pray from morning to noon without success. Elijah ridicules their efforts. They respond by cutting themselves and adding their own blood to the sacrifice (such mutilation of the body was strictly forbidden in Mosaic Law). They continue to pray until evening without success. Elijah orders the altar of the God of Israel to be drenched with water from "four large jars" poured three times (*I Kings 18:33–34*). He asks God to accept the sacrifice. Fire falls from the sky and ignites it. Elijah seizes the moment and orders the death of the prophets of Baal. Elijah prays earnestly for rain. The rain begins, signaling the end of the famine.

Jezebel, enraged that Elijah has ordered the deaths of her priests, threatens to kill Elijah (*I Kings 19:1–13*). He flees to Beersheba in Judah, continues alone into the wilderness, and finally sits under a juniper tree and prays for death. He falls asleep under the tree. An angel touches him and tells him to wake and eat. When he wakes, he finds bread and a jar of water. He eats, drinks, and goes back to sleep. The angel returns and again tells him to eat and drink because he has a long journey ahead of him.

For forty days and forty nights Elijah travels. He arrives at Mount Horeb and seeks shelter in a cave. God speaks to Elijah (*I Kings 19:9*): "What doest thou here, Elijah?" Elijah does not answer directly, but equivocates, implying that the work begun by the Lord centuries earlier has come to nothing, and that his own work has been fruitless. Unlike Moses, who tries to defend Israel when they sin with the golden calf, Elijah complains about the Israelites' unfaithfulness and says that he is the "only one left." Until now, Elijah has had only the word of God to guide him. He is told to leave the cave and "stand before the Lord."

A terrible wind passes, but God is not in the wind. A great earthquake shakes the mountain, but God is not in the earthquake. A fire passes the mountain, but God is not in the fire. A "still small voice" comes to Elijah and repeats the question, "What doest thou here, Elijah?" Elijah again evades the question and does not revise his lament. He fails to understand the importance of the divine revelation he has just witnessed. God sends him out again, this time to Damascus, to anoint Hazael as king of Syria, and Jehu as king of Israel, and Elisha as his replacement.

Elijah encounters Ahab again in I Kings 21. Ahab has murdered in order to claim a vineyard. He now wishes to acquire a vineyard owned by Naboth of Jezreel. He offers a better vineyard or a fair price for the land. Naboth tells Ahab that God instructed him not to part with the land. Ahab accepts his answer with sullen bad grace, but Jezebel plots to take the vineyard. In Ahab's name, she writes to the elders and nobles who live near Naboth. She instructs them to arrange a feast, invite Naboth, and make false charges against him. The plot is carried out, and Naboth is stoned to death. When word comes of Naboth's execution, Jezebel tells Ahab to take possession of the vineyard.

God sends Elijah to confront Ahab with a question and a prophecy: "Have you killed and also taken possession?" and, "In the place where dogs licked up the blood of Naboth shall dogs lick up your own blood" (*I Kings 21:19*). Ahab calls Elijah his enemy. Elijah tells Ahab that he has made himself the enemy of God. Elijah further tells Ahab that his entire kingdom will reject his authority, Jezebel will be eaten by dogs within Jezreel, and Ahab's family will also be consumed by dogs (if they die in a city) or by birds (if they die in the country). When Ahab hears this, he repents to the extent that God decides not to punish him, but still punishes Jezebel and their son Ahaziah.

Elijah leaves Ahab to encounter Ahaziah. As the scene opens, Ahaziah has been injured in a fall, and has sent his messengers to Ekron to ask the priests of Baalzebub if he will recover. Elijah intercepts Ahaziah's messengers, and sends them back to him with the question: "Is it because there is no God in Israel that you are sending to inquire of Baalzebub, the god of Ekron?"(II Kings 1:6). When Ahaziah asks who sent the message, they describe a man in a hairy coat with a leather belt, whom Ahaziah recognizes as Elijah the Tishbite. He orders three groups of soldiers to arrest him. Elijah calls fire down from Heaven, which kills the first two groups of soldiers. The leader of the third group asks for mercy. Elijah agrees to accompany the remaining men to Ahaziah, where he delivers his prophecy in person.

The biblical story of Elijah's departure is unique. Elijah, in company with Elisha, approaches the Jordan River. He rolls up his mantle and strikes the water (II Kings 2:8). The water parts, and Elijah and Elisha cross together on dry land. A chariot of fire and horses of flame appear. They lift Elijah to Heaven in a whirlwind. As he is lifted, his mantle falls to the ground. Elisha picks it up.

Elijah is mentioned once more, in II Chronicles 21. A letter is sent to Jehoram in Elijah's name. The letter accuses Jehoram of leading the people of Judah astray, just as Israel was led astray. The letter ends by predicting a painful death. Readers are often puzzled by this letter because it goes to the southern kingdom; Elijah has been concerned with the northern kingdom. The letter begins, "Thus says YHVH God of your father David...," instead of the more usual "... in the name of YHVH the God of Israel." Furthermore, the letter arrives after Elijah's ascension into the whirlwind. One possible reason for the discrepancy is that the books of I and II Kings are told largely out of sequence, in order to depict one individual or event at a time. The letter may be attributed to Elijah because the better-known prophet's name has been substituted for that of a lesser-known prophet. Some readers reject the notion that Elijah authored the letter. Others argue that the letter is authentic because it addresses a similar set of circumstances.

The final mention of Elijah in the Hebrew Bible is in the Book of Malachi. "Behold, I will send you Elijah the prophet before the coming of the great and terrible day of the Lord." The day is described as the burning of a great furnace,"... so that it will leave them neither root nor branch" (*Malachi 3:19*). In the traditional interpretation of the verse, Elijah will return before the Messiah.

According to a recent researcher, the Elijah stories were added to the *Deuteronomistic History* in four stages. The first stage dates from the final edition of the History, ca. 560 BCE, when the stories of Naboth's vineyard, Ahaziah's death, and Jehu's coup were included to illustrate the reliability of God's word, as well as the cycle of Baal worship and religious reform in the northern kingdom. Narratives about the Omride wars were added shortly afterward, to show that the attitude of the king toward the word of the prophets determines the fate of Israel. I Kings 17–18 was added in early post-Exilic times (after 538 BCE) to demonstrate the possibility of a new life with God after the time of judgment. In the fifth century BCE, I Kings 19:1–18 and the remaining Elisha stories were inserted to give prophecy a legitimate foundation in the history of Israel.

Jewish legends about Elijah abound in the Aggadah, which is found throughout various collections of rabbinic literature, including the Babylonian Talmud. This varied literature does not merely discuss his life, but creates a new history of him, beginning with his death, or 'translation,' and ending with the close of the history of the human race. As with most figures in Jewish folklore, the Biblical account of Elijah becomes the basis of later accounts. Forerunner of the Messiah, zealous in the cause of God, helper in distress: these are the three leading notes struck by the Aggadah, which endeavors to complete Biblical accounts of the prophet. Elijah's career is extensive and colorful. He appears the world over in the guise of a beggar and a scholar. In Jewish consciousness, from the time of Malachi to the later stories of the Chasidic rabbis, Elijah is associated with reverence, love, expectation, and hope.

In spite of Elijah's many miracles, the mass of the Jewish people remain as godless as before. According to the Midrash, they even abolish the sign of the covenant. The prophet appears as Israel's accuser before God (*Pirkei R. El. 29*). God then summons Elijah to the cave in which He appeared to Moses. Elijah perceives that he should appeal to God's mercy on behalf of Israel, but remains relentless in his zeal and severity. God commands him to appoint his successor (*Tanna d' Eliyahu Zuta viii*).

During his vision in the cave, God communicates to him the destinies of humanity. Humankind will pass through "four worlds." Our world is shown to the prophet in the form of the wind, since the world disappears as the wind. A storm represents the day of death, before which man trembles. Fire is the judgment in Gehenna. The last day is stillness (*Tan., Pekude, p. 128*).

Three years after he receives the vision (*Seder 'Olam R. xvii.*) Elijah is 'translated.' Concerning the place to which Elijah is transferred, opinions differ. In the old view, Elijah is received among the Heavenly inhabitants, where he records the deeds of men (*Talmud Bavli Tractate Kedoshim 70; Midrash Beresheit, Rabbah. xxxiv. 8*), a task which, according to the apocalyptic literature, is entrusted to Enoch. As early as the middle of the second century CE, when the notion of translation to Heaven was changed by Christian theologians, the assertion was made that Elijah never entered into Heaven as such (*Talmud Bavli Tractate Sukkah 5a*). In later literature, Paradise is generally designated as the abode of Elijah (*Pirkei R. El. xvi*), but because the location of Paradise is uncertain, Heaven and Paradise may be identical.

At Jewish circumcision ceremonies, a chair is set aside for the use of the prophet Elijah. Elijah is said to be a witness at all circumcisions when the sign of the covenant is placed upon the body of the child. The custom stems from the incident at Mount Horeb (*I Kings 19*): Elijah arrives at Mount Horeb after the demonstration of Jehovah's presence and power on Mount Carmel (*I Kings 18*). God asks Elijah to explain his arrival, and Elijah replies, "I have been very jealous for the Lord, the God of hosts; for the people of Israel have forsaken thy covenant, thrown down thy altars, and slain thy prophets with the sword; and I, even I only, am left; and they seek my life, to take it away" (*I Kings 19:10*). According to Rabbinic tradition, Elijah's words are patently untrue (*I Kings 18:4 and I Kings 19:18*), and because Elijah accuses Israel of failing to uphold the covenant, God requires Elijah to be present at every covenant of circumcision.

The Aggadah describes Elijah's origin more precisely than the Bible's vague, "Elijah, who was of the inhabitants of Gilead" (*I Kings 17:1*). Three different theories regarding Elijah's origin are presented in the Aggaddic literature: (1) he belonged to the tribe of Gad (*Midrash Genesis Rabbah lxxi.*); (2) he was a Benjamite from Jerusalem, identical with the Elijah mentioned in I Chron. 7:27; (3) he was a priest. In later works, some rabbis speculate that he is Phinehas (*Pirkei R. El. 47, Targum Yerushalmi on Num. xxv. 12*).

Mention must also be made of a statement which, though found only in the later Kabbalistic literature (*Yalkut Reubeni, Beresheit, 9a*) seems nevertheless to be very old. According to this particular legend, Elijah was really an angel in human form, and had neither parents nor offspring.

In the Talmudic literature, Elijah visits rabbis to help resolve difficult legal problems. Malachi cites Elijah as the harbinger of the Messianic Age; when confronted with conflicting laws or rituals, the rabbis postponed making a decision "until Elijah comes."

One such question was whether the Passover Seder requires four or five cups of wine. Each serving of wine corresponds to one of the "four expressions of redemption" in the Book of Exodus:

> I am the Lord, and I will bring you out from under the burdens of the Egyptians, and I will deliver you from their bondage, and I will redeem you with an outstretched arm and with great acts of judgment, and I will take you for my people, and I will be your God; and you shall know that I am the Lord your God, who has brought you out from under the burdens of the Egyptians.
>
> —Exodus 6:6–7

The next verse, "And I will bring you into the land which I swore to give to Abraham, to Isaac, and to Jacob; I will give it to you for a possession. I am the Lord" (*Exodus 6:8*), was not fulfilled until the generation following the Passover story. The rabbis could not determine whether this verse counted as part of the Passover celebration (deserving of another cup of wine), thus, the question was left for Elijah's return.

In practice, the fifth cup has come to be seen as a celebration of future redemption. We reserve a place at the Seder table and a cup of wine for Elijah. Traditionally,

Elijah's cup is used for no other purpose. During the Seder, the door of the house is opened and Elijah is invited in.

Havdalah is the ceremony that concludes the Sabbath Day (Saturday evening, in Jewish tradition). As part of the concluding hymn, an appeal is made to God for Elijah to come during the following week: "Elijah the Prophet, Elijah the Tishbite. Let him come quickly, in our day with the messiah, the son of David."

Far more references are made to Elijah in Jewish folklore than appear in the TaNaK.

"At the appointed time, it is written, you are destined to calm the wrath of God before it breaks out in fury, to turn the hearts of parents to their children, and to restore the tribes of Jacob." (*Sirach 48:10*).

In the Wisdom of Joshua ben Sira (*Sirach 48:10*) Elijah's tasks are altered to: 1) herald the Messiah, 2) calm God's fury, 3) restore familial peace, and 4) restore the 12 tribes.

Elijah's miraculous transfer to Heaven led to speculation about his true identity. He is equated with Phinehas, the grandson of Aaron (*Exodus 6:25*). Because of Phinehas' zealousness for God, he and his descendants were promised, "a covenant of lasting priesthood" (*Numbers 25:13*). Therefore, Elijah is a priest as well as a prophet. Elijah is also equated with the Archangel Sandalphon, whose four wingbeats carry him to any part of the Earth. When forced to choose between death and dishonor, Rabbi Kahana leaps to his death. Before he can strike the ground, Elijah/Sandalphon appears to catch him. Yet another name for Elijah is "Angel of the Covenant."

References to Elijah throughout Jewish folklore range from short observations (e.g. it is said that when dogs are happy for no reason, it is because Elijah is in the neighborhood) to lengthy parables on the nature of God's justice.

In one such story, Elijah asks Rabbi Joshua ben Levi if there is a favor he might grant. The rabbi asks to join Elijah in his wanderings. Elijah says he may come if he agrees not to question the prophet's actions. The rabbi concedes to this, and they begin their journey.

The first place they visit is the house of an elderly couple who are so poor they have only one old cow. The old couple gives of their hospitality as well as they can. The next morning, as the travelers depart, Elijah prays that the old cow will die, and it does. The second place they visit is the home of a wealthy man. The man has no patience for his visitors and chases them away with the admonition to get a job and not beg from honest people. As they leave, they pass his wall and notice it is crumbling. Elijah prays that the wall be repaired, and it is. Next, they come to a wealthy synagogue. They are allowed to spend the night with only the smallest of provisions. When they leave, Elijah prays that every member of the synagogue will become a leader. Finally, they visit a very poor synagogue. Here they are treated with great courtesy and hospitality. When they depart, Elijah prays that God might give them a single wise leader. At this, Rabbi Joshua can no longer hold back. He demands an explanation.

At the house of the old couple, Elijah knew that the Angel of Death was coming for the old woman. So he prayed that God might send the angel to take the cow instead. At the house of the wealthy man, a great treasure lay hidden in the crumbling wall. Elijah prayed that the wall be restored to keep the miser from finding the treasure. The story ends with a moral: a synagogue with many leaders will be ruined by arguments. A single wise leader will guide others to success and prosperity. "Know then, that if thou seest an evil-doer prosper, it is not always unto his advantage, and if a righteous man suffers need and distress, think not God is unjust.'"

The Elijah of legend does not lose any of his ability to afflict the comfortable. The case of Rabbi Eliezer son of Rabbi Simon ben Yohai is illustrative. Once, when walking a beach, the rabbi happens upon a hideously ugly man—the prophet in disguise. The man greets him courteously, "Peace be with thee, Rabbi." Instead of returning the greeting, the rabbi cannot resist an insult, "How ugly you are! Is there anyone as ugly as you in your town?" Elijah replies, "I don't know. Perhaps you should tell the Master Architect how ugly is this, His construction." The rabbi realizes his error and asks for pardon. Elijah does not forgive him until the entire city has asked for forgiveness on his behalf, and the rabbi himself promises to mend his ways.

As Elijah is seen as deeply pious, it is only natural that he is pitted against the equally evil Lilith. In legend, Lilith is the first wife of Adam. She rebels against Adam, the angels, and even God. She comes to be seen as a demon and a witch. When Elijah encounters Lilith, he recognizes and challenges her: "Unclean one, where are you going?" Unable to avoid or lie to him, she admits that she is on her way to the house of a pregnant woman. She intends to kill the woman and eat the child. Elijah pronounces his malediction, "I curse you in the Name of the Lord. Be silent as a stone!" Lilith strikes a bargain with Elijah. She promises to forsake her evil ways if Elijah will remove his curse. To seal the pact, she gives Elijah her names, so that they can be posted in the homes of pregnant women or newborns, or used as amulets. Lilith promises, "Where I see those names, I shall run away at once. Neither the child nor the mother will ever be injured by me."

Elijah cheated death and entered Paradise alive because he was a proponent of God, and of God's justice.

Eliezer the bondsman of Abraham

Eliezer, the servant of Abraham, is mentioned by name only in Gen. xv. 2. Abraham describes Eliezer as "possessor of my house" and as "Dammesek-Eliezer." The phrase 'ben meshek' (steward; comp., Zeph. xi. 9, and Job xxviii. 18) is the subject of the sentence, which reads "and the steward of my house is this Damascene, Eliezer". 'Damashek' is used intentionally for the adjective 'Damashki'.

Abraham may well have passed through Damascus on his way from Haran. Nachmanides connects him with that city, as do various traditions (*Josephus, "Ant." vii. 1, viii. 2*).

He may have acquired Eliezer there (who is also spoken of in Gen. xxiv., although the name is not given, in connection with the commission to choose a wife for Isaac).

The rabbis felt the difficulties of the text. According to Eleazar b. Pedath, Eliezer is one who "draws and gives others to drink"—that is, imparts to others the teachings of his master (*Yoma 18b*). Others find in the word 'meshek' an allusion to coveting Abraham's possessions. Herein lies the indication that Abraham pursued the kings (*Gen. xiv.*) to Damascus, and the *Targum Pseudo-Jonathan* and *Yerushalmi* read: "through whom many miracles were wrought for me in Damascus" (*Midrash Genesis Rabbah. xliv*).

The rabbis find in gematria an indication that Eliezer took part in that battle, or may have been the only combatant at Abraham's side. The number (318) of the soldiers (*Gen. 9:14*), and the numerical value of the letters in his name are the same, i.e. $1 + 30 + 10 + 70 + 7 + 200 = 318$ (*Genesis Rabbah. xliii. and xliv. Talmud Bavli Tractate Pesachim 70a, 70b, Talmud Bavli Tractate Nedarim 32a*). Kabbalists have held that this 318 refers to the number of days in the year that the moon is visible. In Genesis 14, when Sodom and Gomorrah are attacked and Lot is taken captive, we read (*Gen. 14:14*) "And when Abram heard that his brother was taken captive, he armed his trained servants, born in his own house, three hundred and eighteen, and pursued them unto Dan."

The very next chapter of the TaNaK tells us (*Gen. 15:2*) "And Abram said, Lord God, what wilt thou give me, seeing

I go childless, and the steward of my house is this Eliezer of Damascus?" Eliezer, written in Hebrew and reading from right to left, contains the letters *Alef, Lamed, Yod, Ayin, Zayin* and *Resh*. The gematria values are as follows:

Alef: Gematria of 1
Lamed: Gematria of . 30
Yod: Gematria of 10
Ayin: Gematria of 70
Zayin: Gematria of 7
Resh: Gematria of .. 200
Total..................... *318*

Eliezer is presented to Abraham by Nimrod. Eliezer saves Abraham's life by disclosing to him the devices for his destruction that have been prepared by Nimrod (*Pirkei R. El. xvi*). At Sodom, Eliezer witnesses a native's maltreatment of a stranger. Taking the side of the wronged man, he is himself severely wounded. He brings suit against his aggressor, but the judge condemns Eliezer to pay restitution to the native of Sodom. Thereupon Eliezer inflicts a severe wound on the judge, saying: "Pay to the man who bled me the amount you owe me for having bled you."

The men of Sodom used to place a guest on a bed, and if his length exceeded that of the bed, they cut off the excess, but if the man was shorter than the bed, he was stretched. Asked to lie in the bed, Eliezer replies that at the death of his mother he vowed never to sleep in a bed.

Another custom in Sodom was that he who invited a stranger to a wedding should forfeit his coat. Eliezer, who is very hungry, enters a wedding celebration, but can get nothing to eat. He sits down next to one of the guests. When asked who invited him, he replies: "By you." Afraid he will lose his coat, the guest leaves the house. Eliezer then sits near another man, on whom he plays the same trick, with the same result, until at last he succeeds in driving all the guests out of the house. He then secures a meal for himself (*Sanhedrin 109b*).

Eliezer is credited with having acquired all the virtues and learning of his master (*Yoma 28b*). It is even said that his features resembled so closely those of Abraham that Laban mistook him for his kinsman. When Abraham leads Isaac to Mount Moriah to offer him as a sacrifice, Eliezer hopes to become Abraham's heir. A discussion on the subject transpires between him and Ishmael (*Pirkei R. El. xxxi*). On completing the mission of selecting a wife for Isaac, Eliezer is freed. God rewards him with the kingdom of Bashan, over which he reigns under the name of Og. It is he who refuses to allow the Israelites to go through his territory on their way to Palestine (*Masseket Soferim*).

Eliezer's merit was loyalty in the Torah, a trait tarnished in later Rabbinic literature. He developed all the virtues, ethics, and spirituality of Abraham. He defended the vulnerable in Sodom, but discussed with Ishmael who would inherit Abraham's lot if Isaac was sacrificed. Obviously in the case of Eliezer, his good deeds overcame his less attractive traits.

Hirom the king of Zor, also known as King Hiram of Tyre

Hiram I (in Hebrew, 'high-born') according to the Bible, was the Phoenician king of Tyre (now Lebanon). He reigned from 980 BCE to 947 BCE, after his father Abibaal. Hiram was succeeded as king of Tyre by his son Baal-Eser I. Hiram is also mentioned in the writings of Menander of Ephesus, preserved in Josephus' *Against Apion*. Information here which does not appear in the Bible includes his age, 53 years, and the length of his reign, 34 years.

During Hiram's reign, Tyre grew from a satellite of Sidon into the most important Phoenician city, and the center of a large trading empire. Hiram suppressed the rebellion of the first Tyrean colony at Utica, near the later site of Carthage (*Against Apion* i:18).

The TaNaK says that he allies himself with King Solomon of Israel, the upcoming power of the region. Through the alliance with Solomon, Hiram acquires access to the major trade routes to Egypt, Arabia, and Mesopotamia. The two kings also join forces to start a trade route over the Red Sea, connecting the Israelite harbor of Ezion-Geber with a land called Ophir (*II Chronicles 8:16,17*).

Both kings grow rich through trade. Hiram sends arch-itects, workmen, and cedar wood to Solomon for the construction of the First Temple in Jerusalem. II Chronicles 2:

> "Solomon sent this message to Hiram king of
> Tyre: "Send me cedar logs as you did for my
> father David when you sent him cedar to build
> a palace to live in…Send me, therefore, a man

skilled to work in gold and silver, bronze and iron, and in purple, crimson and blue yarn, and experienced in the art of engraving, to work in Judah and Jerusalem with my skilled craftsmen, whom my father David provided. Send me also cedar, pine, and algum logs from Lebanon, for I know that your men are skilled in cutting timber there. My men will work with yours, to provide me with plenty of lumber, because the temple I build must be large and magnificent. I will give your servants, the woodsmen who cut the timber, twenty thousand cors of ground wheat, twenty thousand cors of barley, twenty thousand baths of wine and twenty thousand baths of olive oil."

Hiram king of Tyre replies by letter to Solomon, "Because the Lord loves his people, he has made you their king." And Hiram adds:

"Praise be to the Lord, the God of Israel, who made Heaven and earth! He has given King David a wise son, endowed with intelligence and discernment, who will build a temple for the Lord and a palace for himself. I am sending you Huram-Abi, a man of great skill, whose mother was from Dan and whose father was from Tyre. He is trained to work in gold and

silver, bronze and iron, stone and wood, and with purple and blue and crimson yarn and fine linen. He is experienced in all kinds of engraving and can execute any design given to him. He will work with your craftsmen and with those of my lord, David your father. Now let my lord send his servants the wheat and barley and the olive oil and wine he promised, and we will cut all the logs from Lebanon that you need and will float them in rafts by sea down to Joppa. You can then take them up to Jerusalem."

Hiram also extended the Tyrean harbour, enlarged the city by joining the two islands on which it was built, and constructed a royal palace and a temple for Melqart (*Against Apion i:17*). The period of Hiram's reign is derived from Josephus, who cites both Tyrian court records and the writings of Menander. Josephus states that Hiram's reign began 155 years and 8 months before the founding of Carthage. Temple construction began in Hiram's twelfth year, 143 years before the building of Carthage. All extant copies of Josephus/Menander that contain these passages give 155 years and 8 months between the start of Hiram's reign and the foundation of Carthage (one copy has 155 years and 18 months, but this is an obvious error.) Modern historians therefore have confidence in the 155-year figure and have used it to date Hiram's reign.

Classical authors, however, give two dates for Carthage's founding: 825 BCE and 814 BCE. The 814 date is derived from the Greek historian Timaeus (c. 345–260 BCE) and the 825 date from the writings of Pompeius Trogus (1st century BCE). The 814 date is more generally accepted. Earlier historians calculated the beginning of Hiram's reign as 814 + 155 = 969 BCE. Some say 825 BCE was the date Dido left Tyre (but she did not start construction of Carthage until 11 years later, in 814 BCE.)

In 1951, an inscription was published that showed that Shalmaneser III of Assyria received tribute, in 841 BCE, from a certain Baa'li-maanzer of Tyre. The name Baa'li-maanzer was interpreted by eminent philologists as referring to Baal-Eser II/Balazeros, grandfather of Pygmalion. According to Josephus/Manetho, it was during Pygmalion's seventh year that Dido fled from Tyre. Consequently, the dates of Pygmalion have always been computed based on the date calculated for Dido's flight, which was assumed to have taken place when she founded Carthage. But when 814 was taken as Pygmalion's seventh year, the dates for his father and grandfather (based on the best texts of Josephus/ Manetho) were not compatible; his grandfather could not have been on the throne in 841 BC or have given tribute to Shalmaneser in that year. Consequently, several scholars reexamined the 825 date for Dido's flight (Pygmalion's seventh year) and found that 825 BC was consistent with the Assyrian inscription.

Measuring 155 years from 825 BCE gave a new date for the first year of Hiram: 825 + 155 = 980 BCE. 980

BCE also proved an excellent match with another date, one calculated from the Scriptural texts related to the reign of Solomon. Based on the widely accepted date of 931/930 BCE for the division of the kingdom following Solomon's 40-year reign, Solomon's fourth year, when construction of the Temple began (*I Kings 6:1*), begins in Tishrei (roughly October) of 968 BCE. Josephus, citing both Tyrian court records and the writings of Menander, says that in Hiram's 12th year, Hiram sent assistance to Solomon for construction of the Temple. If 980 was the beginning of Hiram's reign, his twelfth year would have been 969 or 968 BC, which corresponds to the Biblical date.

The beginning date for Temple construction, using the Tyrian data, is derived independently from the derivation of the date using the Scriptural data. This factor, plus the evidence of the tribute from Baa'li-maanzer/Baal-Eser II to Shalmaneser III, has led to the adoption of the chronologies of the Tyrian kings. Hiram's first year is therefore accepted as 980 BC, instead of 969 BC, a date favored before publication of the Shalmaneser inscription.

The alleged sarcophagus of Hiram is located a two-hour walk southeast of Tyre. It is a colossal limestone sarcophagus on a high pedestal, known as Qabr Hiram, not to be confused with the famous Ahiram sarcophagus.

Hiram merited entrance to Paradise while he was still alive because he helped Solomon build the first Temple, and praised God by doing so. While this was not an altruistic gesture, as he accepted Solomon's fees and trade routes, Hiram was not an enemy to the Hebrews.

Ebed-melech the Cushi

Ebed-melech's name literally means 'servant of the king.' He was an African eunuch.

Now when Ebed-melech the Ethiopian, one of the eunuchs which was in the king's house, heard that they had put Jeremiah in the dungeon; the king then sitting in the gate of Benjamin; Ebed-melech went forth out of the king's house, and spoke to the king saying, "My lord the king, these men have done evil in all that they have done to Jeremiah the prophet, whom they have cast into the dungeon; and he is like to die for hunger in the place where he is: for there is no more bread in the city."

Then the king commanded Ebed-melech the Ethiopian, saying, "Take from hence thirty men with you, and take up Jeremiah the prophet out of the dungeon, before he dies." So Ebed-melech took the men with him, and went into the house of the king under the treasury, and took thence rags and worn-out garments, and let them down by cords into the dungeon to Jeremiah. And Ebed-melech the Ethiopian said to Jeremiah, "Put now these old cast clouts and rotten rags under your armholes under the cords." And Jeremiah did so. So they drew up Jeremiah with cords, and took him up out of the dungeon: and Jeremiah remained in the court of the prison.

Then King Zedekiah sent and had Jeremiah the prophet brought to him at the third entrance that is in the house of the Lord and the king said to Jeremiah, "I am going to ask you something; do not hide anything from me." Then Jeremiah said to Zedekiah, "If I tell you, will you not certainly put me to death? Besides, if I give you advice, you will not listen to me." But King Zedekiah swore to Jeremiah in secret saying, "As the Lord lives, who made this life for us, surely I will not put you to death nor will I give you over to the hand of these men who are seeking your life." Then Jeremiah said to Zedekiah, "Thus says the Lord God of hosts, the God of Israel, 'If you will indeed go out to the officers of the king of Babylon, then you will live, this city will not be burned with fire, and you and your household will survive. But if you will not go out to the officers of the king of Babylon, then this city will be given over to the hand of the Chaldeans; and they will burn it with fire, and you yourself will not escape from their hand.'"

Then King Zedekiah said to Jeremiah, "I dread the Jews who have gone over to the Chaldeans, for they may give me over into their hand and they will abuse me." But Jeremiah said, "They will not give you over. Please obey the Lord in what I am saying to you, that it may go well with you and you may live. But if you keep refusing to go out, this is the word which the Lord has shown me: 'Then behold, all of the women who have been left in the palace of the king of Judah are going to be brought out to the officers of the king of Babylon; and those women will say, 'Your close friends have misled and overpowered you; while your feet were sunk in the mire, they turned back.' They will also bring out all your wives and your sons to the Chaldeans, and you yourself will not escape from their hand, but will be seized by the hand of the king of Babylon, and this city will be burned with fire.'"

Then Zedekiah said to Jeremiah, "Let no man know about these words and you will not die. But if the officials hear that I have talked with you and come to you and say to you, 'Tell us now what you said to the king and what the king said to you; do not hide it from us and we will not put you to death,' then you are to say to them, 'I was presenting my petition before the king, not to make me return to the house of Jonathan to die there.'" So Jeremiah stayed in the court of the guardhouse until the *day that Jerusalem was captured. Now when Jerusalem was captured in the ninth year of Zedekiah king of Judah, in the tenth month, Nebuchadnezzar king of Babylon and all his army came to Jerusalem and laid siege to it; in the eleventh year of Zedekiah, in the fourth month, in the ninth day of the month, the city wall was breached.*

—Jer. 38:7–39:2

On Tammuz 17 in 70 CE, the Romans breached the wall of Jerusalem. Tammuz 10 was folded into Tammuz 17, and it is now a fast day. True to form, King Zedekiah and the nobility of Judah fled, and were captured. All were killed except for Zedekiah, who was blinded and taken in chains to Babylon.

Of Jeremiah, Nebuchadnazzar says (*II Chron. 39:12–14*), "'Take him and look after him, and do nothing harmful to him, but rather deal with him just as he tells you.' They took Jeremiah out of the court of the guardhouse and entrusted him to Gedaliah, the son of Ahikam, the son of Shaphan, to take him home. So he stayed among the people."

From II Chron. 39:16 onward, God says to Jeremiah:

Go and speak to Ebed-melech the Ethiopian, saying, 'Thus says the Lord of hosts, the God of Israel, Behold, I am about to bring My words on this city for disaster and not for prosperity; and they will take place before you on that day. But I will deliver you on that day, declares the Lord, and you will not be given into the hand of the men whom you dread. For I will certainly rescue you, and you will not fall by the sword; but you will have your own life as booty, because you have trusted in Me, declares the Lord.'"

Ebed-melech saves Jeremiah, which gives Jeremiah another chance to warn the last Hebrew king of Judah to report to Nebuchadnazzar, so that Jerusalem, the people, and the Temple may live on. Like other Hebrew kings, Zedekiah does not listen to prophecy. Jerusalem and the Temple are destroyed, King Zedekiah's household is killed, and the king is blinded and taken captive. God rewards Ebed-melech by saving him from death at the hands of the Babylonians.

Jabetz, the son of R' Yehudah the Prince

There is no Talmudic reference to a son of Rabbi Judah Ha Nasi, Rabbi Yehudah the Prince, named Jabetz or Jabez. This is probably an error, which frequently occurs with names in oral transmission. It should be Jabez the Yahudahite.

The clan of the Kenite family of the Rechabites merged into the tribe of Judah. I Chron. 2:55 refers to "families of scribes" (*soferim*) dwelling at Jabez; while in I Chron. 4:9–10 Jabez is described as "more honorable than his brethren." His name (*Ya'bez*) is derived from his mother's words: "I bare him with sorrow" (*ozeb*). I Chron. 4:9–10, says:

Jabez was more honorable than his brothers. His mother had named him Jabez, saying, 'I gave birth to him in pain.' Jabez called on the God of Israel, saying 'Oh that You would bless me indeed and enlarge my border, and that Your hand might be with me, and that You would keep me from harm that it may not pain me!' And God granted him what he requested.

Jabez was honorable and trusted God. He was prominent, particularly after the Exile, among those Kenite clans who embraced Judaism and became scribes and teachers of the Law. Rabbinic tradition identifies Jabez with Othniel the Kenezite, the head of the beit ha-midrash after the death of Moses (*Temurah 16a*). Hence, the vow of Jabez was understood to refer to his schoolhouse: "If Thou wilt bless me with children, and give me many disciples and associates" (*Sanhedrin 106a*). "The whole tribe of Jethro, the Kenites as well as the Rechabites, left their habitations near Jericho and went to Jabez to learn the Torah from him" (*Sifre on Numbers 78*).

In the *Syriac Apocalypse of Baruch* (v. 5), Jabez is mentioned together with Jeremiah and Gedaliah among the saintly leaders of the people at the destruction of the Temple. He is one of the deathless mentioned in rabbinic tradition.

Jabez was a righteous convert. His ancestor was Moses' father-in-law Yitro. He was a Kenite who joined the tribe of Judah. Like many converts, he was more spiritual than those born Hebrew or Jewish. He taught Torah, was a scribe of Torah, and he had faith in God. He is only mentioned in two verses of the entire TaNaK, yet his faith, integrity, honesty, and teaching earned him the privilege of seeing Paradise while still alive.

Bothiah (Bithiah) the daughter of Pharaoh

> The sons of Ezrah were Jether, Mered, Epher and Jalon. And these are the sons of Bithia the daughter of Pharaoh, whom Mered took, and she conceived and bore Miriam, Shammai and Ishbah the father of Eshtemoa. His Judean wife gave birth to Jered the father of Gedor, Heber the father of Soco, and Jekuthiel the father of Zanoah. These were the children of Pharaoh's daughter Bithiah, whom Mered had married.
>
> —I Chron. 4; 17–18

Pharaoh's daughter did not follow her father's wicked ways, but converted, and ceased to worship idols. She was highly praised by the rabbis. The Midrash includes her among other devout women converts: Hagar, Asenath, Zipporah, Shiphrah, Puah the daughter of Pharaoh, Rahab, Ruth, and Yael, the wife of Heber the Kenite (*Midrash Tadshe, Ozar ha-Midrashim*).

The Midrash specifically praises Pharaoh's daughter for rescuing Moses, thereby aiding in the exodus of the Israelites from Egypt. Some Midrashim attest to her longevity and claim that she entered the Garden of Eden while still alive.

The Midrash calls her 'Bithiah,' identifying her as the woman mentioned in I Chron 4:18, one of Mered's two wives. The rabbis deduce from this passage that Pharaoh's daughter was married to Caleb, son of Jephunneh. They maintain that Caleb was given the name "Mered" because he rebelled (*marad*) against the counsel of the spies (when they spoke ill of the land of Canaan in Num. 13–14). God said: "Let Caleb, who rebelled against the counsel of the spies, marry the daughter of Pharaoh, who rebelled against the idols of her father's house" (*Megillah 13a*). The rabbis conclude that, although she was an Egyptian, Chronicles refers to her as "his Judahite wife" because she repudiated idolatry.

The Midrash relates that Pharaoh's daughter received her new name, Bithiah (bat-yah; literally, the daughter of God), from God directly, as reward for her actions. God tells her, "Moses was not your son, yet you called him your son; you are not My daughter, but I call you My daughter" (*Midrash Lev. Rabbah 1:3*).

The Midrashim about Moses' rescue are replete with wondrous acts and miracles, and graphically illustrate the threat to the infant's life and the necessity of Divine intervention. The reader gains the impression that Moses was not like all men—that his qualities were evident while he was still a child. The miraculous deliverance of the infant Moses symbolizes the future salvation of the people of Israel from Egypt, during which miraculous events also occur.

The Torah explains that Pharaoh's daughter finds Moses when she goes down to bathe in the Nile (*Ex. 2:5*). The Midrash expands upon this to say that she goes to cleanse herself from the idols of her father's house—in other words, to perform the immersion of conversion (*Megillah 13a*). This exegesis illuminates the spiritual qualities of the Pharaoh's daughter, by merit of which God chooses her to find and raise Moses.

The rabbis magnify the test to which she is put when she sees the floating basket. In the Midrash, when her handmaidens realize that she intends to rescue Moses, they attempt to dissuade her, and encourage her to heed her father. "Our mistress, it is the way of the world that when a king issues a decree, it is not heeded by the entire world, but his children and the members of his household do observe it, and you wish to transgress your father's decree?" Gabriel appears and beats them to the ground, and they die (*Sotah 12b*). These handmaidens represent the Pharaoh's daughter's yetzer ha ra. She might have been undecided as to whether she should disobey her father's edict. The angel Gabriel removes this obstacle and reinforces her resolve to draw Moses from the Nile.

An additional miracle is performed when the basket is drawn from the water. Exodus 2:5 attests, "and she sent her slave girl [*amatah*] to fetch it." The word *amatah* has two possible meanings: 'her slave girl' or 'her hand.' According to one view, she sends her slave girl to retrieve the basket. Although the angel Gabriel has killed her handmaidens, he leaves one alive for her, because it is not customary for the daughter of a king to stand unattended. The remaining slave is sent to rescue Moses. When *amatah* is interpreted as 'her hand,' the daughter of Pharaoh herself brings Moses from the river. Since the daughter of the Pharaoh should not have to trouble herself and go down into the river to catch the floating basket, a miracle is performed: her arm stretches until she can reach it (*Midrash Exodus Rabbah 1:23*). In one tradition, her arm extends to a length of sixty cubits (*Sekel Tov on Ex. 2:46*). This exegesis emphasizes her personal involvement in Moses's rescue, as she attests in Ex. 2:10: "I drew him out of the water."

After the basket is drawn from the Nile, the Torah recounts that, "when she opened it, she saw that it [*va-tire-hu*] was a child….She took pity on it" (*Ex. 2:6*). The rabbis ponder the reasons the Pharaoh's daughter would ignore her father's wishes and keep Moses alive. The Midrash says that she sees the Shechinah (the Divine Presence) with Moses, and the words 'va-tire-hu' allude to the name of God (*Midrash Exodus Rabbah 1:24*).

Another perspective is based on the continuation of the verse, which says that the child's weeping motivated Pharaoh's daughter: "She saw that it was a child, a boy crying. She took pity on it." The rabbis maintain that Divine intervention was needed for the infant to cry, which they learn from a close reading of Verse 6. The beginning of the verse refers to Moses as a "child [*yeled*]," and then calls him a "boy [*na'ar*]." Moses is a *yeled*, that is, an infant, but he conducts himself as a *na'ar*, an older child. Thus, when the daughter of Pharaoh opens the basket, Moses, unlike other babies, does not cry. The angel Gabriel immediately comes and hits Moses so that he cries, thereby arousing the compassion of Pharaoh's daughter (*Midrash Exodus Rabbah 1:24*). One tradition claims that the Pharaoh's daughter suffers from leprosy, and goes down to bathe in the water to be cured of her disease. When she touches Moses' basket, she is miraculously cured, which leads her to take pity on the child and love him so strongly (*Midrash Exodus Rabbah 1:23*).

When the Pharaoh's daughter sees Moses, she declares: "This must be a Hebrew child" (*Ex. 2:6*) to which the Midrash adds that Moses is born circumcised (*Midrash Exodus Rabbah 1:20*). When she finds that the infant is circumcised, she realizes that he is a Hebrew child (*Midrash Exodus Rabbah 1:24*).

Another Midrash explains that when Bithiah makes this statement, she is unconsciously prophesying. 'This' child falls into the Nile, but none of the others. She prophesies that Moses will be the last Hebrew child to be cast into the river, and is correct, because Pharaoh's astrologers see in the stars that the one destined to save Israel will be punished through water. They advise Pharaoh to issue the decree: "Every boy that is born you shall throw into the Nile" (*Ex. 1:22*). Once Moses has been placed in the water, the astrologers say: "We no longer see that sign," and they cancel the decree (*Sotah 12b*). The Midrash adds that the astrologers are somewhat correct, in that Moses is punished by water when he sins at the Waters of Meribah (*Num. 20:7–13*).

In the Midrash depiction, the Pharaoh's daughter sees that Moses is hungry when she draws him from the Nile. She takes him to all the Egyptian women, but Moses will not nurse from any of them. Moses says, "The mouth that will speak with God will not suckle something impure" (the milk of non-Jews). Miriam offers Pharaoh's daughter the services of her mother Yochebed, who is "a Hebrew" (*Ex. 2:7 and Sotah 12b*).

In yet another interpretation, Moses rejects the breasts of the Egyptian women because he says, "God will speak with me. The next day the Egyptian women would say: 'I nursed the one who speaks with the Shechinah" (*Midrash Exodus Rabbah 1:25*).

Pharaoh's daughter tells Yochebed (*Ex.2:9*), "Take [*helikhi*] this child and nurse it for me," which, according to the rabbis, is an instance of unwitting prophecy, since the word *helikhi* conceals the truth—"*shelikhi hu* [he—the infant—is yours]" (*Midrash Exodus Rabbah 1:25*). Yochebed nurses Moses for twenty-four months (*Midrash Exodus Rabbah 1:26*). The Midrash asserts that although Yochebed gives birth to Moses, he is called the son of Bithiah the daughter of Pharaoh, because she raises him (*Sotah 19b*).

The Midrash tells that Bithiah kisses and hugs Moses as if he is her own son, and she will not take him out of the royal palace. Because of his beauty, everyone desires to see him, and no one can tear his eyes away from the child. Moses' life is in danger, even though he is protected by Pharaoh's daughter.

In one account, Pharaoh holds Moses and hugs him. Moses takes Pharaoh's crown and puts it on his own head, as he will do again when he grows up. Pharaoh's magicians say, "We fear that this child will take your crown and place it on his own head, lest this be the one who we prophesy will seize the kingdom from you." Some of the magicians advise the Pharaoh to kill the child, and others suggest that he be burnt.

Jethro, who sits among the magicians, tells them: "This child is witless. In order to test him, set before him two bowls, one containing gold, and the other, a coal. If he stretches his hand to the coal, he is witless and does not deserve to die; but if he stretches his hand to the gold, he did this with intelligence, and he is to be put to death." They immediately set before him the gold and the coal. Moses reaches to take the gold, but Gabriel pushes his hand away. Moses takes the coal and puts his hand and the coal into his mouth. His tongue is burnt, which causes him to be (*Ex. 4:10*) "slow of speech and slow of tongue" (*Midrash Exodus Rabbah 1:26*).

The names of Pharaoh's daughter's six offspring in I Chron. 4:18 are six different appellations for Moses: "And his Judahite wife bore Jered, father of Gedor; Heber, father of Soco; and Jekuthiel, father of Zanoah." The Midrash notes that she does not actually give birth to him, as the verse states, but only raises him. From this the rabbis learn that anyone who raises an orphan in his house is accounted by Scripture as if he were the child's birth parent (*Megillah 13a*).

Another Midrash lists ten names given to Moses: Jered, Avi- [father of] Gedor, Heber, Avi-Soco, Jekuthiel, Avi-Zanoah, Tobijah, [Tovya} Shemaiah, Levi, and Moses. God tells him: "By your life, of all the names by which you are called, I will call you only by the name given you by Bithiah the daughter of Pharaoh" (*Midrash Lev. Rabbah 1:3*). Pharaoh's daughter treats Moses with loving kindness, and is rewarded by God's decision to call him only by the name she chooses for him (*Midrash Exodus Rabbah 1:26*).

The rabbis apply to Bithiah the verse from the Woman of Valor poem. "She sees that her business thrives; her lamp never goes out at night" (*Prov. 31:18*). The 'night' refers to the plague in which all the firstborn of Egypt die, including the females, with the exception of Pharaoh's daughter. Moses advocates for her; she is saved by his prayer on her behalf. Where Solomon declares: "She sees that her business thrives [*ki tov*]," *ki tov* is an appellation for Moses: "she saw how beautiful [*ki tov*] he was" (*Ex. 2:2*). Her lamp 'never goes out' because she does not die on that night (*Midrash Exodus Rabbah 18:3*).

The Midrash asserts that Bithiah is among those who enter the Garden of Eden while still alive, as did Enoch, Serach daughter of Asher, Elijah, the three sons of Korach, King Hiram of Tyre, Jabez, Jonadab son of Rahab and his descendants, Ebed-melech the Ethiopian, Abraham's servant Eleazar, the slave of R. Judah ha-Nasi and R. Joshua ben Levi (*Midrash Kallah Rabbati 3:23*). This list differs from the one in *Derek Eretz Zuta*, by adding the three sons of Korach,

Rahab's son Jonadab, and a slave of Judah ha Nasi. Also, Jebez not identified as a son of Judah ha Nasi.

Bithiah was privileged to enter the Garden of Eden because she rescued Moses and raised him (*Midrash Eshet Chayil—Woman of Valor—31:15*), thus facilitating the redemption of Israel from Egypt. In another exegetical tradition, God says: "Since this one brought salvation to Israel and brought them forth to life, I shall prolong her life. I shall reward this one, who left her father's royal house and adhered to Israel" (*Midrash Kallah Rabbati 3:23*). She placed life, *pekuah nefesh*, over the royal decree of her father.

Serech (Serah) the daughter of Asher

Asher was one of the twelve sons of Jacob. Serah was Jacob's granddaughter. She is mentioned in the list of seventy Israelites who went down to Egypt (*Gen. 46:17*) and in the enumeration of the Israelites at the steppes of Moab (*Num. 26:46*). Nothing more is said about her in the Bible; she takes no part in any narrative.

Yet the faceless Biblical character becomes a fascinating personality in numerous Midrashic traditions. Her history is intertwined with the story of the migration to Egypt and enslavement, and also with redemption and the return to Eretz Israel. She lives to an extremely old age and is blessed with much earthly wisdom and knowledge. She helps the people of Israel as needed, even into the time of the rabbis.

According to the Midrash, when Joseph is reunited with his brothers and sends them to Canaan to move Jacob to

Egypt, he orders them not to alarm their aged father. The brothers ask Serah to play the lyre for Jacob, and thus to reveal to him that Joseph is still alive. Serah plays well and sings gently: "Joseph my uncle did not die, he lives and rules all the land of Egypt." She plays this for Jacob two and three times. He is pleased by what he hears. Joy fills his heart, the spirit of God rests on him, and he senses the truth of her words. He bids her, "Continue to play for me, for you have heartened me with all that you said." While he is speaking with her, his sons bring horses, chariots, royal garments, and slaves. They say, "We bring glad tidings, for Joseph still lives and he rules all the land of Egypt." When Jacob sees all that Joseph has sent, he knows they are telling the truth. He is exceedingly happy, and says (*Gen. 45:28*), "This is enough for me! My son Joseph is still alive! I must go and see him before I die" (*Sefer ha Yasher, Vayigash, Chapter 14*).

Although Gen. 46:17 lists Serah among the seventy members of Jacob's family who go to Egypt, the rabbis note that only sixty-nine names appear in Genesis 46. Logic would dictate that Jacob himself completed the count of seventy souls, but the Midrash maintains that Serah was the seventieth member of the Israelite party (*Midrash Genesis Rabbah 94:9*)

According to this view, she is intentionally not enumerated among the seventy because she enters the Garden of Eden while still alive. This exegesis may be based on a tradition preserved only in the late Midrash, which identifies her as the daughter of Malchiel son of Elam and Hadorah, the granddaughter of Eber, who was adopted by Asher after the death of her father and her mother's marriage to Asher. Serah is raised in Asher's home as his daughter, but since she is adopted, she is not listed among Jacob's seventy descendants (*Sefer ha Yasher VaYeshev, Chapter 14*).

The rabbis assign to her an important role in identifying Moses as the one who delivers the Israelites from Egypt. The Midrash relates that the secret of redemption is given to Abraham, who conveys it to Isaac, Isaac to Jacob, and Jacob to Joseph. Joseph transmits the secret of redemption to his brothers, telling them (*Gen. 50:25*): "When God has taken notice of you [*pakod yifkod*], you shall carry up my bones from here." Asher passes the secret to his daughter Serah.

When Moses and Aaron perform miracles, the Israelite elders go to Serah and tell her that a man has come to them and performed wonders. She replies, "There is no substance to him"—that is, he is not the deliverer. They say, "He also said: 'When God has taken notice of you' [*pakod yifkod*]." She replies, "This is the man who will redeem Israel from Egypt, for I heard from my father 'He will take notice' [*pakod yifkod*]." The people believe in God and His agent, as it is said (*Ex. 4:31*), "and the people were convinced when they heard that the Lord had taken note [*pakod*] of the Israelites."

In the Midrashic account, Serah helps Moses fulfill the oath sworn to Joseph. When the Israelites are ready to leave Egypt, they are occupied with collecting booty. Moses alone searches for Joseph's coffin throughout the land, to no avail. Serah is the only person from Joseph's generation who is still living. Moses asks her, "Do you know where Joseph is buried?" She answers, "They placed him here. The Egyptians made for him a metal coffin and sunk it in the Nile, so that its waters would be blessed." Moses stands on the bank of the Nile and shouts, "Joseph, Joseph, the time has come for the oath that God swore to our father Abraham, that He will redeem His children. Give honor to the Lord, the God of Israel, and do not delay your redemption, because we are delayed on your account. If you show yourself, it will be well; and if not, then we are free from your oath, if you will not raise your coffin, we will go forth from Egypt and leave you here." Joseph's coffin rises to the surface, and Moses takes it (*Sotah 13a*). The rabbis state that Serah delivered "the faithful one to the faithful one," because she gave Joseph to Moses when they departed from Egypt (*Midrash Genesis Rabbah 94:9*).

According to the Rabbis, not only is Serah among those who came to Egypt and those who left it, she also entered Eretz Israel. They use Numbers 26:46 as a proof text; Serah is among the names of those entering the land (*Seder Olam Rabbah 9*).

Another tradition indicates that Serah is alive in the time of King David. She is identified as the wise woman of Abel-beth-maacah. When Joab, David's military commander, asks her, "Who are you?" she replies (*II Sam. 20:19*), "I am one of those who seek the welfare of the faithful [*shelomei* emunei] in Israel." In the Rabbinical exegesis, she says to Joab, "I am one of the Israelites who went down to Egypt with Jacob. I completed [shelumai] the count of Israel [emunei Yisrael]." The root shlm refers to peace, welfare, and completion. Emunei Yisrael indicates that she is one of the seventy souls who went down to Egypt. "Do you want to kill the entire city, and also me, an important woman?" Serah saves the lives of all the inhabitants of her town (Midrash Eccl. Rabbah 9:18:2).

One exegetical tradition goes even farther and declares that Serah never dies. Her immortality is reflected in a narrative set in the time of the rabbis. Serah resolves a disagreement in the academy. R' Yochanan is expounding on the verse Exodus 14:22, "the waters forming a wall for them on their right and on their left." R' Yochanan says the wall of water was a sort of impervious net. Serah appears and explains, "I was there, and the water was not as a net, but as transparent windows" (Pesikta de Rav Kahana 11:13). In this Midrashic vignette, Serah is an extremely old woman who testifies, in the first person, to the miracle of the parting of the Reed Sea. In her wisdom she is capable of comprehending and participating in the aggadic discussion conducted in the academy. Her statement is preferred to that of R. Yochanan, since she has firsthand knowledge of the facts.

The traditions that cite Serah's extreme longevity appear to be based mainly on the accounts of those who went to Egypt with Jacob and those who entered Eretz Israel. Her singular name may also have contributed to these traditions, since the expression (*Ex. 26:12*) '*serah ha-odef*' means 'something left over,' or 'the overlapping excess.' In the late Midrash, Jacob blesses Serah so that she will live forever: "My daughter, because you revived my spirit, death shall never rule you" (*Sefer ha Yasher, Vayigash, chap. 14*).

Serah embodies the history of the people of Israel. She is linked with leaders, and expedites the realization of the Divine plan. When she convinces Jacob that Joseph still lives, he goes down to Egypt. She identifies Moses as the true redeemer of Israel, thus leading the people to heed him. When she helps Moses find Joseph's bones, she prevents a delayed departure from Egypt. Her appearance seems to confirm that God's promises will be fulfilled, that the people of Israel will leave Egypt, and will reach the Promised Land.

Rabbi Yehoshua ben Levi, also known as Rabbi Joshua ben Levi

Rabbi Joshua is the hero of nearly all the paradise legends. He meets Elijah before the gates of paradise (*Sanhedrin 98a*). He obtains permission from the Angel of Death to visit paradise so that he can inspect his assigned place. He reports the result of his investigations to Rabban Gamaliel (*Seder ha-Dorot*). The original accounts of his report appear in the Zohar, which contains the elements in fragmentary documents (*Zohar Beresheit, 38a–39b, 41a,* and *Zohar Leka 81a, b*). One of these accounts is credited to Enoch. The first compilation and elaboration of these fragments is Midrash Konen, which reads as follows:

The Gan Eden at the east measures 800,000 years (at ten miles per day or 3,650 miles per year). There are five chambers for various classes of the righteous. The first is built of cedar, with a ceiling of transparent crystal. This is the habitation of non-Jews who become true and devoted converts to Judaism. They are headed by Obadiah the prophet and Onkelos the proselyte, who teach them the Law. The second is built of cedar, with a ceiling of fine silver. This is the habitation of the penitents, headed by Manasseh, King of Israel, who teaches them the Law.

The third chamber is built of silver and gold, ornamented with pearls. It is very spacious, and contains the best of Heaven and of earth, with spices, fragrance, and sweet odors. In the center of this chamber stands the Tree of Life, 500 years high. Under its shadow rest Abraham, Isaac, and Jacob, the tribes, those of the Egyptian exodus and those who died in the wilderness, headed by Moses and Aaron. There also are David and Solomon, crowned, and Chileab [II Sam. iii. 3; Talmud Bavli Tractate Shabbat 55b] as if living, attending on his father, David.

Every generation of Israel is represented except that of Absalom and his confederates.

Moses teaches them the Law, and Aaron gives instruction to the priests. The Tree of Life is like a ladder on which the souls of the righteous may ascend and descend.

In a conclave above are seated the Patriarchs, the Ten Martyrs, and those who sacrificed their lives for the cause of His Sacred Name. These souls descend daily to the Gan Eden, to join their families and tribes, where they lounge on soft cathedras studded with jewels. Everyone, according to his excellence, is received in audience to praise and thank the Ever-living God; and all enjoy the brilliant light of the Shechinah. The flaming sword, changing from intense heat to icy cold and from ice to glowing coals, guards the entrance against living mortals. The size of the sword is ten years. The souls on entering paradise are bathed in the 248 rivulets of balsam and attar.

The fourth chamber is made of olive-wood and is inhabited by those who have suffered for the sake of their religion. Olives typify bitterness in taste and brilliancy in light [olive-oil], symbolizing persecution and its reward.

The fifth chamber is built of precious stones, gold, and silver, surrounded by myrrh and aloes. In front of the chamber runs the River

Gihon, on whose banks are planted shrubs affording perfume and aromatic incense. There are couches of gold and silver and fine drapery. This chamber is inhabited by the Messiah of David, Elijah, and the Messiah of Ephraim.

[Note here Judaism's version of two Messiahs, one of war, and one of everlasting Shalom]

In the center are a canopy made of the cedars of Lebanon, in the style of the Tabernacle, with posts and vessels of silver; and a settee of Lebanon wood with pillars of silver and a seat of gold, the covering thereof of purple. Within rests the Messiah, son of David, 'a man of sorrows and acquainted with grief' (Isa. 53:3), suffering, and waiting to release Israel from the Exile. Elijah comforts and encourages him to be patient. Every Monday and Thursday, and Sabbath and on holy days the Patriarchs, Moses, Aaron, and others, call on the Messiah and condole with him, in the hope of the fast-approaching end.

One Midrash describes three fire-walls of different colors that border Paradise. The section for the pious of the heathen nations is placed outside the outer wall. The dimensions are miniscule (e.g., 600 ells between the walls, and 120 ells' space between the entrances), and in this version, Paradise is said to have existed 1,361 years, 3 hours, and 2 minutes before the creation of Heaven and Earth. A tall musical pillar plays beautiful songs automatically. There are seven sections for pious souls, within which there are segregated areas for the souls of pious women, headed, in the order named, by Bithiah, the daughter of Pharaoh; Yochebed, wife of Amram; Miriam; Huldah the prophetess; Abigail; and, in the highest sixth and seventh sections, the Matriarchs.

In another version of Paradise there are seven sections, but twelve grades of souls: "those (1) who feared God, (2) who were charitable, (3) who buried the dead, (4) who visited the sick, (5) who dealt honestly, (6) who lent to the poor, (7) who cared for the orphans, (8) who were peacemakers, (9) who instructed the poor, (10) who were martyrs, (11) who learned the Law, (12) David, Solomon, and other righteous kings, such as Josiah and Hezekiah."

The following Midrashic narrative is attributed to R. Joshua b. Levi, though written in a style that appears much later, perhaps in the ninth century CE:

> Paradise has two diamond gates, and there are 600,000 attending angels with shining faces. Immediately on the arrival of the righteous, they divest him of his shroud and clothe him with eight garments made of clouds of honor. They put a double crown of fine gold and jewels on his head, and place

eight myrtles in his hand. The angels salute him, saying, 'Go eat thy bread with joy,' and lead him along valleys of water in which grow 800 species of roses and myrtles. Each of the righteous has a canopy as is befitting his excellence. Connected with each canopy are four rivulets of milk, wine, balsam, and honey. Over each canopy grows a golden vine studded with thirty pearls, each glittering like Venus. Under the canopy is a table of onyx set with diamonds and pearls. Sixty angels guard every righteous one and ask him to partake of the honey as compensation for his study of the Law, which is likened to honey (Ps. 19: 10), and to drink the wine, which has been preserved in its grapes ever since the six days of Creation, the Law being likened to spiced wine (Song. 8:2). The most uncomely of the righteous becomes as beautiful as Joseph and as R' Yochanan. Exiguous silver pomegranates reflect the sun, which is always shining; for 'the path of the just is as the shining light' (Prov. 4:18). There are three stages through which the newcomer has to pass: (1) the section of the children, which he enters as at child; (2) the section of the young; and (3) the section of the old. In each section he enjoys himself as befits his state and age."

—Midrash Seder Gan Eden

At the feast that is prepared for the righteous, the main courses to be served are the Leviathan and "the wine preserved in its grapes since the six days of Creation" (*Bava Batra 75a*). The Almighty invites the righteous into Paradise. King David asks God to join the company. The angel Gabriel brings two thrones, one for God and one for David, as the Scriptures say, "his throne as the sun before me" (*Ps. 84:36*). Everyone feasts and drinks three goblets of wine. The toast (grace before meals) is offered to Abraham, 'the father of the world,' but he declines because he had a son (Ishmael) who antagonized God. Isaac, in turn, declines because one of his descendants (an Edomite) destroyed the Holy Temple. Jacob declines because he married two sisters (against the Law). Moses declines because he did not cross the Jordan into Palestine. Joshua declines because he left no issue. Finally, King David accepts the toast, saying: "I will take the cup of salvation and call upon the name of the Lord" (*Ps. 116:13*). After grace, the Law is produced, and God, through the interpreter Zerubbabel ben Shealtiel (*Ezra 3:2*), reveals the secrets and reasons for the commandments. David preaches from the Haggadah, and the righteous say, "Let His great Name be hallowed forevermore in paradise!" The wicked in Gehinnom, upon hearing the doxology, take courage and answer "Amen!" The Almighty orders the attending angels to open the gates of Paradise, and to permit the wicked to enter, as the Scriptures say, "Open gates, that the righteous nation which keeps the truth may enter" (*Isa. 26:2*). The word *emunim*, truth, means those "who observe to answer 'Amen'" (*Tanna d' Eliyahu Zuta 20*).

There are two levels of Gehinnom, which rest against the lower and upper portions of Gan Eden. Curiously enough, Hell and Paradise join each other. R' Yochanan claims that a partition of only a hand-breadth, or four inches, separates them. The rabbis say the width is but two fingers (*Midrash Kohelet*).

R' Akiba said: "Every man born has two places reserved for him: one in Paradise, and one in Gehinnom. If he be righteous he gets his own place and that of his wicked neighbor in Paradise; if he be wicked he gets his own place and that of his righteous neighbor in Gehinnom" (*Talmud Bavli Tractate Chagigah*).

If the majority of an individual's acts are meritorious, he enters Paradise; if wicked, he goes to Gehinnom; and if they are equal, God mercifully removes one wicked act and places it on the scale of good deeds. R. Jose b. Hanina quotes, "Who is a God like You, that pardons iniquity" [lifts a sin] (*Mic. 8:18; and Talmud Yerushalmi Tractate Peah 1:1*).

The Talmud deduces the immortality of the soul from the Scriptures. "The spirit shall return to God who gave it" (*Eccl. 7:7*); the body of the righteous "shall enter into peace" (*Isa. 57:2*); and the soul "shall be bound in the bundle of life with the Lord" (*I Sam. 25:29*), which is under God's "throne of honor" (*Shabbat 152b*). The haggadic dimensions of Paradise and names of the attendants, as well as the materials and articles described, have kabbalistic value and meaning. The feasting and enjoyment are spiritual.

Rab distinctly says: "In Paradise there is no eating, no drinking, no cohabitation, no business, no envy, no hatred or ambition; but the righteous sit with crowned heads and enjoy the luster of the Shechinah, as it is written: 'They saw God and did eat and drink'" (*Ex. 24:11*). The sight of God is considered to be the equivalent of food and drink (*Berachot 18a*).

Rabbi Joshua ben Levi (or Yehoshua ben Levi) was an amora (rabbi of the Talmud) who lived in the land of Israel in the first half of the third century. He headed the school of Lydda in the southern Land of Israel. He was an elder contemporary of Yochanan bar Nappaha and Resh Lakish, and presided over the school in Tiberias (*Genesis Rabbah 94*). Joshua often engaged in homiletic exegetical discussions with Yochanan bar Nappaha (*Bava Batra 116a; Megillah 27a; and Shavuot 18b*). It is unclear whether the name 'ben Levi' means the son of Levi, whom some identify with Levi ben Sisi, or a descendant of the tribe of Levi.

Rabbi Joshua ben Levi studied under Bar Kappara, whom he often quoted. But Joshua considered his greatest indebtedness to Rabbi Judah ben Pedaiah, from whom he learned a great number of legal rulings (*Midrashim Exodus Rabbah 6; Ecclesiastes Rabbah 7:7; and Genesis Rabbah 94*). Another of his teachers was Rabbi Phinehas ben Jair, whose piety and sincerity must have exerted a powerful influence. Joshua himself had a gentle disposition. He was known for his modesty and piety, and whenever he instituted public fasting and prayer, it was said that his appeals were answered (*Talmud Yerushalmi Tractate Taanit 66c*).

His love of peace prevented him from attacking the emerging Christian theology. He was tolerant of Jewish

Christians, though they often annoyed him. He forbore cursing one, pronouncing instead Psalm 145:9, "God's mercies extend over all His creatures" (*Berachot 7a; Avodah Zarah 4b*). His love of justice and his fear that the innocent might suffer on account of the guilty (*Yoma 19b*) led him to oppose the removal from office a leader who, by omitting certain benedictions, had aroused the suspicion of heresy (*Talmud Yerushalmi Tractate Berachot 9c*).

Joshua devoted much of his time to furthering public welfare (*Midrash Ecclesiastes Rabbah 7:7*). His wealth and alliance to the patriarchal family through the marriage of his son Joseph (*Kiddushin 33b*) must have added to his authority. He was recognized as a representative of Palestinian Jewry. In the company of his friend Rabbi Hanina, he interceded on behalf of his people before the proconsul in Caesarea. They accorded Joshua and his colleague much honor and respect (*Talmud Yerushalmi Tractate Berachot 9a*).

When Lydda was besieged because the city harbored a political fugitive, Joshua saved the inhabitants by surrendering the refugee (*Talmud Yerushalmi Tractate Terumoth 46b; and Midrash Genesis Rabbah 94*). He also made a journey to Rome, but his mission is not known (*Midrash Genesis Rabbah 33*). Although Rabbi Joshua was connected through family ties with the patriarchal house, and exhibited high esteem for its members (*Kiddushin 33b*), he is largely responsible for the diminished friendship between the southern schools and the patriarchal house. (For evidence that such friendship once existed, see Talmud Bavli Tractate Eruvin 65b; and Talmud Yerushalmi Tractate Pesachim 32a.)

Joshua was the first to ordain his own pupils in cases where ordination was requisite (*Nedarim 42b*), thus assuming a power hitherto held only by the head of the Sanhedrin.

In the field of legal interpretation, Joshua's decisions were generally declared valid even when disputed by his contemporaries Rabbi Yochanan and Resh Lakish. He was lenient, especially in cases concerning cleanliness and the preservation of health (*Talmud Bavli Shabbat 121b; Talmud Yerushalmi Tractate Yoma 44d*). He devoted himself to the elucidation of the Mishnah. His own legal interpretations resemble in their form and brevity the writings of the Tannaim in the Mishnah.

In homiletic exegesis (aggadah), however, he was even more influential. He had a high opinion of that study, evidenced by his explanation that in Psalm 28:5, "the works of God," refers to homiletic exegesis (*Midrash Tanhuma 28:5*). Similarly, in Proverbs 21:21, he identifies "glory" (*kavod*) with homiletic exegesis (*Bava Batra 9b*). Joshua disparaged the recording of homiletic exegesis, however. A reference to a book ('pinkes') by Joshua ben Levi is assumed to have been the work of another rabbi of the same name (*Talmud Yerushalmi Tractate Shabbat 15c; and Midrash Tehillim 22:4*). Nonetheless, homiletic exegesis occupied an important place in his teachings. His disciples and contemporaries quoted many of his propositions. His interpretations often enabled him to arrive at legal rulings. Some of his explanations were accepted by later commentators (*Midrash Exodus Rabbah 23*).

Joshua ben Levi asserted the value of study when he observed that God told David (*Psalm 84:11*) that God prefers one day of study of the Law to a thousand sacrifices (*Makkot 10a; and Midrash Tehillim 122:2*). Though learning was of paramount importance (*Megillah 27a*), he also insisted on piety. He believed that those who attend the synagogue service morning and evening will have their days prolonged (*Berachot 8a*), and those who move their lips in prayer will surely be heard. (*Midrash Leviticus Rabbah 16; Talmud Yerushalmi Berachot 9d*). He instituted a number of rules regulating the reading of the Law in the synagogue on weekdays (*Berachot 8a*) and other matters relating to the service, many of which are observed in synagogues to this day (*Sotah 39b*). Speaking of the attributes of God, he describes God as "great, mighty, and awe-inspiring."

He conceived the relationship between Israel and God as most intimate: "Not even a wall of iron could separate Israel from his Father in Heaven" (*Pesachim 85b; Sotah 38b*). In his doctrine of future reward and punishment, he says that Paradise receives those who have performed the will of God, while the nether world becomes the habitation of the wicked (*Eruvin 19a*). In Psalm 84:5 he finds Biblical affirmation of the resurrection of the dead (*Sanhedrin 91b*). In Midrash Genesis Rabbah 26 he expresses the liberal view that immortality is the portion not only of Israel, but of all other nations as well.

In one legend, Joshua asks the Messiah when he will arrive. Elijah answers that the Messiah will come when Israel heeds God's voice (*Psalm 95:7, Sanhedrin 98a*). He also speaks of the futility of estimating when the Messiah will come (*Midrashim Tanhuma 9:1; Leviticus Rabbah 19*). Many of the legends relating to Joshua have been collected in separate small works entitled *Ma'aseh de-Rabbi Yehoshua' ben Lewi* and *Masseket Gan Eden we-Gehinnom*.

The list of those who entered Gan Eden while still alive includes Hebrews, Jews, non-Hebrews, non-Jews, men, women, Asians, Africans, converts, and people of high and low status. Some were rich, and some were poor. What they had in common is righteousness. They helped others come to spirituality. They made peace, fought for the common person, displayed humility and loyalty, got along well with others, made teshuvah when they were wrong, and went beyond the letter of the law. They demonstrated extreme ahavath chesed, loving kindness.

The righteous of all nations, all religions, have a share in the World to Come. Judaism is pluralistic. We are taught that God gave Moses the path for the Hebrews, but God gave a different and equal prophet and path to all of the other religions (*Sanhedrin 105a*). This is the central lesson of Chapter One, Verse 6, in *Derek Eretz Zuta*.

References for the above include: *The Encyclopedia Judaica*, the Jewish Women's Archives, Wikipedia, and the teachings of Rabbi Buchwald.

Appendix B

As outlined in *A Spiritual and Ethical Compendium to the Torah and Talmud*, the Talmud consists of the Mishna (Oral Law) and the Gemara (rabbinic teachings and discussion about the Mishna). The Mishna contains six sections called orders, or *sederim*. When the Gemara is added to the Mishna, each of the sederim is divided into subsections called Tractates.

Many published editions of Talmud do not contain the Tractates of Derek Eretz, which were composed 1500–2000 years ago. The first time they were printed with other Tractates of Talmud was in the third Venetian edition (1546–1551). Because they were not compiled and edited until after the Talmud Bavli was closed (ca. 500 C.E.) they are considered 'minor' Tractates, *mashechtot qutanot*, along with Avot of Rabbi Nathan and a few others. Derek Eretz appears in Seder Nezikin (Damages) after Tractate Avodah Zarah (Strange Worship) and Pirkei Avot (Ethics of the Fathers).

A reference from Talmud is properly identified by its *daf* (folio, or page number.) The words of Derek Eretz are referred to by chapter only. In this volume, the chapters have been broken into subsections labeled as 'verses,' in order to simplify the study process; they do not appear as such in the original text. A brief summary of Talmudic development is as follows:

Zugot: 515 BCE–70 CE

During the first generation of the Zugot, supporters of Hellenism gained control over the position of the *Kohen HaGadol*, the High Priest. Greek sympathizers were appointed to fill that role. The people elected a *nasi*, or chief of the courts, as an alternative to the corrupt Temple priests. Thus began the split between the Sadducees (AKA Hebraism) and the Pharisees (AKA Rabbinic Judaism). Pairs of religious teachers, or *zugot*, led the Sanhedrin. One fulfilled the role of *Nasi*, and the other *Av Beit Din*, father of the court, who oversaw the judges.

Following the Hashmonean rebellion, religious authority shifted from the priests to the courts. After the destruction of the Second Temple in 70 CE, the *Beit Din HaGadol*, High Court, no longer existed. The Romans allowed the Sanhedrin to be reestablished at Jamnia, but as the influence of Christianity grew, the Romans shut down the Sanhedrin in order to marginalize Judaism. Hillel (traditionally b. 110 BCE, d. 10 CE) and Shammai (b. 50 BCE, d. 30 CE) were the last pair of leaders of this period, and served at the time of King Herod (b. 74 BCE, d. 4 BCE).

Tannaim, 10–220 CE

Following Hillel and Shammai, the last generation of Zugot, the 'House of Hillel' and the 'House of Shammai' emerged, representing divergent perspectives on *halakhah*, Jewish law. Disagreements between the two schools of thought appear throughout the Talmud.

According to tradition, the Tannaim were the final transmitters of the Oral Law, which had been passed from teacher to student from the time of Moses. The Tannaim consist of approximately 120 sages whose views are recorded in the Mishna. The root *tanna* corresponds to the Aramaic word for the Hebrew *shanah*, which is also the root for the word Mishna, and means 'to repeat' or 'to teach.' The Tannaim lived and taught from the time of the Roman occupation of Judea, through the destruction of the Second Temple and the periods before and after the Bar Kokhba rebellion. Among them are Rabban Yohanan ben Zakki, who lived ca. 40 BCE–80 CE, Rabban Gamliel of Yavneh, Rabbi Eliezer, Rabbi Yehoshua, Rabbi Akiva, Rabbi Meir, Rabbi Yehuda, and Rabbi Judah haNasi.

Amoraim, 200 CE–500 CE

Amoraim is an Aramaic word meaning 'those who say,' denoting the Jewish scholars who taught the Oral Law in Babylonia and Israel, and whose debates were codified in the Gemara. 761 amoraim are mentioned in the Talmud Bavli and Talmud Yerushalmi. 367 lived in Israel from circa 200–350 CE, and the other 394 lived in Babylonia from 200–500 CE.

Savora'im, 500 CE–700 CE

Savora, which means 'reasoner', is a term used in Jewish law and history to signify the rabbis who are credited with having given the Talmud much of its current structure, i.e. the editors. Modern scholars also use the plural term *stammaim* for authors of unattributed statements in the Gemara.

Classical rabbinic literature holds that the Babylonian Talmud was redacted into its final form circa 550 CE. Some statements within classical rabbinic literature, and later analysis thereof, have led many scholars to conclude that the Babylonian Talmud was smoothed over by the Savora'im, although very little was altered.

Geonim, 589 CE–1038 CE

Geonim is the plural of Gaon, which means 'pride' or 'splendor' in Biblical Hebrew and 'genius' in modern Hebrew. The Geonim preserved the transmission of Torah and halakhah, taught Talmud, and made legal decisions on issues for which no prior ruling existed.

The rabbis of the medieval period were the leaders of the Babylonian Talmudic academies of Sura and Pumbedita in the Abbasid Caliphate. These schools were the centers of Jewish learning. The geonim were consulted from abroad on matters of Jewish law. Their questions and answers were compiled to form what is known as the responsa literature. Later geonim consulted not only the Mishnah and Talmud, but decisions made by their predecessors, whose traditions were generally regarded as authoritative. By the 10th century, as learning spread to other regions, Jewish communities consulted experts in their own countries.

Rishonim, 11th–15th centuries

Rishon means 'the first ones' and refers to rabbis who lived before the publication of The Shulkhan Arukh of Yosef Karo in 1563.

Acharonim, 16th century–present

The publication of *The Shulkhan Arukh* marks the transition from the era of rishonim to that of the *acharonim*, or 'last ones.' According to Orthodox Jewish tradition, the acharonim cannot dispute the rulings of rabbis of previous eras unless they find support from other rabbis of previous eras. The question of which prior rulings can and cannot be disputed has resulted in a need to precisely determine which rulings fall within the Acharonim era. Some rabbis hold that Rabbi Yosef Karo's *Beit Yosef* has the halakhic status of a work of a Rishon, while the later *Shulkhan Arukh* has the status of a work of an Acharon.

The above information summarizes multiple articles on Wikipedia. An in-depth description and list of influential rabbis from each period may be found there.

About the Authors

Rabbi Dr. Arthur Segal

Rabbi Arthur Segal graduated *cum laude* from the University of Pennsylvania in the 1970s, where he completed BA and DMD degrees, Specialty, and post-doctoral studies in psychology. His love of Judaism and his Ahavath Israel led him on a personal quest for Jewish spiritual renewal. Following his retirement from a successful oral medicine practice, he began ten years of intensive study, culminating in Rabbinic ordination with Semikah.

Rabbi Segal was the first to bring weekly Torah and Mishna classes to one of the oldest synagogues in America, at which he held the position of Scholar-in-Residence for a year. He has written internationally acclaimed texts and essays on Jewish Spiritual Renewal, Mussar, Ethics, Torah, and Talmud. He offers free online classes on the spiritual and ethical teachings of the Torah, TaNaK and Talmud. In his home town, he teaches Talmud, TaNaK, Midrash and other great texts, such as *Duties of the Heart* by Ibn Paqudah. Rabbi Dr. Segal offers rabbinic counseling using the step-by-step process of Jewish Spiritual Renewal to help his fellow Jews achieve a spiritual life.

His activities include conducting holiday and Shabbat services on cruise ships and for international congregations that do not have a rabbi. He officiates at customized weddings and other life cycle events. He also works with Jewish prisoners who wish to effect change in their lives. He is active in his local community, serving on a variety of Arts and Cultural Diversity boards.

Rabbi Segal, and his beshert, Ellen Freedman Segal, have traveled together to over 150 countries, visiting and aiding Jewish communities where they exist. Ellen and Rabbi Segal enjoy a life of shalom, shlema and gratitude, with their parrot, Avivit Keter.

Sara Davies

Sara provides graphic design and editing services for architects and non-profit organizations, and is a LEED AP in Building Design & Construction. Her background in fine arts includes group shows at the Bellevue Art Museum and the SOIL Artists' Cooperative. Sara's desire to cultivate a personal relationship with God brought her to Jewish spirituality. She lives with her husband and two children in Seattle, where she is working on her first novel.

ALSO BY RABBI DR. ARTHUR SEGAL

The Handbook to Jewish Spiritual Renewal: A Path of Transformation for the Modern Jew

RABBI DR. ARTHUR SEGAL DISTILLS millennia of sage advice into a step-by-step process to reclaim your Judaism and your spirituality, with a concise, easy-to-follow method. If you find yourself wishing for the strength to sustain you through the ups and downs of life; if you want to learn how to live life to its fullest without angst, worry, low self-esteem, or fear; or if you wish that your relationships with family, friends and co-workers were based on love and service and free of ego, arguments, resentments, and feelings of being unloved... this book is for you.

Paperback: $24.99
254 Pages
Published by: Amazon's BookSurge

Praise for *A Handbook to Jewish Spiritual Renewal*:

Searching thru Amazon looking for a decent book, I came upon this title. Having read countless "self-help"/motivational books, I expected to be seriously disappointed. The perfect attitude to begin this book! Having lived thru many trials, and currently battling my most recent challenge—Multiple Sclerosis, I was searching for understanding, searching for something, anything to hold on to and aid me in rising above this latest time of darkness. I had no idea this book would be so incredible, so powerful, so life changing! Reading this book, one truly cannot help but feel that the author wrote this book specifically for "me". The love, compassion, understanding is clear, loud and present on every page. Refusing to accept or embrace cheap excuses, cop outs, or finger pointing, the author creates a loving and completely safe forum for one to truly and really look at ones' life. I cannot even come close to properly describing how powerful, how dead on this book is. I felt as if I had gained a "best friend" while reading this book. This may sound far out, ridiculous, even possibly delusional, but I assure you, I am sane! I have read thousands of books in my lifetime and by far, this book will always be on my top 10. I am Jewish but have shared this treasure with many non-Jewish friends and all came away with the same benefits. You do not need to be Jewish to grow, to gain, to benefit from this book. If I had this book 10, 15 or 20 years ago, my story would be substantially different. I am so grateful, so thankful that I was led to read this book and highly recommend it to anyone who has ever struggled, questioned, felt lost. I recommend this book to anyone who has led a great life. Regardless of your story, your burdens, your joys, this is a comforting "hug" that will truly enhance your life and bring you comfort. I hope and pray this author will pen more amazing blueprints to life!!! Thank you for this gift!

—*T. Gove, Vancouver, B.C.*

The Handbook To Jewish Spiritual Renewal by Rabbi Arthur Segal has given me the foundation to approach each day with honesty, reverence, hope and gratitude. I feel like I am having a personal conversation with a wise prophet with a jovial sense of humor.

—*Diane Weinberg, Washington, D.C.*

I couldn't have written the book or expressed my pain and concern for the Jewish people returning to Judaism. Thank God that He put this desire in your heart.

—*Janelle Vechi, California*

The Handbook to Jewish Spiritual Renewal is an invaluable resource for anyone who is searching for more in their life. I was involved with organized Jewish religion, but something was always missing. Using this guide, and taking each chapter to heart, has transformed my views and put me on the track my life is supposed to be on, filled with love, trust and emunah (faith). Thanks, Rabbi Segal!"

—*Ben Pincus, Houston, TX*

A Spiritual and Ethical Compendium to the Torah and Talmud

DR. RABBI ARTHUR SEGAL DISSECTS each of the Torah's weekly sections (*parashot*) using the Talmud and other rabbinic texts to show the true Jewish take on what the Torah is trying to teach us. This companion to *The Handbook to Jewish Spiritual Renewal: A Path of Transformation for the Modern Jew* brings the Torah alive with daily relevance to the Modern Jew. All of Torah can be summed up in one word: Chesed. It means kindness. The Talmud teaches that the Torah is about love for our fellow man and that we are to go and study. The rest is commentary. This compendium clarifies the commentary and allows one to study Torah and Talmud to learn the

Judaic ideals of love, forgiveness, kindness, mercy, and peace. A must-read for all Jews, and deserves a place in every Jewish home.

Paperback: $29.99
454 Pages
Published by Amazon's BookSurge

Praise for *A Spiritual and Ethical Compendium to the Torah and Talmud*:

Shalom. What a blessing your insights have given me. I am interested in reading more of your writings of Talmud. I find it difficult to find good Talmudic readings. Excellent work, Rabbi!

— *Rabbi Daniel Ben Shmuel*

...most insightful [Torah] essay I could find was written by Rabbi Arthur Segal.

—*Leslie Palma-Simoncek, Staten Island Advance*

Very informative and timely. It allows many people to benefit from Torah lessons, where many of them may not otherwise have an opportunity to receive such content.

—*Mauricio Benzipporah, Founder, Beta Gershom Organization*

Made in United States
North Haven, CT
25 June 2022

20608361R00186